AMERICAN MODERNISM'S EXPATRIATE SCENE

EDINBURGH STUDIES IN TRANSATLANTIC LITERATURES
Series Editors: Susan Manning and Andrew Taylor

With the end of the Cold War and the burgeoning of a global culture, the premises upon which Area Studies were based have come into question. Starting from the assumption that the study of American literatures can no longer operate on a nation-based or exceptionalist paradigm, the books in this new series work within a comparative framework to interrogate place-based identities and monocular visions. The authors attempt instead to develop new paradigms for literary criticism in historical and contemporary contexts of exchange, circulation and transformation. Edinburgh Studies in Transatlantic Literatures seeks uniquely to further the critical, theoretical and ideational work of the developing field of transatlantic literary studies.

Titles in the series include:

Henry James, Oscar Wilde and Aesthetic Culture
Michèle Mendelssohn

Ethnicity and Cultural Authority: From Arnold to Du Bois
Daniel G. Williams

*The Dandy in Irish and American Southern Fiction:
Aristocratic Drag*
Ellen Crowell

AMERICAN MODERNISM'S EXPATRIATE SCENE
THE LABOUR OF TRANSLATION

◆ ◆ ◆

DANIEL KATZ

EDINBURGH UNIVERSITY PRESS

© Daniel Katz, 2007

Edinburgh University Press Ltd
22 George Square, Edinburgh

Typeset in 11/13 Adobe Sabon by
Servis Filmsetting Ltd, Manchester and
printed and bound in Great Britain by
Biddles, Ltd, King's Lynn, Norfolk

A CIP record for this book is available from the British Library

ISBN 978 0 7486 2526 0 (hardback)

The right of Daniel Katz to be identified as author of this work has been asserted in
accordance with the Copyright, Designs and Patents Act 1988.

CONTENTS

Acknowledgements   vii

Introduction   1

1. Native Well Being: Henry James and the "Cosmopolite"   10

2. The Mother's Tongue: Seduction, Authenticity, and Interference in *The Ambassadors*   34

3. Ezra Pound's American Scenes: Henry James and the Labour of Translation   53

4. Pound and Translation: Ideogram and the Vulgar Tongue   71

5. Gertrude Stein, Wyndham Lewis, and the American Language   95

6. Jack Spicer's *After Lorca*: Translation as Delocalization   118

7. Homecomings: The Poet's Prose of Ashbery, Schuyler and Spicer   140

Notes   160

Bibliography 185

Index 193

ACKNOWLEDGEMENTS

In working through the questions that have led to this book, I have profited greatly from conversations with Dina Alkassim, John Culbert, and Thomas Dutoit, who have all marked this project in one way or another. I have also benefited from the perspicacity and erudition of other friends and colleagues who have read parts of the manuscript and unequivocally contributed to its improvement, whatever its present faults may be: Richard Sieburth has been extremely generous with his vast expertise concerning Ezra Pound, and even more, his always astonishing literary intelligence, while David Fussner must be thanked not only for enormous material aid in tracking down texts at the British Library and other like errands, but above all for the critical attention he brought to the text, and the constant intellectual companionship he provided across the channel. That said, the hospitality he and Hannah Fussner provided made research trips to London well nigh irresistible.

Here in France, at a crucial time certain colleagues gave remarkably exhaustive critical feedback to an earlier expression of some of the work done in this book; without their very constructive intervention, I am not sure if it would have been completed. For this, my deepest thanks to Catherine Bernard, Antoine Cazé, Evelyne Labbé, Jean-Michel Rabaté, and above all, Cornelius Crowley. Thanks are due also to series editors Andrew Taylor and Susan Manning, not only for their interest in the book but for having contributed significantly to its improvement through their careful, perceptive, and timely suggestions, and also to general editors Nicola Ramsey, Jackie Jones, and all their staff, who have been a pleasure to work with throughout.

Finally, thanks to my wife, Dorothy Bonnigal-Katz, and daughters Lisa, Daphne, and Esther, for everything.

Some portions of this book have already appeared in print. Chapter 6 appeared in a somewhat different form under the title "Jack Spicer's *After Lorca*: Translation as Decomposition," in *Textual Practice* 18 (1), 2004; certain parts of Chapter 1 appeared in signficantly different form under the title "Aphoristic Patriotics: Henry James and the 'Cosmopolite'" in *La Revue française d'études américaines* 92, May 2002. I thank the publishers for permission to reprint here.

Citations from all works by Ezra Pound are by permission of Faber and Faber, citations from *The Collected Books of Jack Spicer* by permission of the Estate of Jack Spicer, both of whom I gratefully acknowledge. I also thank the research group "Laboratoire de recherche sur les cultures anglophones" (LARCA) of the University of Paris-Denis Diderot, for help defraying costs of the permissions fees.

"Hold to the future. With firm hands. The future of each afterlife, of each ghost, of each word that is about to be mentioned."
                    Jack Spicer, *A Textbook of Poetry*

IN MEMORY OF ELI KATZ, 1928–2006

INTRODUCTION

The association of modernism with expatriation and exile is venerable to the point of being a cliché; around a century after the fact, it might seem strange to revisit the issue now. It is my contention that certain recent developments, critical and historical, make it an especially opportune moment to do so, but it is also worth mentioning that from the inceptions of English-language modernism, exile, exoticism, and expatriation were already being mobilized precisely *as* cliché themselves. Thus Henry James, in his earliest notebook entries concerning what was to become *The Ambassadors*, already worries about the cliché of Paris he intends to employ, "I don't altogether like the *banal* side of the revelation of Paris—it's so obvious, so usual to make Paris the vision that opens his eyes, makes him feel his mistake" (*Notebooks*, 226) only to conclude later in the same entry "I'm afraid it *must* be Paris; if he's an American" (227). As James will put it in his preface, "There was the dreadful little old tradition, one of the platitudes of the human comedy, that people's moral scheme *does* break down in Paris . . . and that I came late in the day to work myself up about it. There was in fine the *trivial* association, one of the vulgarest in the world; but which gave me pause no longer, I think, simply because its vulgarity is so advertised" (*Ambassadors*, xxxvii–xxxviii). James will conclude that this vulgarity furthers his purpose, as "the *likely* place had the great merit of sparing me preparations" (xxxviii). In other words, James seems to recognize how cliché, as a pre-comprehended crystallization of affect, can work as an enabling entry point for that affect's unfolding; a position I too shall adopt, with full cognizance of the banal and the trivial, but also with the confidence that recent critical trends lend this cliché a new legibility at present.

To begin with, the last decade or so has seen a new emphasis on the importance of translation, and to a certain degree, multilingualism, within modernism as a whole. Here, the key figure is largely Pound, and important studies like Daniel Tiffany's *Radio Corpse* and Yunte Huang's *Transpacific Displacement* have done much to establish the centrality not only of "translation" but also of a very closely related ethnographic concern to the entire Poundian project. In a broader context, Steven Yao's *Translation and the Languages of Modernism* shows how crucial the practice of translation and theoretical reflection on it was not only for Pound, but throughout English-language modernism as a whole. Yao unequivocally demonstrates that "from its very inception to even beyond what was normally considered its closing years, then, the age of Modernism, was, quite literally, an age of translations" (5), and his book has given considerable impetus to my own. Every author studied here either engaged in significant translation projects, or meditated on the problem of foreignness, estrangement, and defamiliarization explicitly in the context of the relationship between "foreign languages" and "mother tongues." As I shall argue, when Pound dubs the achievement of Henry James a "labour of translation," the phrase is not idle. For the modernists, "translation" in its most common acceptation is but one mode of the encounter with foreign languages, an encounter which entails the forced re-encounter with the language which is meant to be one's "own"—a problem which shall interest me throughout. My emphasis on the collision of languages dictates detailed readings of instances of language as they are mobilized more than broader synthesizing statements, and my methodology will privilege close readings throughout in its investigation of "internationalism" or "cosmopolitanism" as translation and interference. Building on Yao, I will examine how "translation" of text between languages forms part of a larger modernist project of cultural translation, and the role of the latter for certain modernist textual subjectivities.

In the context of such a question, crucial is the recent growth of transatlantic and transnational studies, which have allowed new ways of configuring the relationship between cultural, "national" or linguistic identifications, and geographical space, and this also "within" the shared but differentiated British-Irish-American linguistic and cultural space.[1] One of my major claims is that for the writers under consideration, expatriation is not a flight *from* American identity, but rather becomes the means for a displaced and dialectical encounter with it, at times conscious and reflective, at others entirely symptomatic, usually both (after all, for Henry James consciousness and reflection are stressed as symptomatic themselves). In this regard, I wish first to call into question an often facile opposition between "nativist" and "internationalist," or "cosmopolitan" and "universalist" forms of American modernism. Regarding "nationality" as context for pedagogy and criticism, I heartily agree with Jahan Ramazani's recent call to apply more "deconstructive pressure . . . not only to mononational narratives but also to the distinction between indigenists and cosmopolitans" (348). Indeed, one task of this book is to insist on expatriation as being in itself a highly venerable *form of* "American identity," an argument which would render impossible the bracketing of the expatriate modernists from the concerns of a somehow more "authentic" or autochthonous group of contemporary writers seen as more integrally "belonging" to "American studies."[2] I hope to demonstrate that the "Europe" and "Europes" of the authors studied here are quintessentially American scenes, that James' Paris, for example, is no less American (and no more a cliché or a construction) than Frost's New England, or Faulkner's South. T. S. Eliot suggested as much in his own 1918 homage to James: "It is the final perfection, the consummation of an American to become, not an Englishman, but a European—something which no born European, no person of any European nationality, can become" ("In Memory," 44). "Europe," in this sense, is nothing if not American, as Robert Crawford points out: "The Eliot who wrote on Henry James is just the person in whose writings we can see that this particular 'mind of Europe' is an American invention" (230).

Regarding the too often restrictive and reified borders of American studies, Paul Giles makes similar points in his illuminating *Virtual Americas*, where he insists that "a virtual American studies should be organized around a more general idiom of dislocation and estrangement, serving to interrogate not only the boundaries of the nation-state, but also the particular values associated explicitly or implicitly with it" (284), while calling for a "transnational" approach which would "acknowledge the necessity for Americanists both inside and outside the United States to rearticulate their field dialogically and comparatively" (284). This means that the "position of estrangement" (3) which Giles advocates and which both the present book and the writers studied herein often adopt, has two implications: first, as Giles rightly suggests, it is necessary to broaden the field of "American" studies and to expand and critically reinterrogate our sense of what is and is not "American."[3] However, the second point to stress, is the danger that this questioning of cultural identity and boundaries be too quickly reappropriated and subsumed under an expanded but structurally similar totalizing structure of cultural appurtenance. That is, while insisting that the authors under study in this book participate in a distinctively American reflection on both American identity and cultural appurtenance in general, I am loath to think that the result of such an argument would be simply the creation of yet another area for area studies—for example, a subcategory of "American studies" now called "expatriate American studies," or "transatlantic American studies" or the like. Regarding certain modernists, Giles points out that if "these cosmopolitan modernist writers tended to cherish exile as generating an alternative form of identity . . . the actual effect of their transatlantic displacement was often to problematize the idea of identity altogether" (123–4). If "transatlantic studies" are to be productive, it will be as an *extension* of such a problematization *into* "area studies" as such, and not as the simple carving out of ever new areas. Thus, I would hope this book would be consonant with Ramazani's eloquent call to reconceptualize the study of modern and contemporary poetry from the assumption—one he brilliantly argues—that for this period "transnationalism" is "primary rather than incidental," which implies a break with contextualizations, in both the classroom and the critical literature, which are all too often facilely "subdivided along national lines" (333).[4]

However, as both Giles and Ramazani are aware, equally unproductive is the abandoning of all emphases on the local in favor of an abstract "universalism" which would fail to address historical context, along with material, cultural differences and specificities, among which figures significantly, for any writer, the bizarre fact of the diversity of human languages.[5] This diversity is at the heart of all questions of literary-cultural appurtenance, and of course the identification of standard literary English with that practiced in southern England is a crucial issue for Irish, American, and as Robert Crawford points out, Scottish writers, particularly in the early modernist period. His entirely fascinating *Devolving English Literature* makes a compelling case for modernism as a "provincial" phenomenon, by which he means one which defines itself in opposition to "Anglocentric identity" (269) and thus yokes together Scottish, Irish

Introduction [5

and American writers. A key element here is of course the registering of non-standard forms of linguistic practice, and Crawford is extremely helpful in establishing the utter centrality to modernism of the "demotic urge" (262), which is also one of my major concerns. At the same time, he is cannily aware of how this urge is in fact entirely allied with what could seem the contradictory modernist practice of "forging a diction so polylingual and sophisticated that it tops and outflanks the English cultural centre" (262). Much like the translation theorist Antoine Berman, Crawford shows a subtle understanding of how "polylingualism" and the "demotic" both work together in the subversion of "standard" or "natural" language proscriptions. Thus, I fully agree when he states, "The 'provincial' and the international are bonded, but not in the kind of cosmopolitan sense that makes a poem's speech as international as nylon" (269). Yet one should not thus infer that such a "provincial" emphasis would run counter to a transnational, transatlantic, or comparatist approach—on the contrary, his study obtains a large part of its force by showing how the Scottish and American situations parallel each other; the insights he offers regarding each take on their full significance only in light of those he offers regarding the other, and Crawford also details many concrete historical examples of cultural exchange between Scotland and America. It is only a transatlantic and transnational perspective that allows him to elaborate "provincialism" in the first place, in a movement which ineluctably shows the need for Scottish, Irish, and American modernists to be read together. In this connection, I would like to add that my own thinking about questions of translation, linguistic interference, bilingualism, cultural appurtenance, and expatriation had its departure in my work on Samuel Beckett, an author in whom many of the questions I will examine here present themselves in hyperbolic form. And if this book restricts itself to the American "domain," if it will emphasize certain questions which historically are particularly American, I would hope that its general tendency would be to make the writers examined here *more easily* studied in the context of Beckett, rather than even more effectively cordoned off from him.

Indeed, by a reading of certain exemplary figures and texts, I shall attempt to explore a series of questions which are also quintessentially Beckettian: to what extent does expatriation allow for a distanced and dialectical re-encounter with the "homeland," now become decentered and uncanny itself? To what extent does this render the relationship to language, even one's "native" tongue, above all one of translation? And to what extent does the massive modernist experience of expatriation represent a seeking out of this space of generalized translation, despite the paradoxical fact that actual practices of translation, emphasizing a grafting of the foreign into the domestic, are often mobilized against this very threat? While emphasizing the elaboration of these questions by Henry James and the generation of expatriate, polyglot, "international" modernists who followed, my final chapters on Jack Spicer, John Ashbery, and James Schuyler will show how their concerns are still actively determinant in these "postmodern" authors.

I will begin with an investigation of James' elaboration of the key figure of the "cosmopolite," as defined in *The Portrait of a Lady* and his travel piece, "Occasional Paris." In these texts, the cosmopolite emerges not as the traveler who has learned to feel at home everywhere, but rather as one who has traveled so much that he or she is no longer "at home" anywhere, including and above all in his or her originary "home." The becoming uncanny of the cosmopolite's relationship to his or her homeland will emerge as a central paradigm for all the writers examined in this study, as will James' trope of the impossibility of a return to the native, as enacted in *The American Scene*. This chapter will also outline Jamesian schemas of seduction, the uncanny, and haunting in relation to questions of translation as psychic phenomenon as discussed by Jean Laplanche, establishing certain theoretical problematics which will recur throughout the book.

In Chapter 2, I will examine two related, fundamental questions, as made evident in *The Ambassadors*: that of exoticism, or the elevation of a foreign "culture" as such to the status of affective object, and that of multilingualism, translation, and "interference," in both specifically linguistic and more generally cultural terms, as the novel's explorations of cultural "authenticity" as a fantasmatic object privilege in particular investments in the "native" language as opposed to multilingualism. Through a close reading of an allusion to Hawthorne's *The Marble Faun*, we shall see how James re-examines Hawthorne's positing of the "mother tongue" as joined to a mystified originary "maternity" in general, itself seen as the ultimate proximate against which any foreign must be defined. At stake is the elaboration of a Jamesian erotics of generalized interference with regard to linguistic "purity" and "cultural authenticity," which by reconfiguring the relationship of the "mother" to the "mother tongue," implies the creation of a subverted Oedipal scenario, in which incest comes to resemble nothing so much as exogamy.

The following chapter on Pound will stress the importance of the precedent of Henry James for Pound's own insufficiently studied attempts at auto-ethnography, and for his sense of American cultural identity. Examining how James' *The American Scene* provides a model for Pound's "Patria Mia," the chapter will focus on Pound's qualification of James' importance as lying above all in what he dubs a "labour of translation" in his crucial essay devoted to the author. This has two major implications, the first of which is that the figure of James as the displaced, cosmopolitan "translator" provides one of the most dominant models of American identity in general for Pound, as he embraces or even extends a Jamesian irony: what makes James most "American" is precisely his distance from any clear and unequivocal sense of his American identity, his fundamental lack of an identity which he is subsequently obliged to reconstruct. It is in James' very estrangement from his American identity and therefore from any other, that James becomes for Pound an archetypal American and in fact, an archetypal investigator of the question of culture.

Chapter 4 examines the second implication of Pound's designation of James as translator: that Pound's own "translations" fully imply the sort of cross-cultural investigations and displacements associated with James. We will see how Pound's translations from the Chinese and Italian are a form of negotiation with the norms of literary London and Victorian Britain which allow him both to affirm and suspend his sense of American difference, while close readings of selected translations will demonstrate how Pound dispenses with the entire question of a "natural" poetic idiom by taking the language of translation as his primary poetic model, in a move which leads Pound to a poetics of interference not unlike those implied by James. However, at the same time, Pound's reflections on Dante and his circle inevitably lead him, through translation itself, to ask the question of the "vulgar tongue" as medium for poetry, and thereby to situate himself in relationship not only to James, but to Whitman, while raising the crucial modernist question of the American idiom.

This question is at the center of Chapter 5 which will address Gertrude Stein's clear dialectic of expatriate estrangement as preservation of cultural identity in the context of Wyndham Lewis' article "The Dumb Ox," a largely negative if ultimately ambivalent account of what Lewis sees as Stein's pernicious influence on Hemingway. Throughout, Lewis recognizes Hemingway's ambiguous achievement—by way of Stein—as that of miraculously capturing an

American language which Lewis views as being in and of itself debased through its contamination by the slovenly speech habits of the mass of recent immigrants. However, the establishment of an independent American idiom and its relation to literary expression is also a key concern of Stein in the 1930s and 1940s, and particularly, in its ramifications regarding the places she believes she and Henry James occupy within American cultural and literary history.

Chapter 6 moves beyond the historical time frame of modernism as conventionally accepted and beyond the biographical frame of expatriation, to see how the legacy of the issues elaborated by the expatriate modernists of the previous generation continues to make itself felt in the work of post-War San Francisco Renaissance poet Jack Spicer, who extends in exaggerated form many of the issues raised heretofore. Fiercely regionalist, Spicer at times prohibited his work from being distributed outside the San Francisco Bay Area, yet at the same time, models of interference, difference, and distance dominate his poetics. Chief among them are metaphors of telecommunication—such as correspondence and radio broadcasting—in addition to the very Jamesian "haunting," and an equally Poundian translation. His *After Lorca* is an adaptation of the Spanish poet explicitly modeled on Pound's *Homage to Sextus Propertius*, in which the relationship between translator and translated is often figured as that of the ultimate interference into the proximate—haunting. Meanwhile, his metaphor for poetic inspiration, "dictation," makes use of the figure of the radio broadcast, only here it is not the poet who "projects" his voice to multitudes, but rather it is an utterly alien radio signal that the poet, reduced to a sheer antenna, must strive to *receive*. For Spicer, "regionalism" means nothing other than a systematic destruction of the intimacy of the proximate, through the interference represented notably by translation.

As a conclusion, we shall look at two works of poet's prose which circle back to wholly Jamesian concerns with home, the native, the unfamiliar, the exotic, and travel as a consistently missed encounter with the authentic. The first is Spicer's unfinished detective novel, which stages the "return" to San Francisco of aspiring poet J. J. Ralston, who after several years of academic work on the east coast comes home precisely to find an origin become unrecognizable. Ralston's journey is undertaken in the hopes of recovering the roots of his creativity, but it is his encounter with an uncanny San Francisco that becomes Spicer's main concern as he wanders through prose in this explicitly Jamesian novel. The second is John Ashbery's and

James Schuyler's co-authored *A Nest of Ninnies*, a remarkable staging and interrogation of many central practices of contemporary tourism and exoticism. Set largely in that new yet indeterminate zone, the suburbs, this novel marks one of the earliest meditations on the future of Jamesian Europhilia in the age of the global village, while reveling in the uncanny kitsch space opened by what Dean MacCannell has called the "staged authenticity" characteristic of the modern touristic consumer experience.

This book has no pretensions to providing a full overview, either historical or literary-historical, of the phenomenon of modernist expatriate writing, or of modernist translation experiments and theory. Rather, I hope to show how certain key problems regarding cultural appurtenance and linguistic identity, expatriation and exoticism, translation and a specifically "American" literary idiom, become intertwined and parsed together, with varying emphases and insistences, in the texts I shall examine here, themselves frequently in explicit or implicit conversation. If I have chosen the above because I find them particularly illustrative and exemplary, this account is in no way exhaustive, and problems found here are also addressed by figures such as W. C. Williams, Djuna Barnes, and T. S. Eliot, to name only a few, all of whom would have cast additional and fascinating light on what concerns me here.[6] Another crucial domain this study will not systematically address is that of African-American expatriate modernism, despite the provocative parallels between expatriated and internal modalities of exile. Racism as material and juridical policing mechanism of identity creates a significantly different set of cultural and political imperatives from the "provincial" anxieties I study here, whereas in terms of exoticist mystification, the African-American situation calls for focus on modernism's intense and ambivalent engagement with discourses of primitivism, while this study focuses more on that exoticism's flipside: Europhilia. If this book at its outset insists so heavily on James, then, it is because he more than anyone else sets American modernism's terms not only for thinking the foreign as such as constitutive of an elaboration of the domestic, but also, the relationship between language, consciousness, and the expressible, while asserting a parallel that will haunt the century's cultural production: that between consciousness, the foreign, and haunting itself. To begin to see how this is played out, let us turn to the Jamesian imbrication of questions of language with those of domesticity, estrangement, and seduction.

CHAPTER 1

NATIVE WELL BEING: HENRY JAMES AND THE "COSMOPOLITE"

Linguistic Position and Expatriation

Let us begin near the end of "modernism," rather than at its beginnings; let us begin forcibly thrust into America, rather than willfully absented from it. In 1944, from the misery of political exile in America, Theodor Adorno extrapolated the following concerning cultural displacement and intellectual life:

> Every intellectual in emigration is, without exception, mutilated, and does well to acknowledge it to himself, if he wishes to avoid being cruelly apprised of it behind the tightly-closed doors of his self-esteem. He lives in an environment that must remain incomprehensible to him, however flawless his knowledge of trade-union organizations or the automobile industry may be; he is always astray. Between the reproduction of his own existence under the monopoly of mass culture, and impartial, responsible work, yawns an irreconcilable breach. His language has been expropriated, and the historical dimension that nourished his knowledge, sapped. (*Minima Moralia*, 33)

Here, under the shadow of the catastrophe of Nazism and the Second World War, Adorno figures his American exile as sheer loss. Given the biographical and historical circumstances, such an attitude is hardly surprising, but still, in its hyperbolic violence and in the context of both Adorno's own intellectual positions and those of the artists and intellectuals who interested him, this statement should give pause. After all, Adorno applies his case to a general condition which he defines not as "forced exile" but simply "emigration," and moreover, resoundingly rejects universalist and cosmopolitan positions which one might imagine quite congenial to him. Adorno's Marxist stance and contempt for what he dubbed the "culture industry" would seem almost to assure that on a theoretical level true intellectual labor would be viewed as international or even universal. Why should the petty *national* context of the "intellectual" be elevated to the rank of enabling "historical dimension" for his labor, and why should "emigration" widen the breach between the "monopoly of mass culture" and "impartial, responsible work"? Even more, given the dialectical method which Adorno constantly asserts to be his philosophical foundation, wouldn't one expect the estrangement of exile to be welcomed for placing the intellectual and her or his unexamined assumptions into the condition of negativity necessary for their true critical elaboration? This is a perspective that Adorno will indeed assume, in various ways, throughout this book which takes as its starting point ". . . the narrowest private sphere, that of the intellectual in emigration" (18). But what I want to stress for now is the *cost* exile must represent for the equation to function: of interest here is precisely the *violence* of Adorno's tirade, the pathos of his sense of lack when severed from the domestic codes of social interaction which he himself so often tends to anathematize as arbitrary, reified, oppressive, and devoid of essential human meaning. The foreign here becomes quite simply "incomprehensible" for the supremely cultured and polyglot Adorno: a negativity that, from the subjective perspective of the exile, even the dialectic seems in danger of failing to recuperate—sheer expenditure in Bataille's sense. The intellectual in emigration, with his language expropriated from him, is as Ralph Ellison might have said, "nowhere," a man without a position.[1] Most important, note that in Adorno's rhetoric, the "foreignness" he bewails seems to have an almost transcendental quality—no amount of actual knowledge about the society will make it any less "incomprehensible," oddly enough, while at the same time, he implies that no form of translation can compensate for the "expropriated" native tongue.

Adorno's sense of mutilation, grown out of the mutilation wrought by the Second World War, might represent an endpoint of a certain form of expatriate or cosmopolitan self-fashioning that will interest me here. At the same time, it serves to illuminate certain anxieties that had already lurked within the High Modernist expatriate stance. Adorno's contrarian position denies and rejects a certain "cosmopolitan" ideal of ease of cross-cultural passage, or the advantages of expatriate distancing, which was entirely characteristic of both Anglo-American modernism and international modernism as a whole.[2] Just as much, the passage wonderfully expresses the underlying anxieties which, I shall argue, rather than simply threaten cosmopolitan affirmation, in fact often serve to provide the conditions which underpin its very attractions. What I am interested in here is "cosmopolitanism" both as a courting of loss and, paradoxically, as a reattachment to the pleasures of cultural positioning—pleasures that Adorno's bereavement here strongly mobilizes.

In the Anglo-American context, both the cosmopolitan position and the imperative to weigh it in terms of artistic and emotional profit and loss are associated with no one so much as Henry James, not least by the generation of American expatriate writers which was to follow him. James' status as mediator of literary London, but also of the cultural heritages of France and Italy, which American and Irish modernists so frequently invoked in an effort to displace "English" cultural authority, is of course unmatched by any of his contemporaries. Yet this in no way abrogated the American turn in his writings, or the continual return of America among his concerns. For these reasons, I would like to compare Adorno's exile's lament with a different yet analogous one, written about forty years earlier, by Henry James. Here, it is not a question of an exile expropriated from his language, but of a language that has been expropriated in and of itself. In James' extraordinary extended metaphor, it is indeed American English—a bewildered, errant immigrant maid—that is, like Adorno's exile, irremediably astray:

> Keep in sight the so interesting historical truth that no language, so far back as our acquaintance with history goes, has known any such ordeal, any such stress and strain, as was to await the English in this huge new community it was so unsuspectingly to help, at first, to father and mother. It came *over*, as the phrase is, came over originally without fear and without guile . . . to find itself grafted, in short, on a social and political order that was both without previous precedent and example and incalculably expansive.
>
> Taken on the whole by surprise it may doubtless be said to have behaved as well as unfriended heroine ever behaved in dire predicament—refusing, that is, to be frightened quite to death, looking about for a *modus vivendi*, consenting to live, preparing to wait on developments. I say "unfriended" heroine because that is exactly my point: that whereas

the great idioms of Europe in general have grown up at home and in the family, the ancestral circle (with their migrations all comfortably prehistoric), our transported maiden, our unrescued Andromeda, our medium of utterance, was to be disjoined from all the associations, the other presences, that had attended her, that had watched for her and with her, that had helped to form her manners and her voice, her taste and her genius. It is the high modernism of the conditions now surrounding, on this continent, the practice of our language that makes of this chapter in its history a new thing under the sun. . . . If you reflect a moment you will see how unprecedented is in fact this uncontrolled assault of most of our circumstances—and in the forefront of them the common school and the newspaper—upon what we may call our linguistic *position*. Every language has its position, which, with its particular character and genius, is its most precious property. . . . ("The Question of Our Speech," 53)

It is, unfortunately, not surprising that James will encourage what were then still his compatriots (he had not yet taken British citizenship) to protect this errant maiden from the grasp of the "American Dutchman and Dago, as the voice of the people describes them" (53)[3], and from the corrupting influence of the newspaper and the "common school" (53), even if he will eventually conclude that a language is only alive when "fed by the very breath of those who employ it, whoever these may happen to be" (55), which induces him to recognize and accept the mongrel and unprecedented fate of American English, provided the "conservative interest" in the language remain as a powerful counterweight (55). But for our purposes, what is crucial to note is the terms in which James sketches what emerges as a transcendental displacement. Here, in contrast to Adorno, it is not a question of a particular individual who has no position, but of a *language* which has no position. And this difference is decisive, for in Adorno's account (and not only his) it is language itself, which, as much as anything, is responsible for giving the individual the position to be conserved or lost. In some sense, a language without a position, a language which does not guarantee this form of positioning, is not really a "language" at all. This is why James insists so strongly on the *unprecedented* character of American English, on the "high modernism" of the situation he evokes: in James' parable, many individuals have emigrated, and thus been torn from their language, customs, and families, but never before has a language itself emigrated and therefore lost the context and associations that ground its meaning. America, in this view, is quite simply a country without a language in the strong sense of the word, and thus Adorno no more than inherits, through the accidents of history, what James defines as the transcendental American condition: that of linguistic homelessness. It is only from this perspective that the question of "our speech" can even be posed.[4] However, a following question which James only seems to approach the verge of asking here, is to what extent does such a condition of linguistic homelessness invalidate the possibility of ever properly having any sort of homeland at all—to what extent, in James' parable, are all Americans doomed to the fate of cosmopolitan displacement, as their own language is itself one which has no place, one which can no longer function as guarantee of origins? The question then is not only that of Adorno—how does one live constantly in translation—but rather, how does one live when one's language is itself a "translation," when the native tongue has been separated from its conditions of nativity? Visiting America after more than twenty years abroad, James is led ultimately to ask how the American writer, in such conditions, can ever return home or even "stay" at a place which could be called "home" in any proper sense.

Of course, James' figuring of language as a young woman is anything but innocent here, insisting as it does all the more strongly on the privileged cultural link between femininity and the domestic in general. The chain linking language to the feminine, the feminine to the family, the family to the "familiar" in every sense, is not only foundational, but arguably founding for the concept of foundation itself. Yet here we do have a noteworthy shift: what James begins by calling "our mother-tongue" (52) quickly evolves into the errant, endangered young virgin. To conceive of our native tongue as an uprooted virgin waif to be rescued and betrothed (almost but not quite an Andromeda awaiting her Perseus, as James puts it) rather than an originary mother whence our essence derives and to whose proximity—be it comforting or stifling—we can always return, represents and entails a rethinking of the native in all its aspects. Naturally, one might object that the equating of a language and the natural propriety of its contours with virgin purity is neither new nor radical; indeed Antoine Berman has provided a brilliant analysis of Herder's objections to the kind of difference introduced by translation, objections which couch in similar terms the threat to the immaculate national tongue which, prior to penetration by translation, would be ". . . like a young virgin who has not yet had commerce with a man, nor borne the fruit of the mixing of blood; she is still pure and unsullied, a faithful image of the character of her people."[5] But this citation already makes the difference clear: James' "virgin" has lost her "purity" in her "coming over," a journey which also, as James was at pains to emphasize, divested her completely of any clear representational link to "her people." She is not the virgin who has never left the patriarchal hearth, awaiting the maternity already programmed for her; rather, she is a waif without lineage, while a mystical, primordial bond to those who speak her is precisely what she has *not*. Rather than the extension of the groundedness of a culture in its wholeness, she is portrayed as *awaiting* that very grounding and domesticity she now lacks, being as James puts it in a litany of negations: "distracted, dishevelled, despoiled, divested of that beautiful and becoming drapery of native atmosphere and circumstance which had, from far back, made, on its behalf, for practical protection, for a due tenderness of interest" (53-4). To what extent, for James and for the modernists who follow, does the relation to the "native tongue" cease to be that of nearly incestuous proximity and oneness, and become rather the space of violation and difference commanded by exogamy?[6] This question can only be addressed through an investigation of the erotics of translation, and their relationship to Jamesian rupturings of the domestic, in every register.

Native Well Being and Uncanny Transpositions: Translation and Seduction

The scene of translation abounds in James; not, of course, in the most literal sense of the word, but certainly in a more extended one: James continually, even obsessively, presents the trauma of the encounter with the radically foreign, and the resulting need to *transpose* that foreign into the comprehensible terms of the domestic. James' so-called "international theme" is often nothing other than the attempts of such a translation of foreign cultural practices into comprehensible form, along with the attempts on the part of characters to hear differently the meanings of their actions within a different system of exchange.[7] Likewise, James' "ghost stories" are often structured around a radical otherness which has to be transferred back into the realm of the familiar and rational. It could be argued that the parable of the governess in *The Turn of the Screw* warns precisely of the violence of what Antoine Berman might call an "ethnocentric" translation.[8] At the same time, both the ghost stories and those belonging to the "international theme" often show how this encounter with difference leaves radically ruptured the "domestic" to which an attempted return is staged. Such a rupturing is, as we shall see, an equivocal and ambivalent goal of James, which he sketches out in his consideration of what he calls the "cosmopolite." For the moment, note that what I am calling James' translation practice—which in terms of biography features prominently the act of expatriation—seems to lead him inevitably to some of the worst dangers that have been traditionally attached to the art of translating, that is, a breach in the domestic. For example, in his classic treatise *On the Different Methods of Translating*, Friedrich Schleiermacher sternly warned that the incursion into foreign tongues makes translators run the risk of rupturing, in their "own" writing, the "gentle sense for the native well-being of the language" (47). Schleiermacher's German phrase, "das heimische Wohlbefinden der Sprache" (cited in Berman, *L'épreuve*, 239; *Experience*, 149), shows that as far back as 1813, the act of translation has been seen as haunted by the specter of the uncanny,[9] an uncanny which, if we follow the connotations of Freud's original German and its emphasis on the domestic, already afflicts the "American" language as James outlines it above. Translators, and I would add ambassadors, cosmopolites, and expatriates, run the risk of finding their own sense of the homely unhoused. "The Jolly Corner" makes this much plain. Indeed, if James is the "uncanniest" of writers, it is less, perhaps, that in his work the repressed returns, as in the Freudian formulation, and more because his writing pressures so intensely the constitutive "ambivalence" which Freud claims applies to the German word "heimlich" (Freud, 347).

In his famous study of "The 'Uncanny,'" Freud traces how the meaning of the word "heimlich" slips and displaces to a point where it is at odds with itself. First meaning "pertaining to the house" and therefore "familiar," "known," and "comfortable," this idea of domesticity is extended so that the word takes on the connotations of something concealed, hidden, or "removed from the eyes of strangers." The progressive emphasis on secrecy and concealment actually leads the word "heimlich" to be used to mean "something hidden and dangerous" (346) or potentially unfamiliar—precisely the meaning of the antonym "unheimlich." Freud concludes, "Thus *heimlich* is a word the meaning of which develops in the direction of ambivalence, until it finally coincides with its opposite, *unheimlich*. *Unheimlich* is in some way or other a sub-species of *heimlich*" (347). Like the old man in the train compartment whom Freud initially fails to recognize as his own reflection in the mirror (371), the word "heimlich" circles back to face itself in non-recognition. James enters into this problematic precisely through his investigations of the constitutive strangeness of nothing other than all forms of domesticity, identity, and familiarity.

One area where these questions are joined by James to the problems of translation is in his concern with childhood and children, those Victorian touchstones of domesticity whose function James was often keen to subvert. In fact, in regard to the native and the domestic—in theory, that from which the expatriate departs, that to which the translator returns—childhood can be shown to be the symmetrical counterpart and supplement to what would seem its contrary, that is, the radical difference of the foreign, and this is due in part to the child's relationship to language as the novelist saw it. Thus, discussing the "technical" problems of the narrative positioning in *What Maisie Knew*, his only novel centered on a child, James suggested that the role he was of necessity obliged to accept was nothing other than that of a kind of translator: "Small children have many more perceptions than they have terms to *translate* them; their vision is at any moment much richer, their apprehension even constantly stronger, than their prompt, their at all producible, vocabulary. . . . even though it is her [Maisie's] interest that mainly makes matters interesting for us, we inevitably note this *in figures that are not yet at her command* . . ." (27–8, my emphases). The narrator is thus a "translator," producing the vocabulary which the child lacks. Yet at the same time, childhood is for James a space of nothing other than the *untranslatable*, a time when there are "fewer names than conceptions" (163), and thus the experience of a namelessness which the Jamesian narrator must nevertheless express, and thereby violate, through his naming. This is made clear by James' specification that he employs his "figures" when treating precisely those parts of Maisie's "experience" which she "rather tormentedly misses" (28). Here we see the violence of translation not only towards the "domestic" to which it must return, but also to the untamable difference of that which is brought over. Etymologically, a child as "infant" is by definition "without speech," and therefore, restoring to it what by its definition it has not, is in some way to destroy it. Perhaps this is partly why James equates the end of Maisie's "wonder" with "the death of her childhood" (28).[10]

If childhood for James is equated with the untranslatability of experience, then the act of translating it necessarily violates what gives it its essential character. In this sense, James' "childhood" would belong among what John Sallis has called the "varieties of the untranslatable," about which he says the following: "In the case of untranslatable feelings it is such that—or at least it is attested to be such that—any would-be translation of those feelings into speech would be not just a bad translation, not just a translation in which much would be lost, but rather no translation at all. Any alleged expression of those feelings in language would prove to be an imposter, something quite other than an expression of those feelings. And yet, the very possibility of attesting to such untranslatability requires that it not be total: in order to identify, name, mark the feelings as untranslatable into speech, it must be possible to say something about them and so to mark a limit of their untranslatability. It must be possible at least to name them. . . . Because at least their untranslatability is translatable into speech, it cannot be total" (114). James' work, with its obsessive interest in the minutest shadings of moral gradation, often articulates itself inside the space of the double-bind Sallis details here. Indeed, I would argue that the classically Jamesian anxiety over the "false position," which Julie Rivkin has shown to be so central for James, is often a variation on the position of the translator as "imposter" which Sallis evokes.

This in turn implies that James' attraction to childhood can be seen less as a raid on the provisionally inarticulate[11] than as a foray into speechlessness itself, a foray into an area of languagelessness, and that childhood therefore mirrors, on the other end of the spectrum, the alienation of the nativity of language evoked in "The Question of Our Speech." Not only does childhood join the "foreign" as a space which poses for James the question of the limits of translation and translatability, and thus the boundaries of the domestic. Even more, the child comes to represent less the keynote of the domestic than its interior limit, that which is short of rather than beyond it, and this would be even more the case regarding those most uncanny children, Miles and Flora of *The Turn of the Screw*. Like the foreign and the ghost, the child at times becomes a key strategic node in James' discussion of the construction of the domestic, and indeed, on the most literal level Maisie's story is that of a young girl who is *without* the domesticity seen not only as birthright, but virtually as ontological origin. Without having lost her empirical parents, who though divorced are both alive and well if utterly negligent in their duties and delinquent in their affections, Maisie has no "home" to speak of, and the novel tells how her presence brings into contact those adults who might marry and subsequently provide a surrogate one. As the novel insists repeatedly, Maisie's story inverts the normal ontology of the family, in which the parents "create" the child, thereby fixing the maternal body and all that is troped as cognate with it as the originary locus of the child's being. On the contrary, it is Maisie who "brings together" her step-parents—it is she who would be the "origin" of the new family to be created—a family which, as a result, could never ground her in myths of the native. Her story is not only about the death of childhood, but about its killing.

Of course, equally central to *What Maisie Knew* and *The Turn of the Screw*, as well as *The Ambassadors*, is the question of seduction—as much a constant of James as "haunting" and the "international theme." To see why this might be so, and how this ties into questions of childhood, speechlessness, the originary domestic, and translation, let us turn to the French psychoanalyst Jean Laplanche, for whom the accession of the languageless infant to adult subjectivity is achieved through nothing other than a process of translation, which he also associates with a "generalized seduction." It is Laplanche who can perhaps best help us to understand the dual prevalence of scenes of seduction and what I have been calling translation in James' work.[12]

In his work on "orginary seduction," Laplanche seeks to restore to "seduction" the importance it had for the early Freud and for Ferenczi, but with crucial modifications. For Laplanche, the scene of seduction is not one occurring between a child and its parents, but more generally consists of the invitation proffered to the child by the entire adult world to enter into a signifying structure charged with unconscious meaning. In other words, not only must the child translate the meaning of the words and gests with which she is constantly confronted, but these "messages" of love and care delivered by the adult world are themselves laden with unconscious sexual energy of which their bearers are unaware. Laplanche explains:

> Par le terme de *séduction originaire* nous qualifions donc cette situation fondamentale où l'adulte propose à l'enfant des signifiants non-verbaux aussi bien que verbaux, voire comportementaux, imprégnés de significations sexuelles inconscientes. Ce que je nomme *signifiants énigmatiques*, il n'est pas besoin de chercher loin pour en donner des exemples concrets. Le sein lui-même, organe apparemment naturel de la lactation, peut-on continuer de négliger dans la théorie analytique son investissement sexuel et inconscient majeur par la femme? Peut-on supposer que cet investissement sexuel, qui peut être dit pervers au sens des *Trois essais sur la sexualité*, n'est pas aperçu, soupçonné par le nourrisson, comme source de cet obscur questionnement : que me veut-il, au-delà de m'allaiter, et, après tout, pourquoi veut-il m'allaiter? (*Nouveaux Fondements*, 125)

> [By the term *originary seduction* we designate this fundamental situation in which the adult offers to the child verbal as well as non-verbal, even behavioral signifiers, loaded with unconscious sexual signification. There is no need to search far and wide to find examples of what I call *enigmatic signifiers*. Can a woman's capital, unconscious sexual investment in her breast, an apparently natural organ of lactation, continue to be neglected in analytic theory? Can it be supposed that this sexual investment, which could be called perverse in the sense of the *Three Essays on Sexuality*, is not noticed or suspected by the nursing baby, as the source of this obscure question: what does it want from me, beyond nursing me, and after all, why indeed does it want to nurse me?][13]

As Laplanche makes clear in many places, the child is therefore forced to attempt to *translate* the sexual content of these messages, which exceeds for both the adult and the child the context of primary care and autoconservation in which they are delivered:

> En effet, le message adulte, adressé à l'enfant sur la base d'un dialogue, d'une réciprocité autoconservatrice, se trouve habité, compromis par la sexualité inconsciente de l'adulte. . . . Le message sexual *habite* donc le message autoconservatif. (*Entre séduction*, 132).

> [In fact, the adult message, addressed to the child on the basis of dialogue, of the reciprocity of a relationship of autoconservation, finds itself inhabited and compromised by the adult's unconscious sexuality . . . the sexual message *inhabits* that of autoconservation.]

For Laplanche, it is this originary situation which gives rise to elements such as the Oedipus and castration complex which, rather than being human universals, become historically and culturally contingent secondary attempts at translating the riddle of the enigmatic signifier:

> Loin d'être des éléments primordiaux du ça, Oedipe et Castration sont des instruments de mise en ordre. . . . La castration . . . permet de traduire sous une forme maîtrisable des angoisses et des messages énigmatiques. (*Entre séduction*, 141–2)

> [Far from being primordial elements of the Id, Oedipus and Castration are tools for creating order. . . . Castration allows the translation of anxieties and enigmatic messages into a form that can be mastered.]

As Van Haute and Geyskens point out, it is the inevitable "failure" of translation, the inevitable unbound remainder, that gives the enigmatic messages, belatedly, their "traumatic or traumatizing character" (129). Or as Laplanche puts it in one of his more schematic pronouncements:

> Ce qui ne peut être traduit, le résidu de la traduction constitue le ça inconscient ; celui-ci échappe à la liaison et devient désormais un pôle de déliaison. (*Entre séduction*, 232)

> [What cannot be translated, the translation's residue, constitutes the unconscious Id, which escapes binding and becomes henceforth a pole for unbinding.]

However, the implications of this schema are not that analysis should then seek to "retranslate" what has been translated badly, in order to "bind" it inside the scope of the ego. Rather, transference should strive to recreate the originary scene—that of the enigmatic address from the other—and the crisis it provokes. Laplanche writes that transference should be seen as the possibility of a

> renouvellement de l'adresse énigmatique de l'autre, prioritaire, instigatrice, voire génératrice d'une néo-genèse d'énergie libidinale. (*Entre séduction*, 146)

> [renewing of the priority of the enigmatic address of the other, the instigator or even the generator of a neo-genesis of libidinal energy.]

and elsewhere he goes on to state:

> Nous ajoutons maintenant que la force motrice nouvelle engendrée par la situation transférentielle et le rapport à l'énigme est précisément cette "pulsion à traduire," renouvelée. (*Entre séduction*, 239)

> [We now add that the new driving force engendered by the transferential situation and the relation to the enigma is precisely this "drive to translate," now renewed.]

Transference, for Laplanche, exists to produce—to reproduce—the "drive to translate" which he sees as originary.

What is key for James, as well as other writers to be studied here, is Laplanche's correlation of this translation drive with libidinal energy, and the paradoxes it produces. For this implies not only the libidinal investment in exoticisms of all sorts, but also, if for all humans the "originary" affective situation is in fact one of translation, as Laplanche suggests, that the desire for the enigmatic novelty of the other—person, language, culture—becomes nothing so much as the desire to *repeat* archaic scenarios depicted as originary. In this light, exoticism is always in part a return, and translation always already constitutive of the construction of the native. Moments of expatriation, in the larger sense, become moments of the *return* of and to the space absented; moments of translation become moments of the slipping away of the domestic to which the foreign is to be brought. Recurrent in this study will be paradigmatic scenes of such uneasy desires, articulated between total reification of the other and total untethering from one's own identifications, and at times through the complicity between the two. An especially revealing scene of this sort is found in Henry James' discussions of what he calls the "cosmopolite," and the economics of estrangement it implies.

The Cosmopolite, The Patriot, The Apparition

That James saw expatriation as being of value to the writer as a form not only of assimilation of otherness but also of invigorating estrangement, leaves little doubt. Note the terms in which James depicted his writerly goals to his brother William in 1888,

> I have not the least hesitation in saying that I aspire to write in such a way that it wd. be impossible to an outsider to say whether I am, at a given moment, an American writing about England or an Englishman writing about America.... (W. and H. James, *Selected Letters*, 208)[14]

The position James ironically eschews is the one that *prima facie* might seem the most desirable: to seem like an American when writing about America, an Englishman when discussing England. On the contrary, the letter to William stresses precisely the *advantage* to be gained from the freshness and critical distance of the foreign perspective—James strives to maintain his American eye when examining English morals, but to put his assumed "Englishness" to good effect when working on his fellow Americans. Expatriation allows for an *enhancement* of the critical gaze. Significantly, this is a position which *The American Scene* begins by repeating, with its stated goal of combining the benefits of the native and foreign perspectives:

". . . if I had had time to become almost as 'fresh' as an inquiring stranger, I had not on the other hand had enough to cease to be, or at least to feel, as acute as an initiated native" (3).

Yet in a less optimistic vein, James could also write, ". . . a man always pays, in one way or another, for expatriation, for detachment from his plain primary heritage" (cited in Lewis, 526). If estrangement and expatriation are strategies of critical perception, "distancing" techniques eminently favorable to the famous Jamesian irony, what then could be the cost, so inevitable, exacted by detachment from a heritage somehow "plain" and "primary"? Or more to the point: is there a place where this cost is not to be paid? For inheriting "clearly" or "plainly," whether economically, linguistically, or patronymically, is not something often witnessed in James, and even James' earliest critics were aware that expatriation could not be designated as the primal cause of this omnipresent Jamesian "detachment" or distance. As T. W. Higginson wryly noted about the younger James, a true cosmopolitan "is at home even in his own country!"[15] Indeed, the question of the "cosmopolite" in James is not primarily that of the foreign, but rather that of the "plain and primary" home in terms of nation, family, language, and custom, for which the foreign "itself" often becomes a figure. Witness Chapter 10 of *The Portrait of a Lady*, and the discussion of national appurtenance engaged in by the novel's most stereotypically and egregiously American character, the journalist Henrietta Stackpole, who is at its center.

Like the novel's heroine, Isabel Archer, Henrietta is young, attractive, and intelligent, but she distinctly lacks Isabel's easy grace and manners. Her journalistic tactlessness and stereotypically American over-seriousness and insensitivity to humor and irony are all played up in the chapter and throughout the book, often to excess. Indeed, James himself in the "New York Edition" preface feels the need to apologize for the "anomaly" represented by Henrietta, "(of whom we have indubitably too much)" (*Portrait*, 13). James explains her prevalence in two ways: first, the "superabundance" of Henrietta is due to an "excess" of "zeal" on James' part, and is symptom of both his tendency to "overtreat" his subject and a perhaps misplaced emphasis on the "cultivation of the lively." But James ends his disclaimer on a different, less technical note:

> And then there was another matter. I had, within the few preceding years, come to live in London, and the "international" light lay, in those days, to my sense, thick and rich upon the scene. It was the light in which so

much of the picture hung. But that *is* another matter. There is really too much to say. (15)

at which point the preface simply ends. As is inevitably the case with James, the disavowal of Henrietta is a double gesture, for James ascribes her inclusion to the very faults for which she herself is condemned by other characters in the book: excessive zeal, lack of a sense of due proportion. In disavowing her James identifies himself with her, and not only had James greatly played the travel-journalist by the time he first wrote the *Portrait*, but he also had with relish taken up Henrietta's role as student of manners and morals in *The American Scene*, written almost concurrently with the New York edition prefaces. This identification works against the belittlement of Henrietta which James himself encourages in the preface, and indeed, Chapter 10 is subtly but insistently devoted to the dangers of misreading her, as the apparently clever Ralph Touchett entirely misconstrues the import of Henrietta's remarks on marriage.[16] If Henrietta is other than a figure of pure fun, then, James' second comment helps indicate on what issues she is to be taken seriously: she is the lamp of the international light, and it is in this role that she so aggressively questions Ralph in the dialogue of interest to us.

When Henrietta first meets Ralph, she begins by asserting that she would like to know if he and his fellow expatriate father consider themselves American or English: "If once I knew I could talk to you accordingly" (80). Through his repartee, Ralph will mock Henrietta's narrow-mindedness, which seems to imply that Americans and English are entirely different species requiring entirely different forms of address. But Henrietta's question is less naive than that: she asks not what "nationality" these two gentlemen "are" but rather what nationality they *consider* themselves to be—in this question, she is not concerned with essences but rather with identifications and positionings. Henrietta clearly feels that Ralph "is" essentially English, but wonders whether he is an Englishman who *considers* himself to be an "American" still: "I don't suppose that you're going to undertake to persuade me that *you're* an American" (80) she pointedly challenges Ralph. Very shortly thereafter, Isabel intervenes in this discussion concerning Ralph's nationality:

"He's what's called a cosmopolite," Isabel suggested.
"That means he's a little of everything and not much of any. I must say I think patriotism is like charity—it begins at home."

"Ah, but where does home begin, Miss Stackpole?" Ralph enquired. "I don't know where it begins, but I know where it ends. It ended a long time before I got here." (81)

At first blush, this passage is yet another example of Henrietta's vulgarity and Ralph's wit. Henrietta, in predictable, journalistic fashion, employs a somewhat inappropriate cliché to make a tautological, jingoistic point: true patriots stay at home. Ralph outplays her by throwing into question the term Henrietta takes as her starting point: "home." It is not so much the "foreign," then, as the "home" which is at issue here. But note the form of Ralph's objection: where does home begin? Let us first imagine the implications of the opposite tactic, that of asking: where does home end? Such a question, while stymieing Miss Stackpole, would extend the "cosmopolitan" element Isabel had suggested, implying that as Ralph is "at home" in so many places he's not quite sure where his "patriotism" should be lodged. The emphasis would be on an ever expanding set of mastered cultural economies and practices, on an endless capacity for identification and comfort. An unending home is perhaps one pole of the Whitmanian narcissistic dream, a microcosmic expression of American expansionism, the Manifest Destiny of individual manners, but here we have something different. Ralph asks where does home *begin*, and a home which doesn't "begin" in any particular, certain site, a home whose locus, whose home base, can no longer be located or situated is precisely not a home. What is a homeless home? Ralph's response is not an affirmation of cosmopolitan assimilation but of the uncanny distancing of everything that might once have seemed perfectly assimilated, entirely "natural." When Henrietta claims that "home" ended a long way away from England she in fact finds herself in a similar position to Ralph, except that for Ralph home has always already ended everywhere, and cannot simply be called "America." For Ralph, homelessness is more than a geographical contingency.

Yet let us look at another aspect of Henrietta's assertion which Ralph seems to ignore—"I must say I think patriotism is like charity—it begins at home." Henrietta's claim is of course based on a proverbial expression—"charity begins at home"—which implies that kindness and concern should be first directed at one's immediate interlocutors, and only subsequently extended to unknown, distant causes. Be just and kind to those you know, before attempting to save the world. "Charity begins at home" is thus a rebuke to self-serving, narcissistic philanthropical projects, designed to buy an easy conscience.[17]

Why should "patriotism" then be compared to "charity"? By appealing to the moral imperative in the proverb Henrietta gives her rather pedantic version of patriotism, certainly, but she also implicitly affirms another possibility: that of considering patriotism as something that might *not* begin at home, that of acknowledging that a displacement to the "foreign" might be a dialectical move in investigating one's relationship to what one considers as familiar. She can be read as offering to Ralph the possibility of asserting that he is indeed a sort of "patriot," examining his relationship to the fatherland precisely by absenting himself from it. This is a possibility that James was at times anxious to claim as his, but which Ralph seems incapable of imagining—he skirts the issue by using one of the classic resources of wit: that of displacing emphasis, and replying not to the term put in question by Henrietta, "patriotism," but rather to that which she had left as a given, "home." If Ralph then bests Henrietta, he also fails to answer her question.

Yet this question was one which was clearly of some concern to James at this time, and in the roughly contemporaneous travel piece, "Occasional Paris," James again juxtaposes the "cosmopolite" and the "patriot." Here, James links what he somewhat archly presents as the slightly dubious habit of "comparing one race with another, and weighing in opposed groups the manners and customs of neighbouring countries" with "the baleful spirit of the cosmopolite—that uncomfortable consequence of seeing many lands and feeling at home in none. To be a cosmopolite is not, I think, an ideal; the ideal should be to be a concentrated patriot" (*Collected Travel Writings*, 721). The word "concentrated" clearly signals the danger besetting the "cosmopolite," which is that of subjective dispersal,[18] for the cosmopolite loses the "sense of the absoluteness and the sanctity" of the "habits" and customs of her or his own "fellow patriots":

> You [the cosmopolite] have seen that there are a great many *patriae* in the world, and that each of these is filled with excellent people for whom the local idiosyncrasies are the only thing that is not rather barbarous. There comes a time when one set of customs, wherever it may be found, grows to seem to you about as provincial as another; and then I suppose it may be said of you that you have become a cosmopolite. (721)

This remarkable passage cannot simply be called "relativist," because it does acknowledge a universal category: the patriot. The irony is that for James, the "patriot" who establishes a binary opposition between the "home" and the "foreign" exactly resembles no one more than the patriot's figure of pure Otherness—the *foreign* patriot who has made exactly the same move. A patriot, then, is not someone who is attached to a particular set of values for their inherent worth, but someone attached to the *arbitrary proximity* of himself or herself to that set, that is, someone attached to attachment itself, and the sharpness of ego identifications such attachment permits. It would seem to be precisely the rupture of the "absoluteness" and "sanctity" of affective investment that James experiences as exhilarating crisis.[19] A cosmopolite, then, having lived through cultural differences, unlike the patriot is poisoned by the desire to "compare" and "weigh," that is, make informed choice. This act of informed choosing is called by James "discriminating" (721), and the word seems to retain both the sense of aesthetic and intellectual judging *and* that of ethnic or cultural prejudice in this context: James emphasizes how for the expatriate, disappointments with one's fellow humans become transformed into a condemnation of the particular ethnic group with whom one finds oneself surrounded. The same idea is expressed clearly in a letter of 1888 to William, with reference to their sister, Alice:

> It is always a great misfortune, I think, when one has reached a certain age, that if one is living in a country not ones [sic] own & one is of anything of an ironic or critical disposition, one mistakes the inevitable reflections & criticisms that one makes, more & more as one grows older, upon life & human nature &c, for a judgment of that particular country, its natives, peculiarities &c, . . . (208)

In "Occasional Paris" James will ironically assert that this unfair displacement has at least the benefit of saving humanity as a whole from opprobrium—one particular ethnic group becomes the scapegoat preserving "humanity" as a category, for such a group does ". . . not represent the human race for you, as in your native town your fellow-citizens do" (722). Whatever the benefits or drawbacks of this procedure, then, it points to a fascinating economy, in which a failure of introjection, where the "absoluteness" and "sanctity" of primary identifications begin to fade, can only be compensated by an exaggerated *projection*, which will then apply to a given cultural group the reification of "natural" qualities the expatriate can no longer identify with himself or herself. The less the cosmopolite is *anything*, the more the cultures among which he or she circulates tend to be stereotyped.

"Cosmopolitanism" here leads not to Enlightenment ideals of "tolerance," but rather creates the conditions for new mappings of cultural prejudice. The vagaries of the "uncanny" are again helpful in understanding this dynamic.

In his investigation of the phenomenon, Freud will fix on Schelling's definition of "unheimlich" as *the name for everything that ought to have remained . . . secret and hidden but has come to light*" (345, original emphasis). In English, we could think of Freud's problematic as a dialectics of the "private," in that this word, like "heimlich," implies both what is most personal and also what is potentially shameful, and to be hidden. In this light, "unheimlich" could also be read as a radical "deprivatization," in the sense of shameful exposure but also of the removal of a space of absolute, sacrosanct identification, creating a situation in which one's affect, though recognizable, is strange to oneself. Suspended against this, as object of resentment, would be the fantasmatic imago of a people inexorably locked into the solidity of their national or ethnic "character." It is within this dialectic that the "cosmopolite" exults and mourns, for even should he or she come to prefer a certain set of "weighed" customs and therefore adopt them, they can never be a source of "concentrated patriotism," as this sort of patriotism comes precisely from *foreclusion* of choice. And this entire problematic of choice, group identity, "home," and the private, is worked through in virtuosic fashion through the character of Henrietta and her aphorism, "Patriotism is like charity, it begins at home."

For this question, concerned with lack of place, with placelessness, frames itself, as we have seen, in reference to a previously existing expression—an expression which can only be called a *commonplace*, and indeed it is the possibility of a commonality of place which is at issue throughout the book, not only in terms of its treatment of the "international theme," but also in its meditations on marriage. Henrietta's appeal to this commonality is one which the profoundly narcissistic Ralph will be compelled to refuse in every form, and in the same vein, it is clear that Ralph's goal throughout much of the novel is to *divest* himself of all forms of inheritance, of every sort of symbolic link or bond, be it the family business, the paternal American accent, the fatherland, or the family money, which, tragically wrong, he hands over to Isabel. This is also of course what is at issue in Ralph and Henrietta's quarrel over the former's refusal to marry. But this quest for the uncommon, the evasion of commonality, is also portrayed as impossible—as Ralph reminds us, after

Henrietta asks him if he considers it right to give up his country, "Ah, one doesn't give up one's country any more than one gives up one's grandmother. They're both antecedent to choice—elements of one's composition that are not to be eliminated" (85). Is this to be read as Ralph finally admitting to us where "home" begins—with the fatherland and the mother's milk? It is not so certain, for what he stresses here is not the *foundational* aspect of these "elements" but precisely their partial, finite quality. They may be "antecedent to choice" but they remain less an essence than a set of traces, impossible to eliminate, try as one might. By treating them as prehensile "elements," what Ralph ironically points to is precisely his *estrangement* from these supposed emblems and indices of "home." Home does *not* "begin" with them as one is not "at home" with, or within, oneself.

Ralph's question, "where does home begin?" certainly points to James as the great meditator on expatriation which indeed he is. But it also points to the later James, the great writer of ghost stories, for as uncanny as it may be to occupy a foreign symbolic space whose laws and objects are at once inscrutable, oppressive, vast sources of anxiety and incomprehension and ineluctably affectively void, as James well knew even more uncanny is that against which the foreign writes itself: the home. James, like Emily Dickinson, tends to stress the contiguity of haunting with houses, and in a tale like "The Jolly Corner" he explicitly posits home as the complex of haunting itself. The point here is that expatriation and haunting are not simply two of James' diverse interests, but two modulations of the same set of questions. Defining where "home" begins means defining subjective boundaries, dividing the within from the without. This implies not only separating the "we" from a "they" in nationalistic or cultural terms but also the "I" from the potentially haunting "it."

Rather than Henrietta's term of "patriotism," James' work calls for a study of what could be called its "patriotics"—the study of the construction of the home and the homely which in James so often begins precisely not at home. On the contrary, estrangement in James seems an allegory of the necessarily uncanny character of all "homes" to begin with, and in this way, leaving becomes itself a way of getting to the essence of the home.[20] To study where home begins in James is at once to emphasize filiation, expatriation, tourism, exoticism and spectography in order to see how the home-effect is itself brought into relief through the trope of the foreign. As Laplanche's work implies, it is to examine how in James the "foreign" itself is used as a trope of the naturalization strategies which mobilize any given "home" in the first place. In this sense, patriotism does indeed begin elsewhere, and one could argue that James spent his life in exile running to America, thus actualizing the distance from "home" he had also felt at home.

Indeed, it is America, this exquisitely mediated home, that Henrietta is somewhat awkwardly made to represent in the early pages of the *Portrait*. When Ralph deems her too "familiar" to Isabel the latter defends her precisely for being "vulgar," with a quibble on the Latin root: "she's a kind of emanation of the great democracy . . . ." (87) Isabel opines, to which Ralph replies: "You like her then for patriotic reasons. I'm afraid it is on those very grounds I object to her" (87)—an objection which leaves unclear whether it is Henrietta's American identity which is at fault or simply her attachment to the patriotic ideal in the abstract. In any event, what follows is the strangest scene in the entire novel. Evoking Henrietta as a kind of emblem of the people, Isabel claims to be impressed less by Henrietta than by what "masses behind her" to which Ralph immediately quips, "Ah, you mean the back view of her" (88). This strange physicalization of Henrietta will continue when Isabel, following a very Whitmanian evocation of Henrietta as a sort of microcosm of the prairies and seas of America, declares: "A strong, sweet, fresh odour seems to rise from it [America], and Henrietta—pardon my simile— has something of that odour in her garments" (88), after which, we are told, Isabel blushes. Isabel's blush is overdetermined both by Ralph's quibble on the "back view" and by the metonymic power of commonplace expressions—already foregrounded by Henrietta's improvised proverb—which leads "garments" ineluctably toward "under garments." Ralph concludes the conversation and the chapter with the assertion that "Henrietta . . . does smell of the Future—it almost knocks one down!" (88). Aside from James' late revision concerning Goodwood and Isabel's kiss, this is by far the most physical and indeed erotic passage in this novel about marriage. The inexpugnable grandmother returns as the granddaughter, as the democratic Fatherland of the common man bowls over Ralph and James with the overpowering odor of the Feminine. The scene could be said to be literally "unheimlich," as Freud points out that the adjective "heimlich" is often used to mean "private" in the sense of the English expression "private parts"—as a euphemism for the genitals. This scene then certainly consists of a bringing to light of what should have remained hidden, and Isabel's blush is justified. But what is "exposed" here, I think, must not be read as a "repressed" yet ultimate and primal "home" of the maternal body, which would allow us to read all of Ralph's cosmopolitan meanderings as the most banal of hysterical symptoms. Rather, Henrietta's body in its very intimacy is an emblem of nothing other than the "Fatherland." America and its leveling democracy is the marriage to be refused, but also the menacing feminized void of indifferentiation. This is the "vulgarity" which begins at home.

It is to this dangerously democratic, dangerously void and indeterminate home that James returns, literally, in *The American Scene*, a book which also echoes the concerns of the discussions concerning the "cosmopolite" which we have studied above, and even more so, its rhetoric in a key passage. James has often been taken to task for what seems to be the anti-democratic and anti-immigrant stance in *The American Scene*, and one can certainly see him as bewailing the invasion of an alien presence denaturing his "homeland" and thereby distancing him from the purity of the sources of his own being.[21] Such a reading, however, profits from its confrontation with certain complexities of James' positionings, both textual and biographical. To start with, for example, James had famously distanced *himself* from this "home" by his deliberate, prolonged absence abroad. Second, if *The American Scene* rails continuously at one prime target, seen as the major factor in the endless destruction of the old New York James loved, this target is not immigration: it is money.[22] But let us go on to examine closely what is often taken as the most incriminating anti-immigrant passage. It is during his visit to Ellis Island that James fully feels the shock of the mere quantity of "aliens" who were becoming American citizens every day, and he argues that this is a shock from which the American visitor to this display will never recover:

> He has eaten of the tree of knowledge, and the taste will be for ever in his mouth. He had thought he knew before, thought he had the sense of the degree in which it is his American fate to share the sanctity of his American consciousness, the intimacy of his American patriotism, with the inconceivable alien; but the truth had never come home to him with any such force. (66)

Such a vision, James continues, leaves a "chill" in the heart, and a "new look" on the face, rendering the visitor like "the questionably privileged person who has had an apparition, seen a ghost in his supposedly safe old house" (66). As readers of "The Turn of the Screw" or "The Jolly Corner" (to say nothing of Freud) well know, however, ghosts only haunt by virtue of an uncanny proximity and likeness to their victim—this is, in fact, the essence of their terror. The "alien" for James is not a simple "foreign body" to be eliminated or quarantined. Rather, the "alien" is at once "inconceivable" *and* "intimate," and as such, an allegory of the subject's own constitution. In a brilliant reading of this passage, Ross Posnock has shown how James' account of Ellis Island "questions and redefines" the meaning of being "at home":

> The "immensity of the alien presence" as the defining fact of American life dissolves the "dividing line" between alien and native and empties the word "home" of positive content. The sense of unity, continuity, and closure the term usually evokes is negated, with home becoming the locus of the alienating, the absent. (278)[23]

Posnock goes on to point out that the "narcissistic fiction" of self-identity, the "supposedly safe old house," is shattered by the alien haunting: " 'American consciousness,' both national and individual, is already violated; the 'ghost' of the other always haunts it" (281). But it is crucial to add that James' passage about haunting here is haunted itself, as James returns to a rhetoric more than twenty years old, for if the "alien" sidles into and repositions the "*sanctity* of his [the visitor's] American consciousness" and the "intimacy" of his "American *patriotism*," in "Occasional Paris" James had already evoked the cosmopolite's loss of the "sense of the absoluteness and the *sanctity* of the habits of your fellow *patriots*" (721, my emphases). In other words, to discuss his own homecoming, James returns to the rhetoric he employed to define the cosmopolite, who by definition has no home, and Ellis Island would seem to indicate the becoming-cosmopolite of *every* American, that is, "Americanness" as an originary cosmopolitanism. Following the logic of James' own chosen terms, the great irony is that the most "patriotic" American must now be nothing so much as what is defined as the "Patriot's" opposite: the cosmopolite. Thus if James is to find himself "at home" in America upon his long-delayed return, it will only be because, having become a cosmopolite himself, he returns to a country whose condition for "patriotism" is that all become as he. What James surprisingly calls the "supreme relation"—the relation to "one's country" (*American Scene*, 67)—has long since been "alienated" for him. But as James makes clear, the challenge of the alien is precisely to admit that which is utterly other *into* what is most intimate: ". . . this affirmed claim of the alien, however immeasurably alien, to share in one's supreme relation was everywhere the fixed element, the reminder not to be dodged" (67). Despite his disorientation, James never disputes this claim.

Of course, James' designation of some sort of "patriotism" as his "supreme relation" may seem somewhat disingenuous, and not only because of his profoundly "cosmopolite" outlook. It seems hard to imagine that for James the "supreme relation" was anything other than that pertaining to writing, to the material inscription of subjective impression. As Adorno noted, "For a man who no longer has a homeland, writing becomes a place to live" (87), yet he also insisted, "Today . . . it is part of morality not to be at home in one's home" (39). In James' case, it is certainly true that the rampant "ethical" and "moral" questions which his works at times almost egregiously foreground need to be considered in light of the question of writing, and thus language, as "home," whether figured either as originary source, or as ultimate destination. As the Ellis Island passages from *The American Scene* illustrate, by the time James was writing that book he was by no means clear as to what was designated by the antecedent of the first-person plural pronoun used in the title, "The Question of Our Speech"—the intimate "we" in question already contained something eerily "not us." But in this, the proprietors do no more than rejoin their object, their "language" itself having "come over," as we have seen, to find itself bereft of its accrued authenticities. As James himself concedes, all European "idioms" are the product of historical mixing, displacement, and change, but the "migrations" of the others are what he calls "comfortably prehistoric" (53). In this sense, part of the "high modernism" ("Question," 53), the scandal of the American idiom, is that it serves to rehistoricize *all* languages, to deconstruct all effects of nativized authenticity. It implies that to the extent that writing is done in language, no one of James' rigor can ever be at home in her or his home. Which only increases the desire to imagine that someone else might be. To further investigate James' exploration of language and cultural practice as marks of authenticity, along with the possibilities of finding oneself at home among them, let us turn to *The Ambassadors*.

CHAPTER 2

THE MOTHER'S TONGUE: SEDUCTION, AUTHENTICITY, AND INTERFERENCE IN *THE AMBASSADORS*

In the previous chapter we examined the curious economy of the "cosmopolite," who seems to compensate for the increasing loss of the "sanctity" of his relationship to his "home," to any sense of originary belonging, by a tendency to reify others into nothing but sheer embodiments of a totalized cultural practice. "Occasional Paris" and Henry's letters to William about their sister Alice explore this dynamic in terms of cultural *prejudice*: living in a space designated as "foreign," all faults, failings and annoyances are read as emblematic of that particular culture, rather than of the human condition. But what I would like to explore in this chapter is the possibility that the cosmopolite's reification can move not only in the direction of prejudice, but also in what might seem the opposite: that of mystified adoration. For as Lambert Strether, protagonist of *The Ambassadors*, becomes increasingly uncertain of the values of "Woollett" which it is his duty to represent, as his European experiences end, as we shall see, by rendering the very concept of "home" largely inoperative, at the same time he increasingly mystifies an authenticity of "Frenchness" against which his own life, experience, and values must be measured. And this mystification is one which the reader is very much encouraged to share, for reading *The Ambassadors*, it is easy to forget that Marie de Vionnet—embodiment of French feminine wiles and touchstone for Lambert Strether of the authenticity of his French experience—is not entirely French at all. Her parentage is a mix of French and English, we are told by Maria Gostrey when she is first introduced, and her schooling Swiss. Our paragon of French ways and traditions, virtues and vices, is by no means the seamless conduit of them, in no way what

Strether through so much of the novel so much wants her to be—his guarantee of real contact with the real thing. Her role in this regard is patent: during his first meeting alone with her, Strether comes to have "the sense that she was—there, before him, close to him, in vivid imperative form—one of the rare women he had so often heard of, read of, thought of, but never met . . ." (178), and she is consistently the culminating mark of Strether's most sublime experiences of Frenchness. When he first enters her house, he finds it to encapsulate "the ancient Paris that he was always looking for—sometimes intensely felt, sometimes more acutely missed" (171), and she is his indispensable companion at one of his most satisfyingly picturesque experiences—an authentic French meal at a charming restaurant by the Seine, where Strether finds "reasons enough" in "the mere way Madame de Vionnet, opposite him over their intensely white table-linen, their *omelette aux tomates*, their bottle of straw-coloured Chablis, thanked him for everything" (213). Indeed, a few pages later Strether will tell Marie that that very lunch has been the culmination of his European excursion, which must now come to a close:

> I've had my rest, my amusement, and refreshment; I've had, as we say at Woollett, a lovely time. Nothing in it has been more lovely than this happy meeting with you—in these fantastic conditions to which you've so delightfully consented. I've a sense of success. It's what I wanted. (218)

The dash here is crucial—the loveliness is not only Marie in herself, but the concatenation of her and the proper "conditions."[1] Strether has succeeded, and gotten what he wanted. But his success in achieving this experience is not obtained without effort, and the efforts are clearly shown to us by James in Strether's exertions to construct the Madame de Vionnet he so desires—his active complicity in his own obfuscation needs to be stressed.

For example, Hana Wirth-Nesher has also noted the mixed background of Marie, and argues that this information plays a role in Strether's increasing demystification of both Marie and France, suggesting, "The touristic tendency to totalize, to see her as a metaphor for France itself, is thwarted when he learns that she is of mixed background, both French and English" (249). However, this thesis is not borne out by the narrative. On the contrary, when Strether first encounters her, before having learned her life story and thus with no reason to think she is anything *but* French, he is almost disappointed at how familiar she seems, wondering if there was anything about her that "would have made it impossible he should meet her at Woollett?" (149), remarking on her "common humanity" with the Woollett types, and concluding, "it would possibly have been more thrilling for him that she should have shown as more vividly alien" (150). Yet *between* this meeting and the next, and *after* learning of her mixed parentage and cosmopolitan personal history, Strether's view of her wholly changes:

> At bottom of it all for him was the sense of her *rare unlikeness to the women he had known*. This sense had grown, since the day before, the more he recalled her, and had been above all singularly fed by his talk with Chad in the morning. Everything in fine made her immeasurably new, and nothing so new as the old house and the old objects (173, my italics).

It is Strether's sense of Marie as responsible for Chad's new continental refinement, along with her old objects and the "ancient Paris" seemingly oozing out of her house, that make her now "new," rather than any perception of her, or exchange with her, whatsoever. Strether has created his own "thrill."

Strether's willful reification of Marie—one which the reader is likely to share—is but one of many projected onto a "Europe," which, as Strether fully recognizes, exists only as it is "performed."[2] "It was indeed as if they were arranged, gathered for a performance, the performance of 'Europe'" (279), he muses, on the arrival of fresh tourists he must entertain. Yet despite this caveat, no audience could be more enthusiastic than Strether for the various "performances" given him by Marie, Chad, or even the artist Gloriani, and the course of the novel mercilessly demonstrates to Strether just what these performances have been covering over. On the most basic level of "Jamesian irony," then, the function of Madame de Vionnet's mixed background is obvious: to remind us to what extent her mythic "Frenchness" is a construct and not "real." In this way it is an obvious parallel to Strether's remarkable foray into the countryside in search of an actual landscape that might resemble the Lambinet painting he remembers from years before, showing that for Strether a pre-constructed *representation* of France is its ultimate reality, the standard against which the authenticity of the country itself will be measured. The ironic reversal could not be more neat: rather than judge a realist painting by its likeness to what it represents, the France in which Strether finds himself is only "real" to the extent that it corresponds to its painting. The Lambinet and Marie are the most powerful of Strether's constructs and for this reason it is hardly coincidental that James has Strether discreetly link the Lambinet-like landscape and Marie's abode as highpoints of his European experience, his experience of the "European." The "conditions" he finds in the Lambinetesque countryside, late in the book, are "*the thing*, as he would have called it, even to a greater degree than Madame de Vionnet's old high salon where the ghost of the Empire walked" (386, original italics). Of course, Strether's idyll in the country will be interrupted by that of Chad and Marie, whose appearance inside the picture or onto what he elsewhere calls the "stage" reveals to him what he had so obstinately refused to see: the sexual nature of their relation. Strether's ironic progress on his path to knowledge is, on this level, complete: just when he is basking most blissfully in his illusions, he is brutally confronted with the reality of Chad, and of Marie. Strether, in this reading, would be seen as finally moving beyond his fond, naive, nostalgic constructions, to confront things quite simply as they are. Indeed, the novel could be seen to end on such a note, with Strether's final statement to Maria, which indicates nothing at all, except a certain enigmatic but ineluctable sense of grounding: "Then there we are!" (438).

However, this reading, as enticing as it is and certainly correct as far as it goes, does not go far enough and indeed, positions us for an ironic comeuppance not unlike Strether's own. First of all, the novel does not leave intact the opposition I have been invoking between construct or representation on the one hand, and "reality" on the other, for if Marie is not "really" French, the landscape into whose frame Strether enters really does perfectly resemble the Lambinet. The pathos of the Lambinet episode is not that a "painting" obscures "reality," but rather that Strether's desire to be in the place the painting represents is due to the painting itself and the cultural economy surrounding its production—its "subject matter" seems increasingly contingent, an appropriated pretext. It is *Boston* that Strether wants to recover outside of Paris, the painting he so wrenchingly did *not* purchase that he wants now to possess by roaming a landscape that refers to it.[3] The painting and the countryside correspond, but for Strether the latter has become the representation of the former, rather than the opposite. Strether's desire for Paris, for Europe, for the raw visual material the Lambinet has built itself out of, is an American desire, a New England desire—it is, like the unmentionable, vulgar product that has enriched the Newsome family, made in Woollett. It is when Strether feels most authentically in France that he is most "American." The France of *The Ambassadors* is an American scene.[4]

Indeed, *The Ambassadors* is very largely the story of Strether's poignant desire to remain *inside* the frame of his desire for Europe, (a desire no less framed than Waymarsh's symmetrical antipathy to "Europe") even as the novel simultaneously refuses to imagine an "unframed" encounter with the continent. To be sure, there is a great deal of variance in the qualities and contours of the mystifications, simplifications, and projections inflicted by Waymarsh, Strether, Jim, and Sarah Pocock, for example, but the book does not propose that Europe could somehow be experienced by these characters other than through the framework of American cultural production; it offers no perspective from which an "unbiased" revelation of a "true" French essence could be revealed. As the title reminds us, the novel's characters are mediators, involved in nothing other than cross-cultural translation. This title thus insists on difference as being *productive* of meaning, not simply a distorting lens, and I would like to suggest that what the novel is most set on dramatizing is not cross-cultural misrecognition. Rather, it would seem that cultural difference implies, to use Jamesian terms, a "point of view" or a "position," and it is only through specific viewpoints and positionings, *through* the frame, that the "differences" can assume their status.[5] Strether deludes himself less because he arrives armed with a set of assumptions, received ideas, and stereotypes which are faulty, than because the defamiliarized space of social, cultural, and linguistic practice on the continent permits his own affect to reinvest the entire domain of experience—his own and that of others. Strether makes this plain enough when he claims Chad and Marie to be the youth he never had, his trip to Europe the great indulgence compensating a lifetime of renunciation. And for the payoff to be valid, Chad and Marie must be virtuous and true, which they are not, and Europe must be, well, Europe. These two affective constructions are of course intimately linked. Regarding the former, Strether suffers two major disappointments: first, that he has been deceived regarding the nature of the lovers' "virtuous attachment," but second, and far worse, that the love Strether feels Marie and all she represents deserves, is not one Chad seems to share. Again, where Strether has most fooled himself is not in his assumptions regarding "European" ways, but in his understanding of Chad's desire, which he had constructed on the model of his own. However, in rejecting Marie de

Vionnet for Woollett and the advertising department of the family business, Chad rejects the entire construct of French refinement which Strether had imagined. Indeed, Chad's great social success in Paris suggests all along that a conflict between American vulgarity and refined French society is only apparent and even more, that Chad's "improvement" as evidenced by his newfound European social graces is entirely consonant with, if not a form of, the unspeakably vulgar "advertising" Chad will be called on to manage.[6] Chad, along with Marie and their circle of friends, have "sold" Strether their "Paris" with total success, have created for Strether a desire from which Chad himself stands aloof. They have also, perhaps, sold him a "Paris" as fantasmatic as the "virtue" Strether believes obtains between the couple. In light of these problems, it seems fair to suggest that the book's interest in the "international theme" consists less of epistemological questions of cross-cultural comprehension, than of affective ones concerning the role of radical difference in the construction of love objects: it is less a question of *how* Strether the New Englander can come to "understand" Europe, than of why he wants there to be "Europe" at all. What is the foreign, what is experience, what is an impression, that their conjugation can reward him so fully for a dull life of petty affairs? This is the question that haunts *The Ambassadors*, and in order to address it is indispensable also to investigate the "foreign" in its dialectic with that to which it must inevitably be opposed: the proximate, native, and familiar. This concern, then, leads us back not only to Marie de Vionnet, but also to her two counterparts: Maria Gostrey, and Mrs. Newsome.

The novel's emphasis on the violence of Strether's affective investment in both Marie and some phantom idea of Frenchness, should lead us to question one implication of an overly straightforward "ironic" reading: that if Marie de Vionnet, with her English mother, is not "really" French, someone else, more thoroughly bred, could be—that the sort of unified cultural authenticity Strether longs to encounter might in fact really exist, in other women, in other haunts. That the novel never presents some sort of "authentic" personage to counterbalance what would then figure as Marie's "charade" speaks against this thesis, as does the fact that to hold on to such a lure is to extend Strether's own perverse desire for the gratification of authenticity, but still, the terms in which Marie's cultural groundlessness are first presented by Maria Gostrey deserve the closest scrutiny, both for the language they employ, and for their insistence on the privileged link between language and cultural appurtenance itself. The propriety of speech, the idea of a speech which is proper, will be seen as crucial not only in establishing someone's "Frenchness," for example, but in being anything at all, and the question of a natural, native language, of a mother tongue, will be linked to the trope of the mother herself as mark of natural belonging, of unconstructed appurtenance. As is so often the case in James, it is the mother and the tongue which make possible the construct of any possible "home" against which a foreign, an other, a difference can be posited. And indeed the introduction of Marie de Vionnet opens with the question of her speech, for it is her multilingualism, her lack of a privileged mother tongue, that for Maria most marks her cultural waywardness, in terms which are anything but uncertain: at school in Geneva, Maria remembers, Marie was

> as polyglot as a little Jewess (which she wasn't, oh no!) and chattering French, English, German, Italian, anything one would, in a way that made a clean sweep, if not of prizes and parchments, at least of every 'part,' whether memorised or improvised, in the curtained costumed school repertory, and in especial of all mysteries of race and vagueness of reference, all swagger about 'home,' among their variegated mates. (162)

The young Marie is thus already an ersatz Jewess (an ersatz of the ersatz, as it were), fully possessing the worrying cosmopolitan propensity for playing roles, hiding one's origins, and shifting identities; this is hardly the "pure product" one might take her for.[7] And as Maria makes very clear, this cosmopolitanism goes well beyond the binary vagaries bequeathed by her Franco-English parentage. The passage continues:

> It would doubtless be difficult today, as between French and English, to name her and place her; she would certainly show, on knowledge, Miss Gostrey felt, as one of those convenient types who don't keep you explaining—minds with doors as numerous as the many-tongued cluster of confessionals at Saint Peter's. You might confess to her with confidence in Roumelian, and even Roumelian sins. Therefore—! But Strether's narrator covered her implication with a laugh; a laugh by which his betrayal of a sense of the lurid in the picture was also perhaps sufficiently protected. He had a moment of wondering, while his friend went on, what sins might be especially Roumelian. (162)

The novel will not expound on either "Roumelian" sins or what Maria's stifled "implication" might be, but the sense of a polyglot "lurid" as developed by the somewhat bizarre analogy of the confessionals of Saint Peter's cathedral deserves some attention. In this comparison, certainly some of the discomfort is created by the depiction of Marie as leaving too many doors open, as it were, of not sufficiently sealing and policing boundaries. She is, by implication, too open to too many comers, but note that the mark of this openness is precisely her multilingual proficiency. It is in fact the barriers of the foreign, of difference, which she does not feel compelled to respect; Marie's mind indulges a sort of cross-cultural miscegenation which, as Maria points out, can at times be quite "convenient." Indeed, it is this over-obliging "convenience" which links her to the Catholic church, so often troped in Protestant tradition as the seductress who under guise of compassion and understanding opens her arms to all and sundry in a never to be escaped embrace. Hawthorne, in *The Marble Faun*, for example, speaks ominously of the "infinite convenience . . . of the Catholic religion" (275) in a passage which, as we shall see, seems to lurk behind this description of Marie. Earlier in *The Ambassadors*, we find the Catholic church, through a metaphorical detour, figured precisely as the insinuating grasper to be denied, as Waymarsh's resistance to all things European is explained:

> The Catholic Church for Waymarsh—that was to say the enemy, the monster of bulging eyes and far-reaching quivering groping tentacles—was exactly society, exactly the multiplication of shibboleths, exactly the discrimination of types and tones, exactly the wicked old Rows of Chester, rank with feudalism; exactly in short Europe. (28)

It is worth noting that in this lengthy, extended metaphor the "Jesuit in petticoats" seducing him towards Europe as others have been seduced by priests to Catholicism is none other than Maria Gostrey. Meanwhile, we see in Marie a monstrous combination of the rootless, essenceless Jewess, and the many-tentacled, multi-faceted Romanist whore. That said, the comparison is elaborate even by the standards of *The Ambassadors*, with the insistence on "Roumelian" making it all the more mystifying. But additional context can help illuminate the passage, however, for beyond its role in explaining Marie's relationship to language, it is also almost certainly a veiled allusion to the novel which represents James' greatest precursor among American "European" novels: Hawthorne's *The Marble Faun*. In one of that novel's climactic scenes, the young New England puritan painter Hilda, alone in Rome with her conscience burdened by a sin not her own, finds herself irresistibly succumbing to the "convenience" of the Catholic rite of confession as she wanders through Saint Peter's:

> She went from one to another of the confessionals, and, looking at each, perceived that they were inscribed with gilt letters; on one, PRO ITALICA LINGUA; on another, PRO FLANDRICA LINGUA; on a third, PRO POLONICA LINGUA; on a fourth, PRO ILLYRICA LINGUA; on a fifth, PRO HISPANICA LINGUA. In this vast and hospitable Cathedral, worthy to be the religious heart of the whole world, there was room for all nations; there was access to the Divine Grace for every Christian soul; there was an ear for what the overburthened heart might have to murmur, speak in what native tongue it would.
>
> When Hilda had almost completed the circuit of the transept, she came to a confessional, (the central part was closed, but a mystic rod protruded from it, indicating the presence of a priest within,) on which was inscribed, PRO ANGLICA LINGUA.
>
> It was the word in season! If she had heard her mother's voice from within the tabernacle, calling her, in her own mother-tongue, to come and lay her poor head in her lap, and sob out all her troubles, Hilda could not have responded with a more inevitable obedience. (276–7)

There is no doubt that James knew this passage well—in fact, in his famous study *Hawthorne* of 1879, he lists this scene as one of the highpoints of Hawthorne's novel.[8] Furthermore, the reference in the *Marble Faun* to the "Illyrica Lingua" might help explain James' odd discussion of "Roumelian," for if "Illyrian" is an obsolete term for Serbo-Croatian while Roumelian indicates dialects of Greek spoken in the Southern Balkans, it is easy to imagine that, given the rarity of the languages involved and their relative geographical proximity, James either remembered wrongly, or chose to package his allusion in a slight displacement. In either event, the passage in *The Marble Faun* is one of the most important in the novel, and clearly relevant to James' concerns in *The Ambassadors*. Obviously, I cannot embark on a detailed analysis of Hawthorne's novel here, but suffice to say that puritan Hilda's relationship with Catholicism is couched entirely in the terms of a seduction, one which culminates, in fact, with an actual abduction. However it is a seduction, as the passage above indicates, effected by the *maternal* agency. Prior to this scene, Hilda has hovered close to Catholic idolatry precisely in her reverence of a Roman shrine to the Virgin, and here, the call of the mother is too strong to resist. But what must be noted is that for the call of the mother to finally exert so strong a pressure, it must also be in the *mother tongue*. For Hawthorne, it is the mother tongue which allows the Mother to speak, while the Mother herself speaks nothing but the pure concentration of the proximate and the proper, so sorely wanting to the wandering expatriate.

These questions are extremely fraught for Hawthorne, for if not surprisingly he firmly opposes Catholicism in *The Marble Faun*, he shows himself quite drawn to certain elements of it. For example, Hawthorne expresses a great deal of sympathy for the cult of the Virgin, as long as it is rationalized into a devotion to the concept of maternity in general—a concept which should be, according to Hawthorne, the normative one for all women, and which remains one the Protestant tradition seems not sufficiently to honor. In *The Marble Faun*, Hilda's radically Protestant chastity, if clearly a virtue, is also a risk, for it necessarily implies the rejection of a relationship with a man as the basis of her life. In the novel, Hilda must be gradually softened into accepting the love of the sculptor Kenyon, and her somewhat idolatrous interest in the Mother of God is a crucial element in this "evolution." As such a conceptualization implies, for Hawthorne it is essential that women accept their secondary, dependent status, and nowhere is this more true than the arts. Indeed, Hilda's feminine modesty is stressed early on precisely through Hawthorne's description of her relationship to her artistic life. Rather than produce daringly original, violent works, like her counterpart, the dark-haired, passionate, mysterious, possibly Jewish Miriam, Hilda chooses to be no more than a "copyist" who, in Hawthorne's words, "sacrifices" herself to reproduce the genius of the Old Masters. The implication could not be more clear: Hilda, as all women should, puts the singularity of great men before her own, and sees her own task as one of "reproduction," in every sense. In case one hasn't gotten the point, Hawthorne contrasts Hilda's decision to remain the "handmaid of Raphael" with a misguided desire to create works the world would call "original," equating this desire disparagingly with "so many feminine achievements in literature!" (49). That the male sculptor Kenyon is never expected to be anything but original shows how much more all this has to do with gender than with aesthetics for Hawthorne, but already the system sketched out above leads to contradictions of which Hawthorne is well aware: the position of submissive devotion and reproduction he prescribes to women is dangerously close, already, to the Catholic idolatry to which Hilda finally succumbs. To a disturbing degree, for Hawthorne to be a proper woman is to be a Catholic, and the novel is partly devoted to working this implication through. Likewise, though Hawthorne despises the stereotypically displayed machinations of the Romanist priests, he shows a clear fondness for the rite of confession as a necessary form of release clearly lacking in puritan New England, while still fearing it as a likely breach in feminine modesty, one to be put in parallel with the constant anxiety the novel evinces towards nude sculpture.[9] It is no doubt partly for this reason that if Hawthorne acknowledges the positive effects of confession for his young virgin, it is on the condition that it be confession to a *mother*, in the *mother tongue*, that is, confession to the origin and the same, confession to an "other" who is assimilated as closely as possible to one's "self." A Protestant form of confession indeed, and a restoration, in foreign lands, of oneself to oneself.

Within this complex network of concerns, we must not lose sight of how Hawthorne pressures the trope of the "mother tongue" in two directions: it is not only that "maternity" is used as a metaphor to guarantee the natural propriety of the native language, but more importantly the reverse: it is one's relation to one's native tongue that provides the template for the maternal relation—it is nothing but the action of the "native tongue" on Hilda that *transforms* the Priest in his confessional into her mother's lap. The phantom immediacy of the native language *creates* the maternal as such, the "mother" relying on an effect which is of itself linguistic. The question we need to ask about *The Ambassadors* is to what extent it too is governed by the matrix of the mother-system, the mother-system *as* matrix, as seen in *The Marble Faun*, with all its implications for an imago of nativeness, indeed of nativity, represented by country, mother, and above all, by native tongue. To what extent is the allusion to *The Marble Faun* an allusion to Hawthorne's construct of linguistic and maternal intimacy, concepts against which Strether's entire journey is delineated? And finally, to what extent is Hawthorne's model of maternal seduction operative in James' work, which pits two mothers against each other in a battle for a prodigal son, and casts Strether's guide into Europe, Maria Gostrey, the "Jesuit in petticoats," in explicitly maternal terms? For if the consummately seductive Marie de Vionnet in no way calls with the immediacy of the mother tongue, as James is at pains to remind us neither does she speak solely with the voice of the exoticized foreign. In fact, despite Strether's over investment in Marie's "Frenchness," it is oddly enough the qualities of her spoken English which represent for him some of her most impressive charms. One of his very first observations concerning her touches on this:

> . . . she had spoken to him, very simply and gently, in an English clearly of the easiest to her, yet unlike any other he had ever heard. It wasn't as if she tried; nothing, he could see after they had been a few minutes together, was as if she tried; but her speech, charming correct and odd, was like a precaution against her passing for a Pole. (147)

On one hand, one must recognize that the contradiction between Strether's mystification of Marie's Frenchness and his liking of her "odd" English is only one of appearance, as the odd English is nothing but an index of her foreignness after all, a reminder of her difference: what makes the English "charming" is the foreign interference it displays. This is certainly true, but at the same time, the very concept of "interference" presents an impediment to the tropes of the mother and the mother tongue as marks of proximity—tropes which the novel is already stressing. It is perhaps for this reason that Maria must linguistically demarcate Marie's maternity: "You must remember that of her—that as a mother she's French . . ." (163). But this exacerbates rather than solves the problem—if the "mother" is the mark of authenticity and wholeness, to be one thing as "mother" and something else otherwise means not to be a "mother" at all. Maria's statement seems to imply that when Marie *functions* as mother it will be as a mark of "Frenchness," that "Frenchness" is the identity her maternity will strive to guarantee, but that this "Frenchness" is one her maternal action produces, and *not*, as in Hawthorne, the grounding itself of her very maternity. Staying with Hawthorne, we might say that when she calls with the tongue of the mother, it will be in French, despite the fact that her "Frenchness" derives from her *father*, her own mother being English. But the obverse of this implication is perhaps more crucial: not whether as "mother" Marie is French, but whether French, with regard to Marie, can be the dwelling of the maternal space. For if Maria succeeds in locating the tongue that speaks her maternity (French), the parable of Saint Peter's seems to indicate that for Marie there is no tongue to speak maternity as such, that maternal seduction, the seduction of the Hawthornian maternal, is denied her. Thus, the question of interference takes on ever increasing importance with regard to Marie, and even enters the language which surrounds her.

For example, in emphasizing the "oddities and disparities" of the people on the English side of Marie's family, Maria wonders "what they really quite rhymed to" (161), while later, discussing how Marie managed after her separation with her husband, Maria tells us, "She had settled in Paris, brought up her daughter, steered her boat" (163). Maria here uses colloquial expressions, but not English ones, as these phrases are quite simply literal transpositions of very common French constructions: "ne rimer à rien" means to make no sense, or to be out of place, and though the expression does not exist in the affirmative it can be used in the interrogative, while "mener sa barque" means to manage one's affairs effectively, sometimes used with a slightly pejorative hint of excessive guile or ambition. The characteristically defamiliarized English of the late James, then, is here rendered such precisely through the pressure of a foreign code, in the midst of a discussion of the homeland, the family, the mother, the native tongue: the most highly charged figures of the proximate, all of which are disturbed or displaced in Marie's case. We saw in the previous chapter James' interest in the commonplace, as evidenced in the exchange between Henrietta and Ralph. Of course, commonplace and proverbial expressions provide one of the most famous practical dilemmas for the translator: either one replaces them with reasonably equivalent alternatives, which means the figural specificity of the original is lost—hardly acceptable when the text pressures this specificity in some way—or one translates them "literally," which makes them resonate in the translated text as deliberate figures and not as conventional, pre-prepared available expressions. James, then, violently opens his text here to the problems of translation, by ripping the "commonplace" out of the commonality to which it could bind and refer. This serves to highlight a notion of meaning as utterly dependent on context, history and praxis: two expressions which have both the same literal *and* the same figural meaning in both English and French, nevertheless occupy an entirely different place and function according to the language they are found in. Marie becomes the center for meditation on the productive violence of translation.

Thus, *The Ambassadors* rewrites many of Hawthorne's concerns regarding the maternal and the mother tongue, but within a space of generalized interference. The English which Maria uses to discuss Marie, tinged with Gallicism, suggests on several levels that Marie's "Frenchness" in general is a product of interference, and this leads to an important observation: that Marie's "Frenchness" is most performed and most intensely felt through its *translation*, through its transposition into English, a transposition which functions exactly as the "frame" of the Lambinet in relation to the landscape. Marie's

Frenchness most charms Strether as a translation effect, an effect which, even if it asserts Marie's maternal grounding as "French", destroys the sanctity of language as template for the maternal. In this way, interference interferes with the mother effect itself. Moreover, this interference allows us to see how differently maternal seduction is structured in James than in Hawthorne; rather than relying on the proximate and the repetition of the same, it works precisely through displacement, incomprehension, and intrigue—the enigma at the heart of Laplanche's seduction theory.

Thus one of the novel's most subtle ironies is that when Marie is most concerned with maintaining a façade, with giving a "performance" (394) and selling an appearance, she shifts into French, for this is the language she uses as she desperately tries to explain away the tryst with Chad that Strether, through the merest accident, has discovered. Yet her linguistic shift, rather than serve as a mark of redeeming authenticity, only heightens Strether's sense of her artificiality and insincerity. This is due in part to the fact that Strether's limitations with the French language give Marie a clear advantage in the steering of the conversational boat, of course, but more than that, the French language now seems to rob Marie of her individuality, an individuality which, as we have seen, is also largely predicated on her Frenchness:

> but the present result [of her speaking French] was odd, fairly veiling her identity, shifting her back into a mere voluble class or race to the intense audibility of which he was by this time inured. When she spoke the charming slightly strange English he best knew her by he seemed to feel her as a creature, among all the millions, with a language quite to herself, the real monopoly of a special shade of speech, beautifully easy for her, yet of a colour and a cadence that were both inimitable and matters of accident. (392)

Again, it is a defamiliarized, "strange" English which lends Marie her charm, and indeed, the charm of her Frenchness is as a pressure upon or interference with the assumed continuities of the "Woollett" cultural space into which she intrudes, by which she is framed. When she simply speaks French, the charm is gone—no longer a figure *for* Frenchness, she becomes simply a symptom of it, and this is of course the flipside of the reification of cultural authenticity which Strether has indulged throughout, and also the familiar reflex of the "cosmopolite" as explained in "Occasional Paris": Marie, no longer *singular* as a glorious incarnation of age-old cultural practice, has her entire being reduced to the level of the typical cultural product. Thus, it is when Marie seeks refuge in the proximity of a mother tongue, of a language less "strange" and tinged by "accident" than her English, that she is swallowed by an authenticity and cultural continuity that render her sadly interchangeable and impersonal. She is undone by her authenticity, and it is at her most "authentic" that she seems most compromised by sham and deception; not because her "Frenchness" here is just an act, but oddly enough, because it is not. Marie's collapse into the mother tongue forms the pendant to Hilda's maternal confession, but turned inside out, as language conceals and proximity flattens.[10] And in this respect, the long critical tradition which reads Marie *not* as a mystified figure of authentic Frenchness but rather as multiplicity and variety itself, be it figured as Shakespeare's Cleopatra, the Whore of Babylon, or both, is also right.[11] This is the dilemma of Strether's desire: just as Marie *must be* French, even "Frenchness" itself, she also *must not be*, so as not to founder into the eminently supplemental position of symptom and sign. For her value as fetish to be maintained, she must not only signify, but also fail to do so, which means her "authenticity" adheres also in its failure. The entire network, in fact, is announced before Marie de Vionnet is even presented to the reader or Strether. The latter, motivated by the sound of the family name, asks Chad if the Vionnets are French: " 'Yes. That is no!' had been Chad's reply" (136)—a reply which, if never explained, also explains much.

In any event, if *The Ambassadors* is a novel which pits three mothers against each other, it is also a novel which refuses the call of the mother in the mother tongue, so crucial to *The Marble Faun*. In fact, the novel can be read largely as the operations of the mother effect within the space of its own desanctification. Here maternal seduction functions not as the call of the proximate, but as the call of difference, which becomes crucially, as we see in the case of Marie, self-difference, and a self-difference which is figured as linguistic. Jamesian erotics imply not the immediacy of the mother tongue but translation in its broadest sense, a mother tongue that must always be displaced, in transit, and whose proximate sounding marks erotic collapse. One element of the Jamesian uncanny in this work is to cast maternal seduction as an exercise in exoticism and exogamy; in its distribution of maternal imagoes, *The Ambassadors* is less a performance of the fantasy of incest, than an exploration of the impossibility of what this fantasy could be said to promise: a negation of the alterity of the sexual relation, an erotic bounding of the familiar. And the question of the familiarity, the "nativity" of language is entirely bound up with this. Certainly, despite what elsewhere in James resembles calls for linguistic purity, the example of Marie shows that he is entirely capable of entertaining the idea of speech reaching charm and distinction through its *lack* of purity, through the elements of strangeness introduced by the pressure of the foreign. I use the word "distinction" advisedly, as in "The Question of Our Speech" it is "differentiation" and "discrimination" which, along with the former term, become the key concepts of good speaking; the favored linguistic practice involves above all the maintaining of differences, and the most exquisite sensitivity to them in all the slightness of their nuance.

One place *The Ambassadors* registers such a concern is by naming two structurally parallel characters Maria and Marie, and thereby allowing them to be distinguished on the most literal level only by the difference of a single a vowel, a difference which also marks a distinction between two different languages. From this perspective, Marie is quite literally the "French" mother, the maternal archetype cast in French, but Maria also is made to carry off a similar role in the "costumed repertory" that James establishes here. For Maria no less than Marie is consistently cast in maternal terms, and she herself tellingly characterizes her relationship to Strether, in her role as his initiator into "Europe" and its ways, in this guise.[12] And as Europe is nothing but an avatar of seduction, our "Jesuit in petticoats" very much needs to be read as a figure of maternal seduction herself, a role of course also played by her onomastic homologue, as Marie is entirely the stereotypical "older woman" (and empirical mother) prying Chad away from his rightful filial devotion to the will of Mrs Newsome.[13] *The Ambassadors* is very much the battle of two mothers over Chad, both of them using Strether to obtain their ends, while Chad's behavior can seem the consummate compromise formation: by leaving his mother for a mother, he nevertheless remains utterly faithful to the maternal bond, and his attachment to Marie remains in this light a form of fidelity to Mrs Newsome. If the individual in question has been provisionally replaced, the structure of the relationship and its predication on debt have not been fundamentally altered, and Chad can return relatively easily to Woollett because in this sense he never really left his mother country. Just as the names "Maria" and "Marie" hover dangerously close to each other, begging the reader to attempt to delineate their difference and perhaps their differing relationship to the archetypal Mary they both invoke, so the name "Chad" is but a scarlet "H" removed from a word that seems possible to apply to him: "cad," which Webster's defines as "a person without gentlemanly instincts: one that deliberately and callously violates the code of decent respectable behavior esp. in relations with women." The word, in its very appropriateness, seems all the more conspicuous by its absence during Strether's final confrontation with Chad: "You'll be a brute, you know—you'll be guilty of the last infamy—if you ever forsake her" (425), and soon after, "You'd not only be, as I say, a brute; you'd be . . . a criminal of the deepest dye" (427). That "her" now refers to Marie, while the words themselves are ones Strether could very easily have used with reference to Mrs Newsome had he fulfilled his mission correctly, points not only to an ironic reversal, but also to an essential interchangeability of the two women and a structural homology between the two situations. Whatever else, Chad is an extremely adept *emotional* businessman, playing two debts off against each other so as to cancel them both.

The novel thus places Marie in a double role, as she at once doubles and opposes both Mrs Newsome *and* Maria Gostrey, in this book which plays at distributing three mothers and two sons among each other. If worries concerning Chad's seduction turn out to be misplaced, those concerning Strether are not: he will succumb to both Maria and Marie, as well as to Chad, albeit in a sublimated form of wishful identification. Certainly, unlike Chad, Strether is eager to honor all his emotional debts rather than refinance them, and this desire seems largely behind his insistence that he must "gain nothing" from the entire adventure.[14] He is, as he is called, "*impayable*"—a word which translates into "priceless," but which literally means "unpayable," and Strether doesn't waver in his devotion to loss, famously refusing the rather enticing offer of Maria's affection, extended to him in the book's final pages, and opting for return to a dreary Woollett, now bereft of the equivocal blandishments of Mrs Newsome. But what Strether most loses, in the catastrophe in the countryside where the masks fail, is two related illusions. The first is that authenticity—of culture, of language, of intention—could in some way be the opposite of a mask, an essence against which the artificiality of performance and lie could be opposed. Rather, it is when Marie is most "authentic" that she most betrays herself, in every sense. Second, and even more important, he loses the ability to let this phantom authenticity be the grounding of his desire. This is why, in his final interview with Marie, following the farce in the country the day before, these categories no longer seem to matter. Noting that Marie is on the occasion "natural and simple" with him, he continues this way: "She had never, with him, been more so; or if it was the perfection of art it would never—and that came to the same thing—be proved against her" (402). If the distinction between the "perfection of art" and "nature and simplicity" is no longer determinant, then all the categories used to understand the relationship between Chad and Marie are rendered inoperative.[15] But more to the point, so are the ones that validate the authenticity of experience and impression which through so much of the book form Strether's main compensation. It is Marie's slide into the position of matrix of Frenchness which spoils Strether's taste for the authentic, for any construction of a home. Maternal seduction operates through the *enigma* of the mother's voice as it is sounded, through the bewildering and unsettling effect of what Cornelius Crowley, in his powerful discussion of *The American Scene*, has dubbed "xenophony."[16] That is, the power of seduction derives not only from the difference of the foreign, as we have seen, but from the self-difference and division figured by the foreign *accent*, the displacement from any proximate call, an ultimate groundlessness that endlessly defers any possible return: " 'Where *is* your 'home' moreover now—what has become of it?'" (406), Marie asks Strether during their final interview. This foreshadows Maria's ultimate question to Strether in the book's last pages, as she hopes to make him stay with her: "To what do you go home?" (437).

In response to Marie, Strether's most fitting home is probably with Maria, in an environment built on what he dubs "selection," a selection itself based on "beauty and knowledge" (438) creating an unmistakably maternal sense of enclosure: "it built him softly round, it roofed him warmly over" (438). But Strether refuses the offer, choosing to return to what Maria, answering her own question, calls "a great difference" (437). It is this "difference" that the novel in the end frames against the depths of the feminine "abyss" of the maternal, certainly, but less in emancipatory jubilation than as the mark of Strether's failure—a failure written into the imperative to elaborate erotic need within a dialectic of homecoming, arrival, or return, along with the negations they dialectically program. Strether will not be allowed to follow the program of restoration which Hawthorne sketches for his Hilda: a program which also dialectically asks her to sacrifice the bodily integrity represented by virginity to Kenyon, in order to achieve *in* her body the maternal status that in her virginity she can do more than cleave to, in displaced, perhaps idolatrous form.[17] This model of maternity becomes impossible even as a *negative* pole that Strether would then reject in some ironic form of "masculine affirmation," consisting of a wholly aggressive maintenance of his famous "passivity." Indeed, the question is not that of deciding whether Strether "frees himself" from successive Circes,[18] or is rather too "emasculated" to accept Maria's proposal. The question is elsewhere, for it is now *Strether's* chastity, not that obtaining between Chad and Marie, which in a notable narrative displacement governs the book's final drama; a chastity which, following what Julie Rivkin has called the "logic of delegation," compensates for the one so sorely lacking between Strether's two chosen paramours. This chastity supplements the novel's dictates of "purity"—dictates policed less by the strictures of Woollett and Milrose, in the end, than by exoticist constructs of authenticity. What Strether refuses is the *consummation* of his "experience," instead settling into a subjective erotics which alights on the moment of prothalamion, a moment which displaces the entire problematics of the encounter, around which so much of *The Ambassadors* revolves. Much like John Marcher in *The Beast in the Jungle*, Strether prefers to postpone, even when—especially when—there is nothing left to wait for. This is his answer to his own famous imperative to "live" before it is too late: when else has life ever really lived?

However, such a position in no way implies that a chastity could also be linguistic, nor that a linguistic grounding could compensate for the mother's own breach—the intrusion of otherness which has made the "son" possible. James' ambassadorial transpositions return to the xenophonic mother, and her unsoundable desire. In contrast to what Hawthorne presents as his ostensible plot, for James it is precisely this remainder within the maternal which takes the place of the object of desire, and which renders translation and all the metasemiotic discussion with which the late James abounds other than a contingent condition of the foreign. This makes the foreign indispensable, while erasing it as such and revealing the extent to which the homelessness of James' "cosmopolite" is also an erotic positioning. The colliding of interlinguistic breaches is also grounding for the poetics of Ezra Pound, for whom to a large extent the translator's position becomes the ultimate model of lyric subjectivity, as we shall see in Chapter 4. In the next chapter, however, we shall investigate how such a poetics parallels and partially evolves from Pound's sense of James' position, or positionlessness, as grounding for that of the American writer, in relation both to Europe and England, but also to his or her own Americanness.

CHAPTER 3

EZRA POUND'S AMERICAN SCENES: HENRY JAMES AND THE LABOUR OF TRANSLATION

"Twenty-five years ago 'one' came to England to escape Ersatz;" Ezra Pound explained in 1933, precisely twenty-five years after having moved to England himself. He continued as follows: "that is to say, whenever a British half-wit expressed an opinion, some American quarter-wit rehashed it in one of the 'respectable' American organs" (*Selected Prose*, 227). The irony, if not particularly subtle, still bears examination. If America, in accordance with the oldest of new-world, expatriate tropes, lags behind England in terms of culture, still one goes to the latter not to shun imitation and obtain the authentic cultural *value*, but rather to encounter the authentic cultural idiocy. One goes to England not for the cure, but rather to treat the heart of the disease instead of a far-flung symptom. Indeed, the word "organs" above needs to be read in all its corporeal and corporatist connotations, as Pound's very next sentence is, "Disease is more contagious than health" (227). Still, Pound's equating of England with the thing itself, the original and authentic rather than the derivation, imitation, and repetition, is unequivocal. No less so is the recourse to a foreign language for a word that expresses the secondary. As is so often the case for Pound, terminological precision demands a term which, neologism or foreign loan word, implies nothing so much as catachresis.[1] "Ersatz" is nothing but the ersatz of a missing English word, invoked in a discussion of English authenticity. Language, authenticity, the foreign, and the question of origins are all neatly woven together here.

But ironic caveats aside, for Pound no less than James the "real thing" was to be sought elsewhere and abroad by the young American. And James becomes crucially strategic in Pound's attempt to work through ambivalences and anxieties the two writers shared: those that inevitably pertain to the locating of authenticity in a space to be thought of as foreign, with its implication that as "Ersatz" European, one's own relationship to this authenticity would be inevitably inauthentic itself, while at the same time one's "aboriginal" roots would be necessarily untethered. Pound's term for the exchanges and risks such a schema demands, as we shall see, is often translation—a term not central to the Jamesian lexicon. How Pound ropes James into a larger trope of translation, and the implications of such a trope for Pound's practice of translation as habitually understood, is what concerns me here. To explore such a question, we must first examine how James becomes crucial for Pound not only in terms of the "siege of London"[2] and the conquest of the European historical and cultural space, but also as an avatar of Americanness, and the cultural negotiations such an identity implies. That is to say, the manner in which James points to translation as an eruption within the native as much as an encounter with the foreign. It is with these questions in mind that I wish to investigate two prose pieces by Pound which engage both the questions of American identity and the American arts, and also the importance of the legacy of Henry James, both as writer in general, and as American writer in particular. "Patria Mia"—chronologically, the first of these two texts—is a long essay, which while mentioning James, is not generally taken as being centrally concerned with him. As I shall demonstrate here, however, the piece seems very largely inspired by James' own exploration of his homeland, *The American Scene*. Indeed, in the other text I wish to consider, "Henry James," Pound gives this work pride of place within the Jamesian canon he is attempting to construct. Let us briefly turn to it here.

Ezra Pound's 1918 article "Henry James," a long homage to and running commentary on the author, who had died two years previously, is well known. First published in the *Little Review* in August, 1918, the piece is largely devoted to defining the extent to which the Master's best work can survive both the test of time and comparisons with the best foreign novelists, such as Flaubert, and the article is habitually read for what it reveals about Pound's conception of "serious prose." But for Pound, James is much more than an example of American excellence in the art of the novel; his life and work become the site of many crucial Poundian reflections on American identity and culture themselves, even as things to be left behind. Thus, when Pound draws up his list of the essential James, the wheat he is separating from the chaff in the section of his article titled "A Shake Down," he singles out for particular distinction *The American Scene* of 1907—not a novel in the least, but a long exercise in travel writing and what might be called auto-ethnography. He writes as follows:

> *The American Scene*, triumph of the author's long practice. A creation of America. A book no "serious American" will neglect. How many Americans make any attempt toward a realization of that country is of course beyond our power to compute. The desire to see the national face in a mirror may be in itself an exotic. I know of no such grave record, of no such attempt at faithful portrayal as *The American Scene*. Thus America is to the careful observer.... (*Literary Essays*, 327)

Key here is the phrase, "the desire to see the national face in a mirror may be in itself an exotic." The statement can be read two ways: first, as implying, paradoxically, that a desire to "reflect" "Americanness" is not in fact a quality that is native to America. But second, and more to the point, is the sense that it is only from the perspective of the exotic, when one has become exotic to others and that one's own country has become exotic to oneself, that one desires to know in what this difference consists, and can even begin to delineate, and therefore to reflect, the "national face."[3] In this way, Pound writes James and as we shall see himself, into the lineage of writers who, however obsessed with "American" scenes, history, idioms, and character, examine the above from the perspective of a dialectical European distancing. What Pound points to here is something as crucial for his own work as for that of James: the extent to which the estrangement of expatriation or even the grand tour in certain versions is in and of itself an American scene; the extent to which *estrangement* from cultural identity is, precisely, American identity.[4] Pound recognizes that James' "cosmopolitanism" is a space from which the question of "American" identity can be asked, and, moreover, as the asking of this question is quintessentially American, therefore a form of hyper-Americanness. This is why, in Pound's own extended sketching of the American scene, "Patria Mia," James joins Whitman as archetypal American writer, the latter literally labeled as the "national face" itself, the former the nation's self-critical mirroring capacity. The implications of such a maneuver must be stressed: they mean that Pound can claim to grasp more firmly his "American" identity thanks to his geographical estrangement from the fatherland, rather than despite it. At the same time, he often seems reluctant to abandon the pretense to a "Whitmanian" cultural indexicality. In certain moods, Pound implies that it is only in oscillation between these poles that his own "Americanness" can come into writerly play, and it is within this spectrum that Pound constructs his own American scenes.

Perhaps the first of these is "Patria Mia." Written several years before the 1918 encomium to *The American Scene*, cited above, and quite probably shortly after Pound had first met James himself, the piece contains in its consideration of James a good deal of language which Pound will echo or even cite in his later essay, and certainly shows him adopting with relish the Jamesian position of the "restored absentee" which James had defined in *The American Scene*. In many respects, it can be seen as a companion piece to "Henry James," and indeed, these two long prose texts, concerned with American artists and American identity, quite neatly bracket the so-called "London Years." The second, elegiac in tone and written in the wake of the catastrophe of the Great War, is as much a "farewell to London" in its way as "Mauberley," as we shall see. The first, however, could well be read as a sort of belated "Greetings to London"—Pound's declaration, after an exploratory journey home, of his intention to settle definitively abroad in furtherance of his literary pursuits.[5]

In June, 1910, after an absence from America of about two years, Pound set sail from London to New York, and remained mostly in New York and Philadelphia until February, 1911, when he returned to Europe. This hardly compares, one might argue, with James' 1904–5 ten-month coast-to-coast tour of the country after twenty-one years abroad—the trip which gave rise to *The American Scene*—but this did not prevent Pound from writing up his observations on cultural difference and the American nation in a vein wholly reminiscent of James' monumental work. Indeed, "Patria Mia" echoes *The American Scene* in various ways—notably, both texts devote a good deal of emphasis to New York City and its architecture, burgeoning immigration, and the American fascination with business.[6] But some of the most "Jamesian" aspects of Pound's project are found in one of the very first paragraphs of the first article of the original series, published September 5, 1912 in *The New Age*, and interestingly omitted in Pound's subsequent revision. Here, Pound writes of his task as follows:

> "America is simple." I am, in the course of about 10,000 words, expected to set forth the simplicity of America, in such fashion that not

only will all foreigners understand implicitly America and its people—all its people; but I am expected simultaneously to bring my fatherland to self-consciousness, to cause America to see its face in the glass. . . .

In vain have I pointed out that this is the labour of a life-time, and that one should have the genius of Turgueneff [sic] rather than the desultory faculties of a lyric poet.

I have been told to tell all I know about "America of the instant." I cry all men grace. (*The New Age*, September 5, 1912, 445)

Particularly noteworthy here is Pound's own double articulation of his relationship to the famous Jamesian "international theme." Certainly, Pound here plays a role, which, to use Jamesian rhetoric, might be called that of "ambassador"—as an American, he will make his country intelligible to foreigners. But this is not the full extent, or even the most vital element of Pound's task, for in addition to making his country intelligible to others, he must make it intelligible to itself. Thus, for Pound the point here is not that what he elsewhere calls "provincial" ignorance prevents one from properly "understanding" foreign cultures and peoples, but that it prevents one from understanding oneself; the inscrutable or badly read foreigner is a *displacement* of the problem, for "provincialism" is less the inability to understand the perspective of the other, than to properly gauge one's own. And the corollary, if banal, is worth pointing out: travel or exile can never be a simple escape to the foreign, without always also being a return to the "native," against which only the "foreign" can inscribe itself. Indeed, it is the "restored absentee" that restores Americans to themselves, for "foreignness" is double in yet another way—that is, if it can obviously be an impediment to understanding, it is also indispensable to it, as James points out in the preface to *The American Scene*, positing that the extent to which he is now "foreign" to his homeland will precisely help him better to see it, in a passage we have already discussed:

> I felt no doubt, I confess, of my great advantage on that score; since if I had had time to become almost as "fresh" as an inquiring stranger, I had not on the other hand had enough to cease to be, or at least to feel, as acute as an initiated native. (3)

Certainly, "Patria Mia" and Pound's homage to *The American Scene* should remind us of the extent of Pound's interest in his homeland even at the most exhilarating moments of his London exile, and of his awareness of the extent to which expatriation is as much an encounter with the native as a distancing from it. Indeed, Pound concludes the first part of "Patria Mia" with this remark:

> If a man's work require him to live in exile, let him suffer, or enjoy, his exile gladly. But it would be about as easy for an American to become a Chinaman or a Hindoo as for him to acquire an Englishness, or a Frenchness, or a European-ness that is more than half a skin deep. (124)

But we should also emphasize the essentially closed economy of this dialectical fantasy, in which it is through the foreign that the "native" may be recovered, through an encounter with the "other" that I find myself, through a Latin title that I write of my homeland, and through cosmopolitan wanderings that my own provincialism is remedied. In analogous fashion, and again having it both ways, throughout "Patria Mia" Pound suggests it is thanks to his very distance from them that he sees the English better than they see themselves, and he thoroughly enjoys playing a double game, using his brash American freshness as a stick with which to beat the English, his London sophistication as an admonishment to his provincial American audience. However, if Pound sees himself both as translating America for "all foreigners" and also promoting an American self-consciousness and self-recognition, the need of the latter task in and of itself, with its presumption of a lack in immediate autoapperception (as James well knew) troubles the very distinction between native and foreign upon which such a project is also structured. It is not surprising that this problematic dialectic of familiarity and difference arises most forcefully in discussions of American art and literature, in a rhetoric of faces, reflection, and recognition.

As we have seen, already in "Patria Mia" Pound identifies his task of causing "America to see its face in the glass" with what will be his subsequent appraisal of the achievement of James the "exotic," who shows "the national face in a mirror." These tropes are also present in the earlier text's discussion of Whitman and James (along with Whistler) as the archetypal American artists. Pound discusses Whitman's American reception as follows:

> One reason why Whitman's reception in America has been so tardy is that he says so many things which we are accustomed, almost unconsciously, to take for granted. He was so near the national colour that the

nation hardly perceived him against that background. . . . He came before the nation was self-conscious or introspective or subjective; before the nation was interested in being itself. The nation had no interest in *seeing its face in the glass*. (124, my emphasis)

So much for Whitman, the "American keynote" (123), or "'The Reflex'" (114, Pound's quotation marks)—a pure product to be contrasted with Henry James as follows:

And if any foreigner is interested in American idiosyncrasies he will do well to read Henry James, who *delineates* these things to perfection. It is true that the more emotional American accuses Mr James of want of feeling, and it is contended that one must know both Continents if one would fully understand or wholly appreciate him. (115, my emphasis)

The rhetorical dialectic clearly emerges: if Whitman is the unmediated "keynote" of the nation, it is James who "delineates" the forms Whitman simply indexes. However, if Whitman is the national face, and James the mirror, as such James is *no less* "American" than Whitman, being the embodiment of America when it becomes "self-conscious," "introspective," and "subjective." Yet what must be stressed is Pound's idea that America is these things precisely to the extent that it achieves a self-estrangement, for which the model is the "exotic," that is, expatriation. Not only the "mirror," James is the prototype of the American desire to have one in the first place, while ventriloquist Pound at this time alternates between the Whitmanian and Jamesian roles for both his English audience, and for his American one. Yet what this mirror most often reflects for both Pound and James, are two phenomena utterly complicit in their assault on identity, despite the apparent contradiction between them: blankness and multiplicity.

A rhetoric of vacancy, absence, emptiness, blankness, and negation is everywhere in the early parts of James' book. In the very first pages, James defines the drama of his visit as that of witnessing "the great adventure of a society reaching out into the apparent void for the amenities, the consummations," and its attempt "to gouge an interest *out* of the vacancy" (13). As the book progresses, this American void seems only to yawn wider. Thus in Cape Cod: "And that was doubtless, for the story-seeker, absolutely the little story: the constituted blankness was the whole business, and one's opportunity was all, thereby, for a study of exquisite emptiness" (30). Boston provides "a town-picture as of extraordinary virtuous vacancy" (45), and the attempt of the higher classes to create an elite culture is "this interesting struggle in the void" (122). Meanwhile, the wealthy neighborhoods off Central Park constitute a "vast, costly, empty newness" (137), and this blanket emptiness, this lack of bounded, defined, and recessed spaces, is captured in a running header which also caught Pound's attention, "The Absence of Penetralia."[7] However, the overarching American blankness is one which James associates not with the lack of history, or new money, or the social and architectural expressions of either of these phenomena, but rather with an institution which is the very essence of America: democracy. James joins his inevitable Doppelgänger, Whitman, in defining "Democracy" as the most imposing factor awaiting the "returning absentee" as "the ship draws near" the harbour (43). The "great presence" is

> the monstrous form of Democracy, which is thereafter to project its shifting angular shadow, at one time and another, across every inch of the field of his vision. *It is the huge democratic broom that has made the clearance and that one seems to see brandished in the empty sky.* (44, my emphasis)

The sense of democracy as the defining American fact is hardly original, as James himself immediately notes. Yet its importance and interest, he insists, is not to be found on the political, civic or economic level, but rather in the way it determines

> manners, feelings, communications, modes of contact and conceptions of life—this is a revelation that has its full force and its lively interest only on the spot, where, when once caught, it becomes the only clue worth mentioning in the labyrinth. (44)

Democracy is the key clue in the vast American labyrinth, but also the broom which sweeps clean and empty. This is a rhetoric which returns as James concludes his one and one-half page-long excursus on the subject:

> The illustration [at hand, of democracy as the central American fact] might be, enormously, of something deficient, absent—in which case it was for the aching void to be (as an aching void) striking and interesting. As an explication or an implication the democratic intensity could always figure. (44)[8]

In "Patria Mia" Pound also often stresses absences and negativities as central American elements, and if they are not entirely the same as those highlighted by James, they certainly tally with his sense of American culture as vertiginously unbounded by the European pieties. For Pound, a morally ambiguous kind of "negative capability" is a crucial component of the American immigrant. "We get from every village the most ruthless and the most energetic. The merely discontented stop in England" (101), writes Pound, and he goes on to define this typical immigrant in terms of what he is *not*:

> . . . the non-constructive idealist, the person who is content with his own thoughts, the person whom it is the fashion to call "sentimentalist," does not emigrate. I mean the person who has "the finer feelings," love of home, love of land, love of place, of atmosphere, be he peasant or no. He may come as an act of heroism, but he returns to his land. (101–2)

This *void* of sentiment regarding one's home, hearth, and nation is extended by Pound as a generalized national characteristic with regard to a few other key objects. First, as Pound continually harps, the "English," as opposed to his compatriots, are governed by a social super-structure based entirely on property: "So far as I can make out, there is no morality in England which is not in one way or another a manifestation of the sense of property" (118). Not surprisingly, this is a sense which Pound feels the Americans are, comparatively, without. They are also without, however, certain other choice elements which go with property and place, to wit, family. Explaining why friendship is so much more important for Americans than for the English, Pound writes: "Our family bond is so slight that we collect another family, not bound to us by blood, but by temperament. And I think it is very hard for Europeans to understand our process of doing this" (120). It is tempting to assume that the portrait of the rootless, "unsentimental" immigrant is one Pound would have been happy to apply to himself, newly expatriated. This portrait is one that will return in *Guide to Kulchur*.[9] In any event, the slightness of the American family bond is clearly felt by Pound as a liberating vacuum more than a lack, while women in general and mothers in particular are seen as those who enforce this bond most powerfully. Pound writes, in language which will resurface in "Henry James":

> The French morale [sic] starts with the belief in the familial unit. "If the family holds, the nation holds," and other details may be considered as

frivolous. We in America are horrified at the French matriarchate, at the tyranny of family ... (119)

When Pound publishes "Henry James" five years later, with certain phrases and evaluations from "Patria Mia" still firmly in mind, it is increasingly the family and above all the "matriarchate" or maternal generally that Pound sees James as militating against, among other evils, when he celebrates James as a specifically ethical writer: "the major James," the "hater of tyranny" (296). However, equally crucial for Pound is it that this Jamesian campaign against tyranny, matriarchal and otherwise, is of essence one fought through displacement, estrangement, expatriation, and ultimately, "translation." These are the modes through which "oppressions" of all forms are resisted.

Indeed, in "Henry James" Pound posits geographical displacement almost as a prerequisite for the reader of James, again echoing *Patria Mia*: "Only an American who has come abroad will ever draw *all* the succulence from Henry James' writings" (332); "I dare say the snap and rattle of the fun... will be only half perceptible to those who do not know both banks of the Atlantic" (337); "Perhaps only an exile... will get the range of the other half of James' presentations!" (302); "No man who has not lived on both sides of the Atlantic can well appraise Henry James" (295). In "Henry James" Pound casts his man as the type of the international artist. However, if comprehension of his works requires transatlantic experience, this is for two somewhat different reasons, which need to be kept in view. First, Pound's insistence arises from the traditional claims of realism: "no one but an American can ever know, really know, how good he is at the bottom, how good his 'America' is" (302).[10] Yet the other side of Pound's claim derives not from the necessity of knowing the local "referents" in order to compare them with James' presentations, but from something rather the opposite: the suspicion that James' genius is not only that of "capturing" a measurable real, but also of capturing the recorder's estrangement from it. Thus, referring to the autobiographical accounts of *The Middle Years*, Pound claims no Londoner will be able to fully appreciate the pages on London, because a Londoner is precisely the person least apt to know what, for a non-native, "it feels like to reach London" (332). In other words, the transatlantic imperative is not based primarily on the need to know, *objectively*, both sides of the pond, but rather on the need to know, *subjectively*, what it means to shift between them, to have one's sensibility constantly reforged through this unstable movement. James' genius becomes less that of capturing the great variety of places than that of capturing how *exposure* to that variety leaves one never quite anywhere, but always in the "aching void." James, the cosmopolite, is also for Pound the categorically placeless. It is in this vein, while still discussing James' portrayal of his installation in London and positing "Apart from the state of James' sensibility on arrival nothing else matters. . ." (332), that Pound arrives at a particularly insightful comment about the Master: "The essence of James is that he is always 'settling-in,' it is the ground-tone of his genius" (332). The keenness of Jamesian perception comes from this: to be settling-in, but never settled, whether in America or on the continent—always "arriving," never quite "there." The "ground tone" is that of being never quite grounded. The question is how this ungroundedness is linked to what Pound considers the explicitly political and anti-tyrannical import of James' work, a valency which in turn inflects the Poundian conception of translation in all its senses, and with it, tropes of the native, nativity, the mother-tongue, and the maternal. Like so much else, Pound's take on Jamesian positioning regarding these issues seems to have been subtly yet violently inflected by the form of rage which his mourning for the losses of the First World War took on. Indeed, the later essay is quick to place James at the center of the war's tragedy, at the center of a reading that casts the war in high tragic terms.

The article printed as "Henry James" in Pound's *Literary Essays* is in fact a compilation of various pieces Pound had strung together to form his contribution to the Henry James number of *The Little Review*,[11] but if some of the writing had been in the production line previously, Pound's commitment to the project and immersion in James in the Spring of 1918 is clearly evidenced in his correspondence with Margaret Anderson. In April, he writes her "I am smothered in the Henry James" (*Pound/The Little Review*, 212), and on June 4, evokes sentiments which many readers of James must to some degree share: "If you want to know what I've been through go look at the collected edition of H.J. in any book-shop, and remember that it dont [sic] contain by any means all of him" (228). It is a note he also sounds as the opening salvo of "Henry James": "This essay on James is a dull grind of an affair, a Baedecker to a continent" (295) and once again to open the section "A Shake Down," which starts three pages later: "I have forgotten the moment of lunar imbecility in which I conceived the idea of a 'Henry James' number" (298). Between these two exasperated grumblings, however, is found the kernel of Pound's encomium for the recently deceased writer and his work, and its terms are noteworthy. Indeed, "Henry James" enacts the shattering of the post-romantic dialectical comedy of estrangement resolving itself into a new self-consciousness, so clearly determining for "Patria Mia," turning instead to a purely twentieth-century tragedy of *translation*, as "translation" now becomes the key term Pound uses to qualify James' entire endeavor. "And the great labour, this labour of translation, of making America intelligible, of making it possible for individuals to meet across national borders" (296), Pounds writes, evoking all that he feels James has striven for in vain. In vain because, according to Pound, the great tragedy of James' final years was his inability to make America enter the Great War in defense of England, leading to his quite literally dying of frustration: "After a year of ceaseless labour, of letter writing, of argument, of striving in every way to bring in America on the side of civilization, he died of apoplexy" (295-6), while his "last public act" (295)—the adoption of British nationality—remained a dead letter, a futile address to an American public who "understood nothing" (295). Not surprisingly, Pound views this death as all the more tragic and ironic, as it was precisely the routing of this sort of message which was James' life's work: "After a lifetime spent in trying to make two continents understand each other..." (296). Crucial here, in Pound's homage and lament, is his decision to dub James' work a form of "translation." After all, given that Pound describes James' task as above all negotiating the differences between foreign countries and cultures, one would think he might seize upon a term James' own work provided him: that of "ambassador." Rather, by dubbing James a "translator," Pound first gives that term a decided inflection in terms of his own work, and second, quite brazenly asserts an unambiguous identification with James, explicitly placing in parallel James's endeavors as a writer with his own, as among Pound's most significant intellectual projects in the years separating "Patria Mia" and "Henry James," translation is extremely prominent, particularly, but far from exclusively, the Chinese poems and Noh plays Pound rendered from Fenollosa's notes. This redefinition and identification carries several important implications.

First, the immersion into the foreign represented by *translation* needs to be read in parallel, in Pound's case, with the foreignness of expatriation, with the more conventional "international theme." Pound's assimilation of China, his renderings of Italian, Latin, and

Provençal, need to be balanced against both his estrangement from America, and his role as an exotic in London—as someone who inevitably speaks a tongue foreign to both his current conditions and his abandoned homeland. Pound's rhetoric here seems explicitly to link the Jamesian trope of the foreign as breach in the sanctity of a "natural" culture, with the interlinguistic torsion of "translation" as breach in the "naturalness" of a given language. Second, the rhetoric clearly shows that "translation" for Pound is more than a simple technical exercise in poetics, but part of the vast battle against provincialism and prejudice—or "tyranny," as he so often puts it in reference to James—in which James himself stands out as a hero. Indeed, in the 1917 essay "Provincialism the Enemy," James again is given a highly strategic role in this regard. This little studied war-time piece is a fascinating defense of "communication" of every kind: it cites Kipling to the effect that "Transportation is civilisation" (*Selected Prose*, 199), calls for the construction of a "Channel Tunnel" (201) linking England and France, and claims "the disease of both England and America during the last century is due precisely to a stoppage of circulation" (200). Not surprisingly, "provincialism," defined as "more than an ignorance, it is ignorance plus a lust after uniformity" (190), finds its prime enemy in James, the great presenter of "human variety" (195) and "the sense of national differences... the slight difference in tone" (189), while the point of joining Paris to London is not to make them more similar but rather "... to accentuate their difference. Nothing is more valuable than just this amicable accentuation of difference, and of complementary values" (202). If this is the task of James, and James is himself a "translator," then it follows that the task of a translation is *not* to create a duplicate or double of the translated text in an extension of "uniformity," but on the other hand, against the background of an apparent similarity, precisely to achieve the "accentuation of difference" or the "slight difference in tone" through the doubling and hence the division of the translated text. Such a project will be examined in detail in the following chapter. For the moment, let us note that this sense of translation as both a fight for communication against provincialism *and* a struggle for the recognition of and preservation of difference is also what motivates Pound's concluding paean to James in the opening section of "Henry James":

> Peace comes of communication. No man of our time has so laboured to create means of communication as did the late Henry James.

The whole of great art is a struggle for communication. All things that oppose this are evil, whether they be silly scoffing or obstructive tariffs.

And this communication is not a levelling, it is not an elimination of differences. It is a recognition of differences, of the right of differences to exist, of interest in finding things different. Kultur is an abomination; philology is an abomination, all repressive uniforming education is an evil. (298)

This assault on "Kultur," like so much else in the passage, is also an extension of "Provincialism the Enemy" which launches an even more extended attack, and Pound's use of the word in these pieces seems largely consonant with this definition from the O.E.D.: "Civilization as conceived by the Germans; esp. used in a derogatory sense during the 1914–18 and 1939–45 wars, as involving notions of racial and cultural arrogance, militarism, and imperialism." Yet it is crucial to note some of the terms in which James' opposition to "Kultur" is couched in "Provincialism," where Pound writes of James as "the crusader, *both* in this internationalism, *and* in his constant propaganda against personal tyranny, against the hundred subtle forms of personal oppressions and coercions" (*Selected Prose*, 189, my emphasis), which clearly states a parallel implicit throughout "Henry James": one obtaining between the oppressions of provincialism, enforced uniformity, and "Kultur" on one hand, and those of personal relations on the other. It is central for Pound that provincialism and "Kultur" have their equivalent on the more restricted personal level, and that part of James' genius is his understanding of this complicity. Thus, as was the case in praising James' internationalism and "labour of translation," in regard to these seemingly less "political" exchanges Pound once again mobilizes his most passionate rhetoric in defense of James as above all an ethical writer: ". . . the major James . . . the hater of tyranny; book after early book against oppression, against all the sordid petty personal crushing oppression. . . . The outbursts in *The Tragic Muse*, the whole of *The Turn of the Screw*, human liberty, personal liberty, the rights of the individual against all sorts of intangible bondage!" (296); "his hatred of personal intimate tyrannies" (299); "What he [James] fights is 'influence,' the impinging of family pressure, the impinging of one personality on another; all of them in highest degree damn'd, loathsome and detestable" (296); and finally, in his discussion of the tale "Louisa Pallant," "a study in the maternal or abysmal relation, good James" (320). As is almost inevitable given James' favored subjects, but hardly coincidentally, Pound's examples of "oppression" focus primarily on the family, even more on mothers or maternal figures, and largely invoke "coercion" as applied to choices of a mate or spouse. Here we return to the disgust of "Patria Mia" for the French "matriarchate" and its approval of the lack of the family bond in America, certainly, but also to an implicit relation between the crossing of borders suggested by translation and questions of exogamy and erotic difference. In Pound's reading, to a certain extent the maternal *is* the unbreached space of enforced uniformity prior to translation, but also the "abysmal" and the abyss, perhaps even the void and pit of the unlocalizable American democratic morass of identity.[12] To what extent is "provincialism" the mother, and the mother, the enemy? Let us remember that Pound's emphasis on communication and circulation is also an insistence on pedagogy—a cause which in Pound's case has consistently phallic undertones.[13] His most notorious remark in this context is probably found in his introduction to Rémy de Gourmont's *The Natural Philosophy of Love*—interestingly enough, a translation—where Pound writes "Even oneself has felt it, driving any new idea into the great passive vulva of London, a sensation analogous to the male feeling in copulation" (viii). Certainly, Pound implies here that the genius in some way "fecundates" popular opinion, from which new art and knowledge is born. Yet on either end of the spectrum, it is both the exogamous foreign female body and the maternal envelope which must be breached, through an opposition to oppression which comprises the trope of "translation."

Thus, if it is hard not to endorse Pound's humanistic enthusiasm for communication and exchange of all sorts, it is important to stress that this phallic positioning of pedagogy, communication, and translation is precisely what will come to dominate Pound's labors as radio broadcaster during the Second World War and indeed, the original meaning of "broadcasting" is the sowing of seed. Ironically, it is through Pound's reflections on provincialism, translation, and ultimately telecommunications, that the seeds of his own abhorrent and botched polyglot ambassadorship for Mussolini's Italy are sown. In this context, let us remember that Pound's use of "translation" to indicate James' labor *against* cultural uniformity or provincialism links him to another figure in the Poundian hagiography—Chaucer, whom Pound notably refers to as "Le Grand Translateur," after explaining Chaucer's anti-provincialist importance in these terms: "Chaucer wrote while England was still a part of Europe. There was one culture from Ferrara to Paris and it extended to England" (*ABC*,

100–1).[14] Indeed, if Pound borrows from the fourteenth-century ballad by Eustache Deschamps when he eschews the contemporary French "traducteur" to dub Chaucer "le Grand Translateur," it is worth noting that in the early twentieth century the word "translateur" reappeared in the French language, but with a new meaning, which the *Robert Dictionnaire Historique de la langue française* qualifies as follows: "appareil intermédiaire entre deux postes télégraphiques éloignés" [an intermediary apparatus between two distant telegraph stations]. This in turn recalls another series of articles Pound published in *The New Age*, not long before those that were to become "Patria Mia." I refer here to "I Gather the Limbs of Osiris," in which Pound famously wrote of facts which are "swift and easy of transmission" and "govern knowledge as the switchboard governs an electric circuit" (*Selected Prose*, 23).[15] Thus, translation, the metaphorics of telecommunications, and the radically synecdochic "luminous detail" (21) all inevitably lead to the Poundian broadcasting project. Yet this project is nothing if not James', as sketched by Pound, turned inside out.

For broadcasting, by dramatizing the distance between sender and receiver, by reducing all to the phonic and the insistence on address, emphasizes nothing so much as the Jamesian obsession with *position*. Implying a generalized poetics of the phatic and debarring the silent emblem of the ideographic real—a crucial underpinning of Pound's theories of translation, as the next chapter shall make clear—it is hardly surprising that broadcasting requires Pound to compensate for these losses with a necessarily logopoetical and caricatural "Amurkan" voice in so many of the performances. It is here indeed that Pound most *em*phatically embarks upon a Jamesian "labour of translation," through the transmission of a message across the most redoubtable barriers to "communication," a message the burden of which was, according to Pound, cross-cultural and transnational understanding, and peace. These etherealized messages, void of inscription and usually multilingual, implying as they do a final deterritorialization, the ultimate positionlessness of the sender, echo what Pound had first elaborated as the artistic privilege and tragic fate of Henry James, forever "settling in."

At the same time, as Pound commits himself ever more forcefully to Italian fascism in the mid-thirties and throughout the war years, "Kultur"—a key term to explain what Jamesian "translation" militated against—returns to the forefront of Pound's concerns, channeled through the German of Frobenius and this time invested by

Pound with an entirely positive valency. However, Pound's reappropriation of the German term is only effected through an aggressively "American" vernacular marking of it, as the spelling of the title *Guide to Kulchur* indicates, or this 1940 letter to Eliot: "Gittin down to thet book," Pound writes, "There is, so far as I know, no English work on Kulturmorphologie, transformation of cultures. Can't use a German term at this moment. Morphology of cultures. Historic process taken in the larger" (*Letters*, 336). This dialect, here also indistinguishable from that figuring in what Michael North has dubbed Pound and Eliot's "racial masquerade,"[16] perhaps provides the alibi for positing "Kultur" as no longer the emblem of provincial prejudice and uniformity, but rather, when rechristened "Kulchur," as quite the opposite: the transcultural investigation Pound saw Frobenius as undertaking, and this at the very "moment" when Nazism was at the apex of its power. Associated by Pound with related terms such as Frobenius' "Paideuma" and Pound's own coinage, "the new learning," Kulchur now can be related to "the gristly roots of ideas that are in action" (*Guide*, 58) as opposed to the moribund dead weight of "philology," which was placed in apposition to the "Kultur" of the James essay of 1918. As Kathryne Lindberg explains in her excellent account, "Pound seems to collapse the general procedures of *Kulturmorphologie* [as found in Frobenius], which analyzes the 'life-cycles' of biological as well as linguistic forms (*morphe*), into the notion of 'paideuma,' which thus covers names of the movements within and between recurrent cultural forms as well as the forms themselves" (178–9).[17] This sense of "Kulturmorphologie" as "the historic process taken in the larger," of "Kulchur" and "paideuma" as historical homing devices, which permit a gauging of *temporal* cultural positionings in a manner analogous to the sketching of synchronous differences in cultural tone for which James stands out, is succinctly expressed in a phrase which punningly if perhaps unconsciously links the siting of one's own home to the invocation of the other: *"A man does not know his own ADDRESS (in time) until he knows where his time and milieu stand in relation to other times and conditions"* (*Guide to Kulchur*, 83, original emphasis).

Thus, through the vagaries of Kultur and Kulchur, and the transpositions of cultural placement such a migration implies, Henry James becomes a key node in the relationship between Pound's sense of "Great literature" as "simply language charged with meaning to the utmost possible degree" (*ABC*, 28), and his own production of language that would be charged *for* its meaning, that is, the treasonous radio broadcasts. Here, electricity and the network come to figure not only energy, power, and poetic production, but also responsibility—the positioning of the sender, with regard to the receivers towards whom he aims. And here James' own eccentricity with regard to the American political scene in the First World War seems to become for Pound paradigmatic. For what is truly astonishing is the extent to which, as Pound increasingly provoked the "incomprehension" of his native country during the Second World War, he had fully *rehearsed* this position in his writings on James as expatriate, American, and "translator"—as the misunderstood expatriate patriot, the foreign eminence who, ultimately unheeded by his former homeland, "abandoned his citizenship out of shame" (*Literary Essays*, 297). More than twenty years before his own diplomatic endeavors, here again is how Pound describes those of James: "After a year of ceaseless labour, of letter writing, of argument, of striving in every way to bring in America on the side of civilization, he died of apoplexy" (295–6). These terms are very much those Pound would unfortunately claim as his own, in his own apoplexy, in the translation tragedy, not only his own but also of his own devising, that the radio broadcasts became. Already in 1918, Pound saw James' fate as encapsulating the destiny he so actively courted: rather than domesticate the foreign, their acts of translation ended by rendering the call of the native unintelligible. This is also their shared achievement, and one which Pound's epochal immersion in translation echoes, through interventions no less destabilizing for any sense of the domesticity of a natural language than the syntactic complexities of the later James.

CHAPTER 4

POUND AND TRANSLATION: IDEOGRAM AND THE VULGAR TONGUE

Recent criticism on Ezra Pound has, quite rightly, been placing an increased emphasis on the importance of translation within both his poetry and poetics—more than ever, translation is being viewed as a fundamental element of Pound's work and thought, and not just as an ancillary activity.[1] However, what particular status to attribute to Pound's work as translator remains as intractable a question as ever. Clearly, we are moving away from an inadequate view of Pound's interest in translation as being mostly a matter of poetic hygiene and calisthenics, undertaken in view of the creation of superior "original" work. The tendency now is more to see the translations *as* a form of original work, as "English poems in their own right," as Ming Xie has said of *Cathay* ("Pound as Translator," 210). If such a view is welcome, however, it still remains problematic, as such an assertion can paradoxically and all too easily *efface* the status of the translations as such, which then simply become more Pound poems. Thus, one "solves" the problem of Pound's translations not by simply occluding them, but by denying that they remain in essence the translations which they are. Even a study as sophisticated as Yao's moves in this direction, when in discussing *Cathay* he stresses what he sees as Pound's concern not to "mark the poem as unmistakably foreign" (43) to an English reader and in the context of the First World War. On the contrary, my argument will be that such a foreignness is not only consistently emphasized by Pound, but that the poems themselves are not even legible as "original" poems in the absence of such markings.

The very real question is how to affirm the "originality" of a work, albeit a translation, within a particular language and culture, while also keeping in view its status as a *negotiation* with a foreign cultural and linguistic text. This is the dilemma posed by the necessary formulation of the translation as "original," a formulation which calls for a new conception of originality itself, one which would also imply new conceptions of literary tradition, linguistic appurtenance, and symbolic debt on the level of both culture and the subject. Lawrence Venuti hints at such a formulation when he writes of Pound's translating practice as follows:

> interpretive translation contradicts the ideal of autonomy by pointing to the various conditions of the translated text, foreign as well as domestic, and thus makes clear that translation can make a cultural difference at home only by signifying the difference of the foreign text. (Venuti, 202)

It is indeed this question of *difference* which is at the core of discussions of Pound's translations, and this is largely why they occupy such a strategic role in recent accounts of Pound's poetics as a whole. That Pound's theories of literature and particularly translation engage with questions of cultural identity, transmission, and reproduction in highly significant but also ambivalent and contradictory ways only increases the notable divergences in the valency attributed to translation, as theory and practice, in his work. Yet the stakes of these divergences are very high, often determining how Pound's relationship to language and politics as a whole will ultimately be assessed.

For example, Yunte Huang insists that Poundian translation is an assertion of interest in cultural difference or "displacement," and therefore "ethnography" and intercultural negotiation. He writes:

> it would be a grave error to assume that Pound's interest was only in poetry. It would be an even bigger mistake to regard his work on Chinese poetry as separable from the ethnographic interest that lies at the heart of Fenollosa's ambitious project. (69–70)

and in this way Pound's work is used to "argue against some nativist trends in literary studies that seek to construct a history of American literature deprived of its transnational character" (5–6). Such a claim must be contrasted with Walter Benn Michaels's view that Pound uses translation from the Chinese not to emphasize cultural positioning and difference but instead to affirm their ultimate inconsequence, thanks to the transmittability of a self-identical, universal, pre-cultural real. Thus, though Michaels might well accord Pound's "ethnographic" interest, it would be one he would see as a means of putting an end to ethnography:

> Pound's deployment of the Chinese ideogram is exemplary in this regard. Rather than serving as a mark of cultural difference, a sign that must be presented in the original because . . . it cannot be translated, the ideogram represents for him a utopian transcendence even of the necessity for translation; this is the meaning of his fantasy about the sculptor Gaudier's ability to understand "the primitive Chinese ideographs" without knowing Chinese and only because "he was so accustomed to observe the dominant line in objects." (109)

For Michaels, translation becomes a centerpiece in his argument that Pound, like Eliot, is part of a strain of modernism notable for "the irrelevance of nationality" (108) to its concerns, "nationality" here seeming to mean cultural identity. Michaels specifies,

> As early as 1917 (in "Provincialism the Enemy" . . .) and as late as 1938 (in "National Culture"), Pound condemned the distinction between native and alien, which is to say, the distinction between nations as such, as a form of provincialism. . . . Ultimately the very idea of a national culture turns out to constitute a kind of oxymoron. A "developed" national culture "must of necessity include criteria which are, as criteria, capable of comparison with the best alien criteria . . ." But since the relevance of the criteria derives from their being the "best," it isn't at all clear what it means to think of them as "alien" (or native); so "in one sense it can almost be said," Pound concludes, "there are no alien criteria." The difference between better and worse renders the difference between native and alien irrelevant; the international becomes the universal. (108)

Michaels is certainly right that Pound abhors all chauvinistic refusal of the "foreign" simply because it is so, but as we saw in the last chapter, Pound also champions the Jamesian "sense of national differences, the small and the large misunderstanding, the slight difference in tone" (*Selected Prose*, 189), the "amicable accentuation of difference" (*Selected Prose*, 202) that would result from joining London and Paris by tunnel; in fact, these passages are found in the article "Provincialism the Enemy," the very text Michaels invokes to make the contrary argument. That is to say, though clearly opposed to patriotic chauvinism, Pound stresses everything that makes "nationality" *more* relevant, rather than less. Indeed, concerning the "irrelevance" of cultural identity to Pound, Michaels's other chosen piece of textual evidence, "National Culture," features statements like these, which should at least give pause: "It can't be said that an alteration on Mr. Eliot's passport has altered the essential Americanness of his work" (*Selected Prose*, 163), and "The American culture is Franco-English, it is at the start the culture in the bone of the one English segment that ever in all history threw off the tyranny of the conquerors of the Island" (164), and "Cummings . . . is indelibly New England" (164). In fact, Pound emphasizes that the very insistence on the *lack* of importance of cultural difference is not in opposition to but rather a form of provincialism, which he defines as ". . . a desire for uniformity—uniformity always based on the temperament of the particular provincial desiring it" (*Selected Prose*, 197), thus showing how provincialism and ethnocentric universalism are entirely complicit. Pound's position regarding these issues is, then, far more complex than Michaels portrays it, but still, Michaels is correct to emphasize the universalist push of some of Pound's work on the "ideogram," with its insistence on mimetic reproduction of the real. And given the ideogram's central position not only within Pound's work as a translator but also in terms of his poetics and politics as a whole, the translations from the Chinese and his theory of the "ideogram" prove an indispensable starting point for any discussion of the questions of cultural and linguistic identity and difference or universalism in Pound's work. Such an inquiry will show that even when Pound's pretensions are at their most universalist, his *practice* speaks to the problematics of cultural and linguistic positioning that come to the fore in his considerations of James; and likewise, that a separation of Pound's poetics from his theories of translation is entirely impossible. As we shall see, for Pound, poetry *is* translation, translation interference, and it is through these interferences that Pound will also negotiate his debt to a poetic tradition from which he was also eager to distance himself: that of England.

∼

Ezra Pound's tripartite division of "great literature," that is, "language charged with meaning to the utmost possible degree" (*Literary Essays*, 23), into phanopoeia, melopoeia, and logopoeia, emphasizing respectively image, sound, and verbal play, has become one of the most enduring and famous statements of modernist poetics. Elaborated in the *ABC of Reading* and even more so in the 1929 essay "How to Read," this charting delimits the following categories:

melopoeia, in which "the words are charged, over and above their plain meaning, with some musical property, which directs the bearing or trend of that meaning" (*Literary Essays*, 25), phanopoeia, "which is a casting of images upon the visual imagination" (25), and the more complex logopoeia, " 'the dance of the intellect among words' . . . [which] takes count in a special way of habits of usage, of the context we *expect* to find with the word, its usual concomitants, of its known acceptances, and of ironical play" (25). If this story is by now quite well known, what has received less stress is that this theory is also and explicitly a theory of *translation*. Immediately after establishing the categories, Pound moves directly to assessing their varying translatability, with rather predictable results. Thus, logopoeia, deriving directly from the chance encounters of the signifier within a particular language, "does not translate," although Pound acknowledges the possibility of finding a translingual "equivalent" (25). Melopoeia, equally dependent on the arbitrary qualities of the signifier, albeit its phonic ones, is therefore "practically impossible to transfer or translate . . . from one language to another, save perhaps by divine accident, and for half a line at a time" (25). Not surprisingly, it is phanopoeia, the poetry of the visual signified, which can ". . . be translated almost, or wholly, intact. When it is good enough, it is practically impossible for the translator to destroy it save by very crass bungling, and the neglect of perfectly well-known and formulative rules" (25).

Phanopoeia seems in many ways the least useful of Pound's categories, returning us to a heliotropic poetics of the primacy of the visual object, with no real interrogation of what seem such unavoidable issues as the positioning of the subject in any act of perception, the relationship between image and trope, or the constitutive role of language in the creation of any form of verbal sense.[2] The visual referent seems to be given the status of an unambiguous pre-expressive "real," whose essential and empirical "thereness" is sufficient to ensure its transfer between languages and translators, save in the case of "very crass bungling." Pound will go on to assert, "In *Phanopoeia* we find the greatest drive toward utter precision of word; this art exists almost exclusively by it" (26), and this very concept of "precision" is only possible because the visual referent provides an external and unequivocal measuring stick. If the transfer of these images into language demands a certain degree of skill, it is only that required to *reduce* sufficiently the linguistic interference between image and perception. In successful phanopoeia, it is precisely because the intercession of language in the *original* is so minimal, that the original can be translated so effectively. The case is entirely different in logopoeia, in which the "referent" is itself only a linguistic fact, and would have no existence outside of language at all. This is why logopoeia "cannot possibly be contained in plastic or in music" (25)—it "refers" to nothing but language and usage itself.

Pound will go on to insist, in the late 1920s and 1930s, that it is Chinese poetry which represents the highest achievement in phanopoeia; this affirmation is based not only on the abstract ethnographic or racialist theorizing with which Pound was increasingly taken, but also on the linguistics of the ideogram he arrived at during the key period of 1913–18, through his editing of the notes of Ernest Fenollosa on *The Chinese Written Character as a Medium for Poetry*.[3] If Pound's interest in Chinese poetry preceded his encounter with Fenollosa's papers, it was only through the latter that Pound's lifelong engagement with the Chinese *language* began,[4] and it is here that Pound theorizes the key components of the Chinese ideogram which would make it the ideal vehicle, or "medium," for phanopoeia. Once again, we are on familiar terrain: Pound, misrecognizing the phonetic component of Chinese characters, will view them not as what post-Saussurians would call arbitrary linguistic signs, but rather as stylized yet legible referential *pictures* of what they represent. Pound's most extreme statement of this position is undoubtedly that to which Michaels refers, his affirmation that sculptor Gaudier-Brzeska was able to "read" Chinese writing simply by staring at the characters and applying his visual genius to "recognizing" what they were pictures of.[5] So for Pound, Chinese is the ideal writing for phanopoeia because the writing itself *mimics* the visual nature of what it represents; to use Peirce's terminology, a Chinese ideogram would be not only conventional or "symbolic," but also "iconic," that is, bearing a clear mimetic link to what it designates. *The Chinese Written Character* puts it this way:

> But Chinese notation is something much more than arbitrary symbols. It is based upon a vivid shorthand picture of the operations of nature. In the algebraic figure and in the spoken word there is no natural connection between thing and sign: all depends upon sheer convention. But the Chinese method follows natural suggestion. (8)

Thus Chinese *writing* would evade even the primal "translation" of visual referent into arbitrary phonic signifier.

What might seem from the preceding a most naive and logocentric form of Cratylism is, however, disturbed by Pound in a number of ways. First, in *The Chinese Written Character*, if the relationship between "sign" and "thing" is unacceptably reductive, it is crucial to note to what extent the conception of "thing" itself, and in itself, is productively problematized. For Fenollosa and Pound, the key flaw of western languages is not their failure to correspond mimetically with "things," but even more their faulty establishment of the abstraction of the "thing" in the first place, whereas in "nature" there is nothing but process, and transfer of energy. Thus, "A true noun, an isolated thing, does not exist in nature. Things are only the terminal points, or rather the meeting points, of actions, cross-sections cut through actions, snap-shots" (10). Yet Fenollosa is also chary of granting ultimate authority to "action" as an abstraction, instead refusing the noun-verb dichotomy as a whole: "Like nature, the Chinese words are alive and plastic, because *thing* and *action* are not formally separated" (17). But perhaps the key to the Chinese language for Fenollosa, along with the roots of the "ideogrammic method" for Pound, lies in a conception of thought as essentially syntax—a morphology and energetics of relationships: "Relations are more real and more important than the things which they relate" (22). The above statements hold two key implications which need to be stressed. First, if the influence of Emerson on Fenollosa, as critics have argued, does seem evident, it is clear that Pound's "Cratylism" is certainly *not* consonant with, for example, the famous Emersonian call for the poet to give each thing "its own name and not another's, thereby rejoicing the intellect, which delights in detachment or boundary" (271).[6] The abstraction of the "thing," and the "detachments" or "boundaries" which such an abstraction implies, are the very target of this poetics. Second, the emphasis on *relations* as the ultimate real leads not to a poetry of mimetic disclosure of pre-existent "things," but rather to a poetry of figure and trope.[7] And this becomes immediately apparent once we consider what Pound actually does in *Cathay*, where he purportedly would be engaging in largely "phanopoeic" translation, that is, concentrating on projecting the image on the retina while minimizing the verbal play of logopoeia and the melopoeic propensity to distract from precise meaning.

Pound's translations in *Cathay*, directly inspired by the Fenollosa notes, comprise some of his most celebrated and anthologized work, and this for many reasons.[8] On the surface, many of these poems are more accessible in terms of formal coherence and diegesis than much of Pound's lyric work, and also are often more in keeping with middle-brow lyric conventions regarding sentiment. But the most impressive achievement of the poems is Pound's invention of a language and a tone that walks the tightrope between supple familiarity and the uncanny alterity which a translation of texts so distant geographically, temporally, and linguistically would seem to require. Thus, if Ming Xie can insist that "The language of *Cathay* was colloquial, prosaic and contemporary" ("Pound as Translator," 210), it is just as accurate to assert that it is overwrought, full of "non-prosaic" parallelisms, inversions, and repetitions, and most importantly, very largely unidiomatic. Witness lines such as the stilted, "We say: Will we be let to go back in October?" ("Song of the Bowmen of Shu"), or "The lone man sits with shut speech" ("Sennin Poem by Kakuhaku"), or again, "The Monkeys make sorrowful noise overhead" ("The River Merchant's Wife"), a line in which colloquial English demands either the indefinite article or the plural "noises." Much of the delicacy of the Chinese poems comes from the strange feeling Pound creates of a language being handled with extreme attentiveness and care, precisely because it is *not* entirely mastered or appropriated. One might be tempted to assert that this is evidence of Pound's willingness to let the alien structures and usage of Chinese "speak" in the English, to preserve in English what makes the Chinese written character such a superlative "medium for poetry," and this is certainly true, up to a point. But what is striking is the extent to which Pound creates his "Chinese" effect precisely through pressuring diction and usage. The poems of *Cathay* derive their power through destabilizing effects of tone and voice, employing a ghostly tongue which is properly uncanny in being at once homely and unpretentious *and* alien to native usage. Whence, perhaps, the disquieting intimacy of their emotional appeal.[9]

In addition to the oddities of usage, however, the poems are perhaps even more notable within the body of Pound's work for their reliance on certain recurring tropes, which are less prevalent elsewhere in Pound. For example, what can one make of the speaker of the "Exile's letter," when he says he " . . . went back to the East Mountains white-headed" (256), and the context does not indicate that he is referring to old age? And among these prime examples of phanopoeia, in "Separation on the River Kiang," can one even determine the referent of the line "The smoke-flowers are blurred over the river" (257)? The informed reader will quickly surmise that Pound here is following Fenollosa's view that Chinese avoids undue abstraction by constructing "general" concepts through the accretion and juxtaposition of particulars, building complex characters through metaphorical agglomerations of simpler ones. As *The Chinese Written Character* puts it, ". . . one must follow closely what is said, not merely what is abstractly meant" (16), and respect the "speaking" etymologies of Chinese "abstractions." Pound lists several examples in his appended notes, for example, "Sun above line of horizon=dawn" or "Speech+grass growing with difficulty (i.e. twisted root and obstacle above it)=appearance of speaking in a confused manner" (39).[10] Thus, "shut speech" would be a transliteration of "silently," and "smoke-flowers," we may learn, would be more idiomatically translated as "river mist." That it is only exoticism which permits the oddities created by such a practice seems evident; it is difficult indeed to imagine a Romance-language translator wishing to perpetrate a similar effect on the English "understand," for example, or foregrounding an emptily grasping hand when rendering "mistake." But the point that needs to be made is that "accurate" translation of phanopoeia, on the level not of what is "meant" but of what is "said," implies nothing so much as *trope*, specifically catachresis. The execution of "phanopoeia" leads us in a circle to its putative opposite: logopoeia, with its emphasis on "habits of usage," displacement of context, and metalinguistic effect. Take, for example, "The Beautiful Toilet":

Blue, blue is the grass about the river
And the willows have overfilled the close garden.
And within, the mistress, in the midmost of her youth,
White, white of face, hesitates, passing the door.
Slender, she puts forth a slender hand,

And she was a courtezan in the old days,
And she has married a sot,
Who now goes drunkenly out
And leaves her too much alone. (*Poems*, 249–50)

The potentially odd "blue" in the first line is in deference to the Chinese character *ch'ing*, which can mean either blue or green, but more important stylistically is the foregrounded *repetition* of "blue," along with "white" in line four, certainly due to the Chinese practice of repeating a character for emphasis.[11] A more idiomatic translation would be "very blue" and "very white," yet much of the structure of the first stanza is built around these two repetitions of a color adjective, each occurring in the same slot in the line. If English too can at least tolerate the repetition of an adjective for purposes of intensification, Pound plays up the strangeness of the technique rather than assimilate it, as the heavily paralleled lines 1 and 4 prepare the way for the doubling of an adjective again in line 5, only here the intensifier dissolves into a complete tautology: "Slender, she puts forth a slender hand." This line so egregiously violates the arch Poundian precept "Use no superfluous word, no adjective which does not reveal something" (*Literary Essays*, 4), that the reader cannot help but pause over the seemingly more innocent adjectival repetitions of lines 1 and 4. In fact, this poem utterly violates the canonical imagist economy, to say nothing of the modernist valuations of a writer like Wyndham Lewis. Here, we have overt adjectival surplus rather than paucity, an emphasis on color rather than line, and, as is so often the case in Pound's Chinese translations, suggestion and connotation rather than precise description and presentation. Why does she "put forth a slender hand"? To reach for the door? And if so, to open it or to close it? Why write the neutral "put forth" over, say, "reached out," "stretched out," or "held out," all of which would more clearly delimit the nature of her action? Continuing to the second stanza, we can see how the key half-rhyme "sot/out" is only made possible by the somewhat unidiomatic inversion "go drunkenly out" (which would be less noticeable were "go out" being used transitively), while the last line reads like a mistaken synthesis between two forms: "And leaves her *too often* alone" with "And leaves her alone *too much*." Word order in Pound's line seems to imply that "too much alone" modifies the object "her" rather than the verb "leaves," which gives us "much" in its qualitative, rather than quantitative, sense, though this too is left strictly indeterminate.

A few points bear pondering here. First, in *Cathay* it seems very much as if the "foreignness" of the Chinese provides an alibi for introducing the sorts of verbal extravagances and liberties that "imagism" often proclaimed to militate against. Second, these extravagances often take the form of noticeably unidiomatic construction and usage, in contrast to the techniques Pound uses elsewhere in both his poetry and translation.[12] Third, the vividness of image, constitutive of Chinese poetry for Pound and Fenollosa, yields catachresis in English. Fourth, due to the preceding, the overall effect of *Cathay* is less the establishment of an exemplar of the poetry of the image, than the invention of a linguistic style which, meant to embody some sort of

"Chineseness," creates a breach in "English" poetic usage. Thus, if one can only agree that "the poems of *Cathay* should indeed be read as English poems in their own right" and not be demoted to a secondary status as "translations," they are not *simply* "English poems in their own right." Their status *as* translation is essential to their success, even when considered as *original* English poems; without the backdrop of the Chinese paratext, without the conceit, fictive or not, of an enacted reference to a foreign language, culture, and literary tradition, their maneuvers are unthinkable. And phanopoeia, the "most translatable" form of poetry, leads inexorably to linguistic interventions which can only be considered as logopoeia, while the theoretically neutral transfer of the visual referent comes to involve nothing so much as issues of usage, voicing, inflection, cultural coding, and therefore context and address—that is to say, the well-known terrain of Henry James, or that of a young American poet trying to "modernize" his idiom in the context and to the taste of literary London.

In this way, translation becomes the pretext for transgression. If, as Saussure says, we inherit language as a law, then the Chinese ideogram and the "laws" of its construction as adduced by Pound and Fenollosa become the alibi behind which Pound rewrites the laws of poetic convention, but also and more importantly, of English usage, in a manner consonant with James' less insistent but still strategic practice of fomenting effects of interference within the standards of novelistic prose. The "ideogrammic method" insinuates itself into the core of English, Pound finding what Antoine Berman might have called the "chinks" and "holes" within English apt to accommodate the foreign pressure Pound feels the Chinese language to exert. In his discussion of the translator's need of such gaps, Berman goes on to say, "That's what translating is: ferreting out what is non-normativized in the mother tongue, in order to insert there the foreign language and its expression." [13] Yet as Berman has elsewhere amply demonstrated, the question of just what the "norms" of the mother tongue might be and the nature of their authority is one no serious reflection on translation can afford to bypass. One cannot translate "idiomatically" without some sense of what one's idiom is, or should be, and how this idiom can accommodate modes that are foreign to it; moreover, historically it is often through the relation to the foreign that "mother tongues" evolve and are codified as such. As an eminent example, Berman emphasizes how Martin Luther's translation of the Bible founded modern German, in a double move: Luther at once insisted that the word of God be rendered in a colloquial German, that spoken by "the mother in the home, the children on the street, the common man in the marketplace" (cited by Berman, *L'épreuve*, 45, *Experience*, 25), yet at the same time, as Germany as a whole was divided into many dialectical regions and was without a single, national common vernacular, Luther also needed to *generalize* his own local dialect through a "subtle labor of purification, of dedialecticalization" (*L'épreuve*, 46, *Experience*, 25, translation slightly modified). He thus founds modern German by refusing both an ossified learned language, with no relation to language as used, *and* the easy familiarity of the native and local. Yet it is the pressure of the biblical text which opens the way for a reconstruction of the "native."

In terms of the construction of a vernacular fit to write in, of course, for Pound it is not Luther who would be the important reference but rather Dante Alighieri, who put that very problem at the center of one of the key texts for Anglo-American modernism: *De Vulgari Eloquentia*, Dante's defense of the vernacular, rather than Latin, as a medium for poetry. Indeed, the single name Dante designates the two key figures behind virtually all of Pound's translations from Italian and Provençal. First, it is almost entirely on the authority of the Italian poet's judgments in *De Vulgari Eloquentia*, the *Convivio*, and the *Divine Comedy*, that Pound chooses the poets he will translate and study most closely, particularly the troubadour Arnaut Daniel and Dante's friend and rival, the Tuscan Guido Cavalcanti. However, in understanding Pound's medievalism another Dante comes into play—pre-Raphaelite poet, painter, and translator Dante Gabriel Rossetti, under whose influence that of the first Dante very largely accrued for Pound's generation, and whose enormously popular translations of "Dante and his circle" set the model against which Pound would always measure his own work in the field of Medieval Italian. The name "Dante" thus becomes the site of a double negotiation for Pound: first, with the Italian poet who both affirmed and created his own "vulgar tongue," and second, with the man Pound called "my father and my mother" in the matter of "my knowledge of Tuscan poetry" (*Poems*, 190). Indeed, this hermaphrodite progenitor, through his *translations* (Pound rarely mentions Rossetti's "original" work) will become a privileged site through which Pound can negotiate his relationship to nineteenth century "English" poetic usage—a heritage Pound usually dodges either by focusing on other languages, or on other periods of English poetry. Medieval Italian poetry becomes a way for Pound to mediate a relationship to a much closer, and more problematic literary idiom: that of Victorian England, at once conventional, stilted, formulaic, euphemistic, and not least, English, as opposed to American. For among his other qualities, Ezra Pound's Dante Alighieri is also an American scene, while Pound's reflections on translating Cavalcanti, for example, are at least as concerned with Victorian poetics as with thirteenth-century Italian.

By way of privileging Dante, rather than, say, Shakespeare, to say nothing of Tennyson, Pound escapes from an American position of marginalization regarding an English "tradition" (which would be no "closer" to Dante than he),[14] while also establishing a parallel between the predicaments of the Florentine writer and Americans of Pound's generation: that of eschewing a conventionalized, normative, essentially "foreign" tongue (Latin or Victorian English) and creating a poetic idiom out of a lively, young, but traditionless and seemingly undignified vernacular (Italian or American English). This is what enables Pound explicitly to equate Dante and Whitman, in revealing terms:

> Personally I might be very glad to conceal my relationship to my spiritual father [Whitman] and brag about my more congenial ancestry—Dante, Shakespeare, Theocritus, Villon, but the descent is a bit difficult to establish. And, to be frank, Whitman is to my fatherland (*Patriam quam odi et amo* for no uncertain reasons) what Dante is to Italy. . . . Like Dante he wrote in the "vulgar tongue," in a new metric. The first great man to write in the language of his people. (*Selected Prose*, 145–6)

Thus, even if Pound in the end cannot help being Whitman's son, rather than Dante's, to be so is to be Dante's after all, given the parallel between them. Meanwhile, in Pound's overly dense "spiritual" and "poetic" family tree, father Whitman must be made to fit next to father and mother Rossetti. All this shows how crucial the two Dantes are for Pound's identity as a particularly *American* poet. Indeed, it is probably Dante's emphasis on the vernacular along with the means he provides for bypassing the authority of the English tradition, which explains why, despite some notable exceptions, he appeals above all to American and Irish modernists: while absolutely crucial for Pound, Eliot, Yeats, Joyce, and Beckett, he holds nowhere near the same importance for Woolf, Lawrence, or even Wyndham Lewis, despite the latter's personal ties to and aesthetic affinities with the aforementioned group. In fact, at almost the same time that Pound was returning with renewed vigor to his translations of Cavalcanti (after a fifteen-year hiatus) and not coincidentally taking up the translating of Confucius, the young Samuel Beckett was linking the Dante of the vulgar tongue not to Whitman, but to the "Work in Progress" of James Joyce.[15]

In his celebrated "Dante ... Bruno. Vico .. Joyce" of 1929, Beckett refers to Dante's precedent concerning the "vulgar tongue" in defense of the language of Joyce's "Work in Progress," as *Finnegans Wake* was then known. But Beckett in no way asserts Dante to be a sort of dialectical regionalist, as Pound's likening him to Whitman might imply. Rather, Beckett emphasizes that Dante's "vulgar tongue" is a *construction*, in a manner which signally likens his project to that of Luther as described by Berman. Beckett writes,

> Dante did not adopt the vulgar out of any kind of local jingoism nor out of any determination to assert the superiority of Tuscan to all its rivals as a form of spoken Italian. . . . His conclusion is that the corruption common to all the dialects makes it impossible to select one rather than another as an adequate literary form, and that he who would write in the vulgar must assemble the purest elements from each dialect and construct a synthetic language that would at least possess more than a circumscribed local interest: which is precisely what he did. He did not write in Florentine any more than in Neapolitan. He wrote a vulgar that *could* have been spoken by an ideal Italian who had assimilated what was best in all the dialects of his country, *but which in fact was certainly not spoken nor ever had been.* ("Dante," 18, last phrase, my emphasis)

Thus, the attention paid to the particularities of local idiom as spoken leads not to regionalist mimesis but on the contrary to a heteroglot language that as a whole would probably never be "spoken" at all; indeed, such a tongue would inevitably pertain only to the discontinuities, spatial and temporal, which are only made possible by the written page, such a language being no less an abstraction than the German which Luther created to receive the Bible. In this way, an insistence on "living, spoken" language leads precisely to those elements of writing—the separation of language from the plenitude of any single, "coherent," time-space moment—which Derrida has shown to have led writing to be associated with death. The Dantesque, Joycean, and Poundian vernaculars are of the book and indeed, the mobilization of the vernacular in the formulation of textual economies which break with all "oral" models of coherence is one of the signal marks of English-language modernism.

Meanwhile, it must be noted that Dante's paradoxical need as adduced by Beckett to *create* a "vulgar" of his own, as opposed to simply "finding" it, was one which Pound saw himself as sharing, as his discussions of translation, and particularly Rossetti's, make clear. On the one hand, Pound is fully capable of lauding the purely contingent and affective relationship of anyone to his or her "mother tongue"—a relationship, following James, we could call "patriotic." Indeed, in "Notes on Elizabethan Classicists" that affect itself becomes a motive force of what Berman might call the drive to translate: "Is any foreign speech ever our own, ever so full of beauty as our *lingua materna* (whatever *lingua materna* that may be)? Or is not a new beauty created, an old beauty doubled when the overchange is well done?" (*Literary Essays*, 235). Yet at the same time, Pound is careful to stress the initial *unavailability* of the *lingua materna* itself, at least as a literary vehicle in which the "overchange" could be "well done." Thus, when Pound looks back in the late 1920s on what he considers to be the failings of his early renderings of Cavalcanti, written almost twenty years previously,[16] he explains as follows:

> My perception was not obfuscated by Guido's Italian, difficult as it then was for me to read. I was obfuscated by the Victorian language.
> If I hadn't been, I very possibly couldn't have done the job at all.
> (*Literary Essays*, 193)

And later he evokes "the crust of dead English, the sediment present in my own available vocabulary—which I, let us hope, got rid of a few years later" (193). Victorian language, if an obfuscation, is also an enabling one, and one can't *simply* divest oneself of it and move on. On the contrary, without it one is forced to invent: "Neither can anyone learn English, one can only learn a series of Englishes. Rossetti made his own language. I hadn't in 1910 made a language, I don't mean a language to use, but even a language to think in" (194).

Several points need to be stressed here. First, it would seem that for Pound, the language that Rossetti "made" is precisely the one he made for and by translating,[17] which leads to the second point—that it was almost entirely by translating, from Italian and Chinese but also from Latin and Provençal, that Pound "made" his own poetic idiom, and presumably, that in which he "thought" also. This is made entirely clear in the passage from "How to Read" discussed above, in which each major "form" of poetry—melopoeia, logopoeia, and phanopoeia—corresponds to the genius of certain particular languages, to wit, Greek and Provençal, Latin, and Chinese, respectively. It is interesting that Italian is absent from this list. But indeed, this absence makes it in certain ways all the more present, as the Tuscan Italian poetic is often figured by Pound as mediating between the Provençal whence it came and the Chinese tradition, with which it shares the insistence on precision of terminology. Italian, largely filtered through Dante and Cavalcanti—in Pound's view, its greatest poets—becomes for Pound a kind of *lingua franca* both in the original and in the idiom into which Pound translates it, the line of communication linking the other tongues, which leads to the third point implicit in the citation above, that is, the plurality not only of languages, but of any given language: "one can only learn a series of Englishes" means that "English" as organic totality has ceased to exist. In this way, the *Cantos*, like *Finnegans Wake*, are in some way "post-English"—not only because they feature many foreign languages, but because no particular English remains against which the foreign tongues can be measured, it too having become an untethered "series of Englishes." Thus, when Pound rails against the "dead English" or "sediment" of his youthful idiom, it would be wrong to identify that solely with archaism, or non-colloquial usage: the new translations of Cavalcanti which Pounds offers in his "Cavalcanti" essay of 1934 are explicitly *more* archaic than those of the *Sonnets and Ballate* of 1912, being written in what Pound dubs "pre-Elizabethan English" (*Literary Essays*, 199). But this ultra-archaizing turn, and the severe break with Rossetti it implies, can only be understood in the context of Pound's parallel gesture of adopting as his main point of focus Cavalcanti's famous canzone, the "Donna mi Prega."

This poem would become, as of the early 1930s, one of Pound's most important touchstones of artistic excellence, particularly through what he saw as its joining of erotic mystery with linguistic precision, and tags and allusions to it recur in highly strategic places throughout the *Cantos*, while a new, full translation of the work comprises by far the better part of *Canto XXXVI*.[18] Yet Pound's engagement with the poem arrives tardily; he does not single it out for praise in the considerations of Cavalcanti in *The Spirit of Romance* of 1910, and, aside from quoting the "envoi," he hardly mentions it in the preface to his early book of translations from Cavalcanti, *Sonnets and Ballate*, in which it does not figure.[19] Certainly, it could be objected that, as the title indicates, no "canzoni" were to be included in the volume, but it is difficult to believe that such a stricture would have restrained Pound had he been interested in the poem. On the contrary, by all appearances in 1910 he was simply following what had been the revisionist judgment when first proffered by Rossetti in his *Early Italian Poets* of 1861, where he claims that Guido's most famous poem, an intricate, highly learned definition of the phenomenon of love, was in fact ". . . a poem beside the purpose of poetry, filled with metaphysical jargon, and perhaps the very worst of Guido's productions" (158). Stray passages from "Troubadours—Their Sorts and Conditions" imply that in 1913, for example, such a position was indeed Pound's: "The second, and to us the dullest of the schools [of late troubadour poetry], set to explaining the nature of love and its effects" (*Literary Essays*, 103). Cavalcanti's "Donna mi Prega" is subsequently listed as a Tuscan extension of this practice, though Pound does, perhaps for the first time, translate the poem's first line: "A lady asks me, wherefore I wish to speak of an accident which is often cruel" (103).

Thus, the shift of interest to the "Donna mi Prega" represents a full-scale repudiation of Rossetti's very sense of the poetic; as Pound's long essay makes abundantly clear, what Rossetti dismisses as "metaphysical jargon" is in fact nothing other than the "speech of precision" (*Literary Essays*, 175), with definitions "as clear and definite as the prose treatises of the period" (161). In short, it is the prime example of "the radiant world where one thought cuts through another with clean edge" (154), and Pound asserts ". . . if ever poem seemed to me a struggle for clear definition, that poem is the *Donna mi Prega*" (177). Ultimately, these are the qualities of the poem and its author which lead Pound to call for a "pre-Elizabethan" English for their translation, this being "a period when the writers were still intent on clarity and explicitness, still preferring them to magniloquence and the thundering phrase" (199).[20] For all these reasons, as has been long known, the evolutions sketched in the "Cavalcanti" essay are absolutely decisive for the future of Pound's poetry and poetics, even as the *Cantos* themselves, in their engagement with history, economics, and philosophy, become increasingly concerned with the sort of "metaphysical jargon" which for Rossetti was of essence non-poetic.

That for Pound the insistence on Cavalcanti's linguistic precision, as evidenced in the "Donna mi Prega," was also of political import leaves no doubt. Pound's harping on the "general precision of terminology" (*Literary Essays*, 177) of the age of Guido, as seen above all in his masterwork, links the poem and its author to the key

Poundian problematic of "ch'ing ming," or the Confucian doctrine of the "rectification of names"—for Pound, another foundational assertion of "precise terminology," and the logical outgrowth of the "precision" of the phanopoeic Chinese ideogram as Pound conceived it. From the 1930s onward, Cavalcanti and the Chinese ideogrammic-cum-Confucian paideuma are joined into a new vortex by Pound, to which is linked, in a more explicitly political key, the Adams dynasty. Thus, one sees part of the ideograph of "ch'ing ming" closely followed by untranslated tags from the "Donna mi Prega" in *Canto LXIII* (352–3), within the series of highly citational *Cantos* on the life of John Adams, and a similar concatenation is found spaced over a few pages in *Canto LXVII* (387, 391). This element of Pound's program is well known, and I do not wish to explore it further here, but rather to note how Cavalcanti forms a thread leading from the "pre-modern," pre-imagist, and perhaps pre-Raphaelite Pound straight through to the very latest, while remaining a crucial component of the political speculations.[21] But in counterpoint to this continuity, Pound's sense of Cavalcanti's true importance, along with his own relationship to Rossetti, pivots decisively on his revalorization of the "Donna mi Prega" and the new yet archaic idiom its translation calls for. Not surprisingly, from the vantage point of the late 1920s and 1930s, and increasingly fixated on a phallicized fascism, Pound situates his earlier differences with Rossetti in terms like these: "I saw that Rossetti had made a remarkable translation of the *Vita Nuova* . . . that he was indubitably the man 'sent,' or 'chosen' for that particular job, and that there was something in Guido that escaped him or that was, at any rate, absent from his translations. A *robustezza*, a masculinity" (*Literary Essays*, 193). The "mature" Pound thus implies that it was to amend Rossetti's insufficient masculinity that he undertook to retranslate poems easily available in the hand of a still extremely popular and respected translator, to whom he knew he would inevitably be compared.[22] However, in his preface to the early book he suggests nothing of the sort, only offering an instance of what he takes to be Rossetti's misreading of Cavalcanti, while carefully acknowledging the former's status as his "father and mother" in terms of Italian poetry, as we saw above.

This rather Oedipal compromise formation of opposing Rossetti by and while emulating him is not particularly original, and Lawrence Venuti has provided a helpful reading of Pound's work as compared to Rossetti's which follows those lines.[23] Clearly, Pound's insistence on maintaining a literal fidelity to Guido's precision precisely by violating the precepts of Rossetti implies a very different mapping of debt than that which obtains in the rather joyful and provocative liberties Pound takes with his *Propertius*.[24] The degrees to which Pound's various modes in fact succeed or fail in preserving this "fidelity" have been the subject of several excellent recent studies, often calling into doubt whether the "pre-Elizabethan" style is substantially more "precise" or faithful than the earlier idiom, albeit significantly different in tone.[25] But the major point of Pound's revalorization of the "Donna mi Prega" through the lens of "precise terminology," is that such a move (already suggested in Pound's preface to the early *Sonnets and Ballate*) will allow Guido to be linked to Pound's Confucian construction, to say nothing of that which he associates with Flaubert and the "prose tradition in verse." Meanwhile, *both* the Elizabethan song mode, associated with Campion and used in the "Cavalcanti" essay translation of the "Donna mi Prega," *and* the "pre-Elizabethan" style, will remain valid for Pound henceforth, in his own work. What I would like to examine in what follows, then, is not only Pound's specific translation strategies, but also how he "translates," as it were, in so-called "original" works, along with how the latter feed back into his subsequent translation. This will allow us to gauge how the dual problems of the construction of a vulgar tongue, and the divided language and positioning of the translator, along with the translator's constant imperative to "recreate" a language through the plundering of the histories of the one in which he is writing, become integral to all of Pound's poetry, through the remodeling of the poetic and authorial positions themselves.

For an even more remarkable gesture than that of doubling Rossetti by adopting his very mask, of voicing Guido so as to echo Rossetti but also drown him out, is perhaps that contained in a book like *Canzoni* of 1911—not a book of translations aiming to attain the stature of "original" autonomous works (as *Cathay* and *Homage to Sextus Propertius* have been described), but a book of mostly "original" poetry, cheerfully adopting the pose of a book of "translations." *Canzoni*, far from an "Oedipal" struggle with either Rossetti or Guido, would seem an effort to divest oneself of authority, in both senses, in favor of the double responsibility and thus servitude of the translator before his or her texts. What has traditionally been the translator's greatest anxiety—how to answer for both the foreign text and author, *and* the contemporary context and constraints of the receiving language—becomes for Pound a liberating force, in which the semiotic and historical clash of translating becomes poetically generative. Rather than face the translator's habitual problem of finding a colloquial, unstilted language nevertheless apt to register faithfully the pressures of foreign idiom and references, Pound turns the problem on its head: how to open *original* poems to the cultural and linguistic discontinuity and clutter effected by translation. To put it another way: it is not enough to say that in Pound translations become pretexts for "original poems"; one must also add that original poems become pretexts for the language and gesture of translation. To call this *pastiche* is insufficient; rather, what becomes apparent is a poetics that generalizes the sorts of interference for which translation is notorious. The translated text, as is well known, is doomed never to be of either the time and place where it was composed, nor of that into which it is rendered, but must hover between, ghostlike.[26] At its worst, the linguistic apparition of such a spirit is called "translatorese." But it is just such a hovering that Pound's writing almost always strives to convey—not in the interest of a transcendent "universality," as Michaels argues, but in order to highlight the different markings of connotation, history, and usage which traverse the poetic utterance. Pound's poetic idiom follows what might be called the inevitable "deterritorialization" of the riven language of translation, creating texts that revel in emphatically *staging* myriad positionings— through regional, sub-group, or class dialect, the use of heavily marked literary styles, archaisms, etc.—while refusing to appeal to any ultimate discursive authenticity whatsoever.[27] If the title "Canzoni" points the way, it is probably not until *Ripostes* that Pound begins to achieve this effect on a regular basis. Let us look briefly at Pound's early "A Virginal":

> No, no! Go from me. I have left her lately.
> I will not spoil my sheath with lesser brightness,
> For my surrounding air has a new lightness;
> Slight are her arms, yet they have bound me straitly
> And left me cloaked as with a gauze of aether;
> As with sweet leaves; as with a subtle clearness.
> Oh, I have picked up magic in her nearness
> To sheathe me half in half the things that sheathe her.
>
> No, no! Go from me. I have still the flavour,
> Soft as spring wind that's come from birchen bowers.

Green come the shoots, aye April in the branches,
As winter's wound with her sleight hand she staunches,
Hath of the trees a likeness of the savour:
As white their bark, so white this lady's hours. (*Poems*, 243)

This poem, from *Ripostes* of 1912, thus published in a book on the cusp of imagism, is remarkable for many reasons.[28] A sonnet, it features a somewhat unusual but by no means transgressive rhyme scheme of abba, cddc, def, fde; indeed, many of the sonnets in the *Sonnets and Ballate* use very similar forms. Meanwhile, in terms of diction, we are confronted less with unequivocal archaisms than with a certain unidiomatic preciosity of vocabulary and construction: thus "birchen" for "birch," "as with" in line 5, "Go from me," or the somewhat archaic use of "straitly" in line 4, or "aether," in addition to "Hath" for "Has" in line 13. More important than this, however, the poem invokes nothing in its range of references, images, or figures that is distinctively contemporary, or even post-medieval. On the contrary, "sheath" and "sheathe," if here used metaphorically, nevertheless connote the world of chivalry, which subsequently colors what would otherwise be more neutral terms, such as "wound" and "staunch." And yet, the poem avoids both kitsch archaism and decorative medievalism, and this for a variety of reasons. First, here Pound follows his own precepts calling for a precision of terminology. The poem is not a series of idle poeticisms, but rather quite concretely describes the transfer of the lady's aura onto the poet and the latter's desire that such remain unalloyed, with language which is both clearly denotive ("aether") and tactile, emphasizing the more fleshly erotic dimension the title implies. Thus, the rhetoric of being "sheathed" in the lady clearly sexualizes the more mystical aura, as does the sense of the poet's subsequently carrying her "flavour" and "savour" with him. At once ensconced in the lady's aura, the poet is also bathed in her taste and smell. The final image of the white bark on the birch trees extends the concern with sheathing, with skin, with forms of wrapping, with which the poem is occupied throughout, while the conceit of April's hands taking on a likeness to the "savour" of the trees is an apt figure for the process of transfer described in the octave. The poem breaks with Victorian preciosity, then, through the sexualization of its tropes, leaving the title ironic: the "virginity" the speaker wants to preserve intact is that brought about by having penetrated the lady in whose traces he is deliciously bathed and insulated—the pure white bark of her skin become his skin, while he therefore becomes in some way feminized himself, "penetrable" as she has been. The fantasy is that of continuing to inhabit her, with such a habitation left intact, while assuming also a position regarding the policing of bodily boundaries traditionally imposed on women, and this as a consequence of the sexual act. Indeed, the poem is a striking literalization of what is merely decorative in a poem like Rossetti's translation of Dante's very famous "Donne ch'avete intelletto d'amore," from the *Vita Nuova*:

> Ladies that have intelligence in love,
>   Of mine own lady I would speak with you;
>   Not that I hope to count her praises through,
>   But telling what I may, to ease my mind.
> And I declare that when I speak thereof,
> Love sheds such perfect sweetness over me
> That if my courage failed not, certainly
>   To him my listeners must be all resign'd. (Rossetti, 203)

In his work, Pound pressures sense out of what in Rossetti is a conventional figure: "Love sheds such perfect sweetness over me," a figure not found in Dante's plainer and more precise, "Amor sì dolce mi si fa sentire" (*Vita*, 30). Rossetti's ornament becomes rhetorically generative in Pound, and the only line in "A Virginal" which feels like rhythmical stuffing is "Oh, I have picked up magic in her nearness," precisely because the term "magic" is not written into the network of auras, sheathes, traces, and barks the poem otherwise works through scrupulously. Pound's poem thus hearkens back to both Victorian sentimentality and "stil novisti" idealization, but the poem desublimates both, while reactualizating what twentieth-century discourse might call the hystericization of desire, so evident in the *Vita Nuova*.[29]

Yet the passage from Rossetti also shows another break on the part of Pound, who in no way follows Rossetti's easy, flowing lines. On the contrary, Pound's rhythm is far more sharply marked than Rossetti's, often using heavily stressed trochaic words or phrases as a bracing counterweight against the generally iambic meter, at times with the help of alliteration. Thus, "lesser brightness," "bound me straitly," "birchen bowers," or "lady's hours." As the preceding examples indicate, this rhythmic brake tends to occur towards the end of the line, and indeed, Pound creates such an effect largely through using exclusively feminine rhymes in this poem, something he never manages in any of the sonnets in the *Sonnets and Ballate*, despite his frequent intermingling of feminine rhymes therein. However, "A Virginal," while departing from the practice of the first translations of Guido, seems to point the way to the later ones, as the piece Pound offers in "Cavalcanti" as a model of "pre-Elizabethan" translations of Cavalcanti sounds in places almost like a pastiche of "A Virginal," whose counter-iambic mode it follows closely in the battle against "magniloquence," and whose rhymes it at times borrows. Thus, the first stanza:

> Who is she that comes, makying turn every man's eye
> And makying the air to tremble with a bright clearenesse
> That leadeth with her Love, in such nearness
> No man may proffer of speech more than a sigh?
> *(Literary Essays*, 199–200)

The "bright clearnesse" of the trembling air seems to have its "paternity" in the "subtle clearness" of the "surrounding air" constituting the sheath in "A Virginal," implying a genealogy other than that deriving from Rossetti. If the later version of the poem then hearkens back to "A Virginal," it is a far cry indeed from the more Rossetti-like version in the *Sonnets*, of which the first stanza reads:

> Who is she coming, drawing all men's gaze,
> Who makes the air one trembling clarity
> Till none can speak but each sighs piteously
> Where she leads Love adown her trodden ways? *(Poems*, 199)[30]

"A Virginal"—an "original" poem—is thus haunted both by Victorian medievalist translation, as exemplified in Rossetti, and by the *stil novisti* demarcations of the amorous subject. By eschewing the "fidelity" Pound insisted on in his translations of Guido through writing an "original" poem, in "A Virginal" Pound is able to lay bare what he will return to as the true literalism of Guido in the later work, and this in an idiom which will also make a reappearance therein. "A Virginal" is in this way translated out of Guido, only to be translated back into him almost twenty years later, in a series of exchanges it is hard not to figure in the procreative terms the title both invokes and denies. At the same time, the poem offers language and figures which can belong wholly neither to a contemporary context, nor to a medieval one, nor to the conventions sketched out by Rossetti for the accomodation of the medieval. "A Virginal" could not be read comfortably as a "contemporary" original poem even in 1912; nor it could it be simply read as translation or pastiche. The poem's authority, in every sense, cannot be placed. A translation of a translation, "A Virginal," as many consider "bad translations" to do, breaks with "coherence" in the traditional sense, haunted by languages, voices, and idioms it cannot claim as its own. Meanwhile, the relationship between translation, haunting, and death, whose importance for Pound has been effectively stressed by Daniel Tiffany, will return as foundational for Jack Spicer in the 1950s. Prior to examining this, however, let us turn to the concerns of Gertrude Stein and Wyndham Lewis regarding the construction of an American literary idiom—parallel to if significantly different from Pound's, and worked through in Stein's case no less than his by a confrontation with the foreign and an insistence on subjective, linguistic, and cultural displacement.

CHAPTER 5

GERTRUDE STEIN, WYNDHAM LEWIS, AND THE AMERICAN LANGUAGE

As much as Henry James before her, albeit in the glare of bohemian rupture rather than the fantasmatic glow of a renewed relationship to unbroken tradition, Gertrude Stein became the archetypal American expatriate artist for her generation, inextricably linking cultural authority to the continent once again. And as much as James if not more, she was to stress in various ways the essentially American aspect of her situation, in a body of writing consistently concerned with siting and situating generally. If her influence was decisive for Sherwood Anderson and Ernest Hemingway, two writers more obviously concerned with representing or perhaps embodying a certain "Americanness," it is by no means coincidental nor reducible to an abstraction called "style." Nor is it an accident that Wyndham Lewis places her at the center of a worried discussion of American literature and the American vernacular, which orients his analysis of Hemingway in his *Men Without Art* of 1934. The expatriate Stein becomes for Lewis a flashpoint of the dangers he sees pertaining to the propagation of American literature as vector of American speech—an idiom which threatens to blur the distinctions on which, for Lewis, subjective identity, social order, and high art all rely. If Lewis' pseudo-Nietzschean, authoritarian, and anti-Semitic account is a travesty of Stein, it is nevertheless one which is far from irrelevant, as the issues and problems Lewis pinpoints are ones that exercised Stein in the 1930s also: geography and identity, influence and originality, speech and writing, repetition and inauguration. Ultimately, for both Stein and Lewis, the question is not only *what* it means to be American or an American writer, but *where* such designations are able to signify. Which leads us to Paris, France.

In 1940, in her short book *Paris France*, Gertrude Stein famously posited a fundamental cultural and geographical displacement as a necessary preliminary for the creative act, particularly writing:

> After all everybody, that is, everybody who writes is interested in living inside themselves in order to tell what is inside themselves. That is why writers have to have two countries, the one where they belong and the one in which they live really. The second one is romantic, it is separate from themselves, it is not real but it is really there.
>
> The English Victorians were like that about Italy, the early nineteenth century Americans were like that about Spain, the middle nineteenth century Americans were like that about England, my generation the end of the nineteenth century American generation was like that about France.
>
> Of course sometimes people discover their own country as if it were the other . . . Kipling for instance discovered England but in general that other country that you need to be free in is the other country not the country where you really belong. (2–3)

If such a dialectic of the domestic and foreign is achingly familiar, a few key elements of it need nevertheless to be stressed, chief among them, the function of French expatriation for Stein: it is not a case of finding one's true home, a more suitable one than the contingent home in which one happened by chance to be born, but rather of forcibly absenting oneself from it. One settles, precisely, where one does not "belong," and in order for the dialectic to continue to function, it is imperative not to lose the original sense of belonging, as it must be continually opposed through proximity to that other country which is "separate" and "not real . . . but really there." Here, in short, is one key element in the logic of the persistence of American identity throughout Stein's writing: only through its maintenance can the French estrangement succeed in protecting the interiority and freedom, built through discontinuity, which is necessary for writing. Writing is an encounter with an "unreality" which nevertheless is "really there," and according to this logic, should Stein come to feel "French," France would no longer occupy this role for her.[1] These are the stakes of her occasional anguished sense of estrangement when visiting her childhood home, as recorded three years earlier in *Everybody's Autobiography*; if Oakland is erased, then so too would be France, in its role as separate other, in its continually present unreality.

Thus, as Stein approaches the moment when "I was to be where I had come from" (250), she writes that the Oakland hills ". . . made me very uncomfortable I do not know why but they did, it all made me uncomfortable it just did" (250). This discomfort culminates in what might seem a crisis of identity, when Stein confronts the absence left by the disappearance of her childhood home, (which had also been the model for the Hersland house in *The Making of Americans*): "Not of course the house, the house the big house and the big garden and the eucalyptus trees and the rose hedge naturally were not any longer existing, what was the use, if I had been I then my little dog would know me but it had not been I then that place would not be the place that I could see, I did not like the feeling, who has to be themselves inside them, not any one and what is the use of having been if you are to be going on being and if not why is it different and if it is different why not" (253). The phrase "who has to be themselves inside them" links these concerns to the definition of the writer as "interested in living inside themselves in order to tell what is inside themselves" which we saw above, and indeed, outside of the context of Stein's writings in the 1930s and 1940s, the passage on Oakland can lend itself to an interpretation which is misleading, to wit: Stein, faced with the ravages of time and forgetfulness, can no longer maintain the link with her former self ("it had not been I") and therefore loses the reassuring and simple sense of identity which is reaffirmed in the homely and material manner in which one is recognized by one's little dog. The problem is that this sort of identity is precisely what Stein repeatedly recuses as antithetical to the production of what she calls "master-pieces," or creative work generally. As she writes in "Henry James": "I am I not any longer when I see. This sentence is at the bottom of all creative activity. It is just the exact opposite of I am I because my little dog knows me" (*Writings 1932–1946*, 149), and if she chooses to stress the normative production and policing of identity by her oft-repeated parable of canine interpellation, it is perhaps also to distance herself from the great modernist trope of the periplus and the homecoming, as evidenced most notably by Ulysses' restoration from exile and wandering to his home, hearth, wife, and true identity, first noted, of course, by his faithful dog Argos.[2] To borrow a key term from "Melanctha," in Stein creativity is not the return to the originary hearth, but "wandering." "What Are Masterpieces and Why Are There so Few of Them," among other texts, offers a helpful elaboration of Stein's thoughts on these questions:

> The thing one gradually comes to find out is that one has no identity that is when one is in the act of doing anything. Identity is recognition, you know who you are because you and others remember anything about yourself but essentially you are not that when you are doing anything. I am I because my little dog knows me but, creatively speaking the little dog knowing that you are you and your recognising that he knows, that is what destroys creation. That is what makes school. Picasso once remarked I do not care who it is that has or does influence me as long as it is not myself. (*Writings 1932–1946*, 355)

Indeed, one of the major issues of both "What are Masterpieces" and the more or less contemporary "Geographical History of America" (both written after the trip to America which takes up so much of *Everybody's Autobiography*, but before that text was composed) is the incompatibility of "identity" with art—"the masterpiece has nothing to do with human nature or with identity" (*Writings 1932–1946*, 358) Stein writes in the former text, and that is why a masterpiece "has essentially not to be necessary" (357). Sounding not entirely unlike T. S. Eliot in "Tradition and the Individual Talent," Stein explains "It is not extremely difficult not to have identity but it is extremely difficult the knowing not having identity," to conclude that masterpieces are "knowing that there is no identity and producing while identity is not" (360). In a similar vein, in one of the many discussions of the parable of the little dog in the "Geographical History," Stein writes, "They [i.e., dogs] would like to get lost and so they would then be there where there is no identity, but a dog cannot get lost, therefore he does not have a human mind, he is never without time and identity" (*Writings 1932–1946*, 464). This sense that being lost, that achieving a therelessness, is a necessary condition in order to escape identity and create masterpieces, again returns us to the account of the "two countries" for the writer which Stein proposed in *Paris France*. And once more, we find ourselves within an obvious dialectic: if the writing of masterpieces depends on the active negating of certain forms of identity, it cannot dispense with identity and its marks entirely. Stein asks "But what can a master-piece be about mostly it is about identity and all it does and in being so it must not have any" (*Writings 1932–1946*, 360–1). It would appear, then, that the "master-piece" must take identity and identities as its matter or material, without embodying, reflecting or expressing any "identity" itself. This means that the "living inside" that *Paris France* posits as necessary for writing is clearly *not* that of the solipsistically infolded and self-identical subject, in need of protection from incursions from a threatening outside, as that is the form of identity which impedes the production of the masterpiece. This helps explain why the interiority which Stein will invoke is one she consistently associates not with a "living speech," as the logocentric heritage might lead us to expect, but with *writing*. In a key passage in *Everybody's Autobiography*, Stein links identity to writing, then writing to that which exceeds speech, and speech to the anti-creative form of identity as policed by the canine:

> All this time I did no writing. I had written and was writing nothing. Nothing inside me needed to be written. Nothing needed any word and there was no word inside me that could not be spoken and so there was no word inside me. And I was not writing. I began to worry about identity. I had always been I because I had words that had to be written inside me and now any word I had inside could be spoken it did not need to be written. I am I because my little dog knows me. But was I I when I had no written word inside me. (49–50)

Earlier in the book, Stein explains that "the spoken language is no longer interesting," and looks forward to the day when speech and writing will differ to the extent of becoming almost two different languages: "So soon we will come to have a written language that is a thing apart in English" (5). This can easily be linked to both the primacy given to abstraction and defamiliarization in Stein, and her esoteric, avant-garde aesthetic generally.[3] Yet, as many have pointed out, a certain relation to spoken English, and in particular marked American vernacular or American-dialect oral practice, is crucial for much of Stein's work, and spans her entire career. Michael North has brilliantly discussed Stein's rewriting of the autobiographical, lesbian love story *QED* as the heterosexual, African-American "dialect" novella "Melanctha" at the outset of her career,[4] but almost forty years later, in 1946, Stein was also insisting on the specificities of spoken "American" in a book like *Brewsie and Willie*. However, this apparent disjunction cannot be dismissed as an inconsistency in Stein's logic, or as the vagaries of a position which changes and wavers over time. On the contrary, the question of the possibility and effects of transfer between speech and writing—the becoming-speech of writing and the becoming-writing of speech—is central throughout Stein's entire project, and the logical outcome of many her concerns. In fact, her short, earlier text "An American and France" explicitly links the *written* to the dialectic of expatriation which opens *Paris France*, whose section on the "two countries" is very largely lifted and adapted from the former text, which evokes the artist's need for "two civilizations" (162). Indeed, in this connection the earlier essay develops at greater length two points which are generally elided in *Paris France*. First it divides expatriation or exoticism generally into two categories, "adventure" and "romance." While "adventure" makes "the distant approach nearer" (62), "Romance is the outside thing, that remains the outside thing and remaining there has its own existing and so although it is outside it is inside because it being outside and staying outside it is always a thing to be felt inside" (64). Naturally, it is "romance" that is necessary to the artist—"adventure has no relation to creation. Any one can realise that" (64)—a point which helps clarify her use of the adjective "romantic" in the passage from *Paris France* cited above.[5]

The second point pertains to the status of the written. Stein goes on to consider situations in which the second "civilization" is not available, for example the modern world which is "less and less different" (65) or the ancient one in which the creator "belonged to his own civilization and could not know another" (65). Here what supplements the unavailable cultural estrangement is nothing other than writing:

> That is really really truly the reason why they always had a special language to write which was not the language that was spoken, now it is generally considered that this was because of the necessity of religion and mystery but actually the writer could not write unless he had the two civilizations coming together the one he was and the other that was there outside him and creation is the opposition of one of them to the other. (65)

Not surprisingly, now that in our little world "the difference between writing and speaking is nothing" (66), Stein goes on to wonder "where are we to find two civilizations" (66)? The absence of cultural estrangement and the absence of the linguistic estrangement of writing are placed in parallel, and this is why not having any word "inside" that "needed to be written" corresponds to no *longer* "living inside" oneself, which in turn hands identity over to the gaze of the little dog, in a process which would seem to mirror that of losing the "romantic" country as the "outside thing." Interestingly enough, in his reflections on Stein and Hemingway, Wyndham Lewis will also equate cultural or what he calls "racial" borders with those that separate writing from speech, but with a very different sense of the implications for "civilization." The spoken, democratic, and demotic for Lewis inevitably lead to the "vulgar" and "vernacular" in the strictest sense, as the American idiom threatens to become a vector of enslavement for all the groups Lewis believes should occupy the position of Master.

The lead article from Lewis' 1934 *Men Without Art*, "Ernest Hemingway: 'The Dumb Ox,'" ostensibly concerned with Hemingway's prose style, quickly becomes a worried consideration of what the arrival of American *speech* will perpetrate upon English letters. However, at the heart of the American problematic for Lewis are not the most stereotypically autochthonous sources (for example, Faulkner, whom Lewis mentions here, and who is the subject of Chapter 2 of *Men Without Art*), but two largely expatriate, internationalist American writers—Hemingway and Stein. Yet such a state of affairs is hardly a contradiction, and this for two reasons which are at the very core of Lewis' anxieties. First of all, Lewis is concerned with nothing other than the *exportation* of the American idiom, with what we might now call globalization—the Americanization of what Lewis calls "Anglo-Saxony" is one of his major subjects. Second, Stein, both the daughter of immigrants and an émigrée herself, is for Lewis supremely exemplary of the difficulties America and its society present for establishing firm and clear boundaries and lines of demarcation on every level, which is what worries him most of all. Throughout, Lewis' key disquiet is in regard to the question of *influence*—first, that of Stein on Hemingway, which Lewis cannot condemn as unequivocally as he would like, and second, that of "American" on English language and literature, and perhaps world culture. In a reading which progressively displays its neo-Nietzschean underpinnings, Lewis will arrive at a position which condemns influence in its very self, in that it runs counter to an ideal of subjective autonomy or self-sufficiency: in terms of subjective exchange, "positive influence" becomes virtually a contradiction in terms. Lewis is thus far removed from Stein's "I do not care who it is that has or does influence me as long as it is not myself," yet be that as it may, his reading of Stein is in many ways more insightful and prescient than its own terms allow it to recognise, in addition to being, as Lewis does partially discern, closer to her positions than it might seem, or he might like.

Lewis nearly begins the article, and therefore, the entire volume *Men Without Art*, with a confession and enactment of weakness: " 'I have a weakness for Ernest Hemingway,' as the egregious Miss Stein says" (19). To a considerable extent, the rest of Lewis' article will be nothing other than a meditation on this phrase, not least of all its status as a foreign graft which Lewis has allowed to implant itself within "his" words, as his quotation marks clearly demonstrate. For if Miss Stein is "egregious" in certain ways for Lewis, his own critical conquest by Ernest Hemingway is no less so, while his compulsion to echo the "Jewish lady," as he later calls her, is most egregious of all. Certainly, Lewis' main concern throughout his study of Hemingway is nothing other than weakness, for his own is but the duplicate of Hemingway's. And in crucial ways, Lewis finds Hemingway to be irremediably "weak"—in terms of his prose style, the narratives he chooses to tell, and the place he assigns to his protagonists within them. Lewis rails throughout against Hemingway's passivity and susceptibility to lesser influence, only to arrive at the same position which he criticizes: one in which weakness is indulged, rather than purged, due to the influence of the weakness of another. Weakness is a form of infection, then, sliding from Hemingway into Lewis, and as Lewis defines the origin and nature of this infection, along with the boundaries it transgresses, a very different resonance is given to the question which originally motivates Lewis' study: that of the "political significance" (19) of Hemingway's work. At the conclusion of Lewis' account, this "significance" is associated with three linked traits of Hemingway: his capacity to suffer influence, itself negative, his capacity to suffer the particular influence of "Miss Stein," which is even more negative, and finally, his capacity to let his own authorial voice be permeated and penetrated by the idiom of the American "urban proletariat." The problem for Lewis, however, and what makes his study fascinating, is that these fatal flaws become inseparable, as he recognizes, from Hemingway's successes, which Lewis judges considerable in spite of all.

According to Lewis, Hemingway's style is notable above all for two elements: its use of the language of the "urban proletariat" (24) and its incorporation of certain techniques derived from Stein. Both these aspects are highly problematic for Lewis, who sees them as related, and in both cases, the key category for Lewis is that of passivity. Thus, while Lewis praises Hemingway's writing as an "art of the surface" (20), which he privileges over "romantic" emphases on interiority, and while he appreciates the work as ". . . almost purely an art of action, and of very violent action" (20), in a very telling passage Lewis nevertheless distinguishes it from the robust kinetic prose of Mérimée, to whom Lewis believes Hemingway can be to some extent compared:

> Between them [Mérimée and Hemingway] there is this deep gulf fixed: that gifted he of today is "the man that things are done to"—even the "I" in *The Sun Also Rises* allows his Jew puppet to knock him about and "put him to sleep" with a crash on the jaw, and this first person singular covers a very aimless, will-less person, to say the least of it: whereas that *he* of the world of *Carmen* (so much admired by Nietzsche for its bright Latin violence and directness—*la gaya scienza*) or of Corsican vendetta, he was in love with *will*, as much as with violence . . . (22)[6]

In fact, this propensity of being knocked out by a "Jew," of allowing, through sheer passivity, the reversal of what Lewis considers to be natural hierarchies, is emblematic of Hemingway's relationship to both Stein and vernacular American. Thus, Lewis feels the need to discuss a "very surprising fact" in relation to Hemingway's style:

> He has suffered an overmastering influence, which cuts his work off from any other, except that of his mistress (for his master has been a *mistress!*). So much is this the case, that their destinies (his and that of the person who so strangely hypnotized him with her repeating habits and her *faux-naif* prattle) are for ever interlocked. His receptivity was so abnormally pronounced (even as a craftsman, this capacity for being *the person that things are done to* rather than the person who naturally initiates what is to be done to others, was so marked) and the affinity thus disclosed was found so powerful! I don't like speaking about this. . . . But there it is: if you ask yourself how you would be able to tell a page of Hemingway, if it were unexpectedly placed before you, you would be compelled to answer, *Because it would be like Miss Stein!* (24)

And in addition, just as Hemingway allows himself to be "like Miss Stein," he also allows himself to be infiltrated, permeated, by the American vernacular language: ". . . with Mr. Hemingway, the story is told in the tone, and with the vocabulary, of the persons described. The rhythm is the anonymous folk-rhythm of the urban proletariat. Mr. Hemingway is, self-consciously, a folk-prose-poet in the way that

Robert Burns was a folk-poet" (23–4). This is why Hemingway is the "dumb ox"—his work possesses a "penetrating quality, like an animal speaking" (19), and that animal is the ox, privileged emblem of that to which Lewis feels Hemingway gives voice: the "*bêtise* of the herd" (20). For Lewis, the problem is the extent to which Hemingway's passivity entails that he himself be penetrated, infected, with this "bêtise," just as he is by Stein. But this problem is complicated for Lewis even further, for, despite his distaste for Stein's work and disgust at the thought that the manly Hemingway has been penetrated by a Jewish lesbian, if one agrees to suspend the question of influence in and of itself, Lewis is forced to conclude that Stein's on Hemingway is largely beneficial:

> If we blot out Gertrude Stein, and suppose she does not exist, does this part of Hemingway's equipment help or not? We must answer *Yes* I think. It does seem to help a good deal: many of his best effects are obtained by means of it. (26)

Lewis's problem here is that he is forced to recognize that the negative elements which are influence and passivity have produced positive effects in Hemingway's prose. To acknowledge such a state of affairs, Lewis feels, is an extremely problematic denial of the "individual" given how "near to communism as we all are" (26). Thus, in a remarkably circular bit of reasoning, Lewis will conclude that Hemingway's receptivity to Stein is indeed negative after all, as it imposes upon him the "Stein ethos," which is in fact one of passive receptivity:

> He passes over into the category of *those to whom things are done*, from that of those who execute—if the latter is indeed where he originally belonged. One might even go so far as to say that this brilliant Jewish lady had made a *clown* of him by teaching Ernest Hemingway her baby-talk! So it is a pity. And it is very difficult to know where Hemingway proper begins and Stein leaves off as an artist. It is an uncomfortable situation for the critic, especially for one who "has a weakness" for the male member of this strange spiritual partnership, and very much prefers him to the female. (26–7)

In other words, the passivity Hemingway inherits from Stein makes him susceptible to a passive position in relationship to Stein, which is supposed to be responsible for the passivity in the first place.

Meanwhile, the danger of becoming one of those "to whom things are done" within a relationship in which boundaries are so fundamentally uncertain that one cannot determine exactly where the "male member" leaves off, despite one's weakness for it, reveals the complicity of anxieties concerning stylistic autonomy, cultural identity, and linguistic integrity with those pertaining to sexual identity and castration in Lewis' tracing of authorial potency.[7] For this blurring of distinctions and boundaries which Stein's prose effects is for Lewis precisely the main failing of the language of the American "urban proletariat"—the vernacular which marks Hemingway's style—and largely, again, due to a "Jewish" influence.

Indeed, the figure of the "Jew" is crucial to Lewis' qualification of Hemingway's use of "American" as necessarily implying passivity, "bêtise", and the voice of the herd. As Lewis has nothing against *local* vernacular, it is essential for him to distinguish regional dialects from idioms tied to social class—writers like Synge and Burns are exonerated for their use of folk dialects because the latter represent "the mixture of English and another language, Gaelic or lowland Scotch" (29), and these "dialects" are opposed to "low-English," "slum-English" and "cockney" (29) which derive from class, as would Hemingway's "American." At this point in his argument, Lewis begins to borrow heavily and tendentiously from H. L. Mencken's monumental study, *The American Language*. Following the latter, Lewis adopts the term "Beach-la-mar" to refer to pidgin Englishes generally, and silently broadening its application far beyond Mencken's, deems it to be Hemingway's language—the new proletarian idiom of America. Lewis goes on to point out that it contains many "immigrant words" (29) which he sees as an advantage over British cockney, but it remains, as Lewis puts it, "fundamentally *a class-jargon*" brimming with misshapen new terms and structures (29), and he bewails the fact that "negro and immigrant pressure" are forcing American English to "simplify itself grammatically" (29). At the same time, here more in line with Mencken, he considers that English grammar is already the simplest to be found among the modern tongues, this making it likely to become the new universal "volapük," or *lingua franca* (30–1). Most importantly, Lewis follows Mencken in suggesting that this immigrant-induced grammatical simplification is mirrored by the reduction of a structural element of English which is on the contrary quite elaborate: its plethora of vowel sounds. Lewis quotes Mencken directly on the new, debased usages cropping up in America: "Many characteristic Americanisms of the sort to stagger lexicographers—for example, *near-silk*—have come from the Jews, whose progress in business is a good deal faster than their progress in English" (30, cited in Lewis), and then again on the question of vowel disorders, concerning which Mencken says this:

> The immigrant, facing all these vowels, finds some of them quite impossible; the Russian Jew, for example, cannot manage *ur*. As a result, he tends to employ a neutralized vowel in the situations which present difficulties, and this neutralized vowel, supported by the slip-shod speech-habits of the native proletariat, makes steady progress. (31, cited in Lewis)

Lewis ends his discussion of the subject with dire if rather arch warnings for England, and a call to discipline: ". . . the above-mentioned 'neutralized vowel' will make its way over here [that is, to Britain] in due course, who can doubt it? These vowels must be watched. *Watch your vowels* should be our next national slogan!" (31). Once again, the "Jew" is depicted as an agent of the dismantling of boundaries, here, of the erosion which transforms a race-language into a class-jargon. Of course, what is crucial to note is that this sort of racism can only be maintained through a simultaneous implicit *denial* of "race," for unlike the Irish or the Scots, the Jews are seen as bringing no new linguistic racial "genius" into English at all, but rather as undermining it from within, neutralizing or neutering the careful distinctions it articulates, and which articulate it. Thus the "Jews" are not simply a "low" race within a complex fantasmatic hierarchy. On the contrary, they are the most horrible thing of all: a race without a racial quality, a people without a category who in consequence erode the categories they find around them. Without essence, the Jews assimilate—citing, repeating, echoing, and finally de-differentiating the "originals" to such a degree that they become no more than citers, repeaters, and echoers themselves, just as Hemingway haplessly echoes Stein, whose very terms of affection for her prey are in turn parroted by Lewis.

For Lewis, then, Hemingway is the supreme smithy of two very troubling sorts of ore: the Stein style and "Beach-la-mar." Hemingway's style is so largely comprised of "the brute material of every-day proletarian speech and feeling" and "the prose of the street-car or the provincial newspaper or the five and ten cent store" (32) that Lewis declares quite simply: "It is not writing, if you like"

(33). Yet Lewis' mobilization of Mencken against Hemingway and Stein demands careful consideration. First of all, Mencken's large and influential work was nothing other than a *defense* of the American language, stressing both its differences from and dignities compared to standard British English. Second of all, Lewis' citations from Mencken give a partial and misleading sense of Mencken's arguments and concerns. For example, if Mencken's anti-Semitism and racism are much discussed and beyond dispute, the centrally strategic role Lewis gives to Jewish mispronunciation and malapropism is quite simply absent in Mencken. Lewis' telling example of the difficulties of the "Russian Jew" with English vowels comes in the midst of a seven-page chapter on "Vulgar Pronunciation," of which only three paragraphs are devoted to "vowel neutralization" (324–6), a process also at work, for other reasons and at a slower pace, in England (324), and one which Mencken sees as in no way threatening to the language, but rather taking its place in the construction of the American accent alongside phenomena such as the "misplaced vowels" which were "brought from England by the colonists," and whose partial disappearance due to the pressures of normative "pedagogy" (323) Mencken regrets. Likewise, Mencken consistently and repeatedly views the disappearance of distinctions and inflections in the course of the history of a language as a largely inevitable and entirely inconsequential phenomenon. In fact, at times he suggests that the grammatical "simplicity" of English as compared to German is actually desirable, and he rails against linguistic "purists" throughout. As Lewis partially acknowledges, his linguistic anxieties are not ones Mencken shares.[8] Rather, Mencken's emphases are two-fold: first, on "American" as a full-fledged and independent native tongue in its own right, second, that as such it become a vehicle for a full-blown literature of which it would be the medium. For Mencken, if American is to some extent ruined it is not by immigrant or class pressures, but by slavish attempts to force it to conform with the alien standards of "English." In his introduction he writes of the predicament facing the American student:

> What their professors try to teach is not their mother-tongue at all, but a dialect that stands quite outside their common experience, and into which they have to translate their thoughts, consciously and painfully. . . . Thus the study of the language he is supposed to use, to the average American, takes on a sort of bilingual character. (4)

In his conclusion, he awaits the writer who, going beyond Whitman's "half attempt," will fully revel in and reveal the American idiom:

> As yet, American suffers from the lack of a poet bold enough to venture into it, as Chaucer ventured into the despised English of his day, and Dante into the Tuscan dialect, and Luther, in his translation of the Bible, into peasant German. (395)

In short, Mencken calls for the American writer capable of successfully *dispensing* with a labour of translation, of making available for literature the vulgar tongue which, despite its evident availability for *speech*, is failing to be *written*. That Mencken goes on to compare such an undertaking with work already done by the "neo-Celts" Douglas Hyde, John Millington Synge, and Augusta Gregory within the "Irish dialect of English, vastly less important than the American" (396), shows that Mencken in no way endorses the distinction between "racial" dialect and "class" dialect which becomes so crucial for Lewis, who is diametrically opposed to Mencken when he asserts

> And the Anglo-Saxon *Beach-la-mar* of the future will not be quite the same thing as Chaucer or Dante, contrasted with the learned tongue. For the latter was the speech of a race rather than of a class, whereas our "vulgar tongue" will really be *vulgar*. (24, Lewis' italics)

For Lewis, the final irony of Hemingway's dubious frequentations is that the Stein element is the only one in his work which is *not* simply the expression of the anonymous, herd-like, proletarian mass voice, speaking the mass-produced world of alienated proletarian labor: "Hemingway's is a poster-art, in this sense: or a *cinema in words*. *The steining* in the text of Hemingway is as it were the hand-made part" (33), though in some way not by Hemingway's hands, as we have seen.[9]

Lewis, to a certain extent, continues the worried interrogations of Henry James—who is also discussed at length in *Men Without Art*, though in a different context—when he evoked dismay at the immigrants' propensity to "dump their mountain of promiscuous material into the foundations of the American [language]" ("Question of Our Speech," 54), and who said of the "Accent of the Future," as voiced in America, "we shall not know it for English—in any sense for which there is an existing literary measure" (*American Scene*, 106). In both cases, however, unlike Lewis, James regards such losses as ones pertaining to the contingencies of his own personal history and habits, and not necessarily as forms of historical decline. On the other hand, elements of Mencken's position join a venerable tradition which can be seen as far back, for example, as in Thomas Wentworth Higginson's "Letter to a Young Contributor"—published in the *Atlantic Monthly* in 1862, and as we know, decisive for Emily Dickinson. There, Higginson exhorts young writers as follows: ". . . do not shrink from Americanisms, so they be good ones" (278), and continues shortly thereafter to specify:

> To the previous traditions and associations of the English tongue we add resources of contemporary life such as England cannot rival. Political freedom makes every man an individual. . . . We unconsciously demand of our writers the same dash and the same accuracy which we demand in railroading or dry-goods-jobbing. The mixture of nationalities is constantly coining and exchanging new felicities of dialect: Ireland, Scotland, Germany, Africa are present everywhere with their various contributions of wit and shrewdness, thought and geniality. . . . Many foreign cities may show a greater variety of mere national costumes, but the representative value of our immigrant tribes is far greater from the very fact that they merge their mental costume in ours. Thus the American writer finds himself among his phrases like an American sea-captain amid his crew: a medley of all nations, waiting for the strong organizing New-England mind to mould them into a unit of force. (278–9)

Though much of this could in turn be traced back to Whitman and Emerson, many of the elements here deserve to be stressed: the contributions of "Africa," glaringly absent from Mencken; the sense that the American obsession with business efficiency is in fact beneficial to writing, rather than its enemy; the assertion that the *greater degree* of "merging" of immigrant "mental costumes" is an advantage, rather than the contrary, and finally, the strange image of the American writer as a kind of Ahab, mobilizing a motley linguistic crew by virtue of his own New England singleness of purpose. For Higginson, the American voice is anything but that of the passivity and lassitude which Lewis detects in Hemingway's mongrel "Beach-la-mar," yet it is also, ultimately, only the white New Englander who will be empowered to speak it. Without denigrating Higginson's courageous commitment, one can hardly be surprised that the piece was written by a man shortly to become the white commander of a black regiment in the Civil War. Indeed, the ultimate appeal to the white hierarchical superior as figure of American *force* might be seen to compensate for an underlying anxiety regarding a potential threat to the "executive will and intelligence," which according to Lewis, the American language itself, as seen in Hemingway, makes unavailable (36). In 1934, Lewis could not have known how sinister his words would sound to our ears, when he delivers on his promise to discuss the "politics" of Hemingway's style and of the language he writes in, compromised by immigrants and Jews:

> Where the "politics" come in I suppose by this time you will have gathered. This is the voice of the "folk," of the masses, who are the cannon-fodder, the cattle outside the slaughter-house, serenely chewing the cud—*of those to whom things are done*, in contrast to those who have executive will and intelligence. (36, Lewis' emphases)

Yet in this discussion Lewis' words resonate in still another way, as Stein's own agency, and questions of influence, passivity, and subjective assertion, also define considerations of her negotiations with Americanness and identity generally at this time, on both a textual and a biographical level.

The ambiguities of Stein's position during the Second World War have been the subject of a great deal of recent discussion, and at the heart of them is an unpublished translation project. For if Stein's rather equivocal stance regarding Vichy and the collaboration has long been known, as well as her close friendship with rabid anti-Free Mason and Vichy collaborator Bernard Faÿ, it has more recently come to general attention that during the war Stein took up the task of translating the speeches of the Maréchal Pétain into English for an American audience, quite probably through Faÿ's offices. Astonishingly, Stein flirted with a role of cultural and political transmitter and translator quite similar to that reveled in by Pound in his notorious radio broadcasts. I do not wish to enter the lively debate as to why a well-known Jewish lesbian would support the Vichy government, nor pronounce on the obvious answer which is often given: to save her skin.[10] Even as a bad faith ploy, such a project raises enormous questions, among them, of course, the extent to which Stein's celebratory writings about G.I.s, written immediately following the liberation, might have been part of a process she hoped would lead to a patriotic rehabilitation. But what the new emphasis on translation in Stein's work can help bring to light, is the odd fact that her theoretical musings on the issue are consistently linked to the figure of Henry James, who is himself crucial to Stein's sense of the evolution of Americanness in literature and language generally. Moreover, all these concerns to some degree echo the anxieties pertaining to responsibility, originality, and the relationship between expression, language, and inaugural or executive will which so troubled Lewis.

Stein's "Henry James," from the posthumously published *Four in America*, devotes a great deal of space to her own only serious venture into translation other than the Pétain project, that is, her rendering of Georges Hugnet's long poem *Enfances*, which resulted not only in a personal break with Hugnet but also in a text so different from the French that it came to be published as an "original" work by Stein, with a title that referred to the quarrel to which it gave rise: *Before the Flowers of Friendship Faded Friendship Faded*. In the James piece as well as elsewhere, Stein links the lessons she learned in translating to her new understanding of the difference between Shakespeare's plays and sonnets, as well as to the achievement of James himself. The exact nature of Stein's arguments is subject to some debate, but they derive from an initial opposition between two ways of writing, which she establishes by placing in parallel the sonnets and *Before the Flowers*, putting them in the category of works that "were written as they were going to be written," as opposed to Shakespeare's plays which "were written as they were written" (*Writings 1932–1946*, 150). Stein unquestionably prefers Shakespeare's plays, and the distinctions she draws in relation to Shakespeare between writing "his way" in the drama as opposed to "some way of somebody's" (160) in the sonnets, make it tempting to assume that Stein places translation and the sonnets into a category of works that are somehow dictated by external demands or "influence," and thus are not consonant with the expression of the author's own individual genius. In this light, translation could be seen to threaten her "own" writing in much the same way Lewis saw her work as threatening Hemingway's. This is no doubt partially true, but only up to a point, as is evidenced by several elements. First of all, the major claim made for James in the essay is precisely his ability to write in *both* of the opposed "ways": "He saw he could write both ways at once which he did and if he did he did" (163).[11] Second of all, we have already seen in terms of expatriation and writing how crucial the relationship to an "outside" can often be for Stein's sense of "creation," and this emerges once again as the operative category governing Stein's thought on these issues in the late "Transatlantic Interview" of 1946, where translation and the sonnets are linked not only to each other but also to the writerly practice she calls "narrative": "A young French poet [Hugnet] had begun to write, and I was asked to translate his poems, and there I made a rather startling discovery that other people's words are quite different from one's own, and that they can not be the result of your internal troubles as a writer" (19). According to Stein, Shakespeare "never expressed any feelings of his own" in the sonnets, which is why they are marked by a "smoothness" unlike the preferable "fullness and violence" of the plays (19). But Stein goes on to insist that what makes "narrative" similar to translation or the sonnets, is that it "is not what is in your mind but what is in somebody else's" (19), with *The Autobiography of Alice B. Toklas* figuring as prime example: "But still I had done what I saw, what you do in translation or in a narrative. I had recreated the point of view of somebody else" (19). Sorting this out, it would seem that the ability to mix the "fullness and violence" of one's own words with the representation of the point of view of somebody else constitutes the two ways of writing of Henry James.

Translation, then, need not be for Stein an essentially passive act, which threatens the autonomy of genius, as some have suggested.[12] On the contrary, it enters into the broader category of the "outside" which is so important for Stein at this time, and she explicitly likens her rendering of Alice's point of view—or any rendering of any point of view, for that matter—to translation. Thus, translation may be seen to take its place alongside expatriation and *writing* as forms of externality which are wholly enabling for "creation,"[13] while no less than for Pound, for Stein too James emerges as involved in a labour of translation. However, Stein links herself to James not only as a notably *American* writer, but also as one who, through her relationship to the *written*, is engaged in the project of constructing the native autonomy of American *speech*. It is this concern that ties her engagement with James to her latest works.

In the American G.I. texts, for example, as Julie Abraham has pointed out, Stein very largely portrays her sense of patriotic kinship with the young soldiers in terms of their shared relationship to a language, and a linguistic and cultural predicament.[14] Notably, in a text like "The Coming of the Americans," a celebration of the American liberation of occupied France, Stein, much like Mencken, stresses the need for Americans to *appropriate* a true American language, while simultaneously positing writing—the true concern of the artist in words, as opposed to speech—as a conservative element inhibiting this development. No less than for Lewis, the relationship between writing and speech becomes a *political question*. In her epilogue to "The Coming of the Americans," Stein closes the work with a discussion of American identity and American speech, the two being intimately linked. "There is one thing one has to remember about America, it had a certain difficulty in proving itself American which no other nation has ever had," Stein writes (*Selected*, 705). A large part of this difficulty is tied to the difficulty of the American language in differentiating itself:

> The trouble of course is or was that by the time America became itself everybody or very nearly everybody could read and write. . . . America as everybody knew how to read and write the language instead of changing as it did in countries where nobody knew how to read and write while the language was being formed, the American language instead of changing remained English, long after the Americans in their nature their habits their feelings their pleasures and their pains had nothing to do with England. (705)

Stein will conclude that the G.I.s of the Second World War "dominate their language" in a way that the First World War doughboys did not, and thus "in dominating their language which is now all theirs they have ceased to be adolescents and have become men" (706). The manner in which Stein argues that this "domination" has been achieved is crucial, and links this piece to many other of her reflections from the 1930s and 1940s. Given the resistance written forms presented to linguistic change, Stein explains: "So the only way the Americans could change their language was by choosing words which they liked better than other words, by putting words next to each other in a different way than the English way, by shoving the language around until at last now the job is done, we use the same words as the English do but the words say an entirely different thing" (705–6). Obviously, this concept of using the "same words" to say "an entirely different thing" would be an excellent description of Stein's own writing practice, which rarely resorts to modernist emphases on neologism or the tortured pursuit of the "mot juste," but rather tends to take a small number of common, banal, and often seemingly inappropriate terms, and through various forms of repetition, decontextualization, and defamiliarization, creates the impression that these now emptied counters are coming to say "an entirely different thing."[15] Thus, Stein would seem to be suggesting that her own writing is quintessentially American, all the more so as this emphasis on the deliberate choosing of words hearkens back to what Stein had defined as the prime characteristics of American literature in "What is English Literature," along with those of a writer she consistently defines as centrally American—Henry James.

"What is English Literature" forms part of her four *Lectures in America*, which, as the title indicates, gathers together talks she gave on her 1934–5 triumphal tour of America. Very early on in the piece she specifies "by English literature I mean American literature too" (*Writings 1932–1946*, 195), yet a fair amount of the text is devoted to distinguishing between the two. For Stein, the main characteristics of specifically "English" literature derive from being "shut up" and "shut in" within the "simply daily island life" (198). Not surprisingly, this insularity produces paradoxical effects, as "the things being shut in are free and that makes more poetry so very much more poetry" (199). Stein will go on to emphasize in various ways that the sense of completeness and totality provided by "island life" precludes an emphasis on the deliberate choosing of words, which she feels marks the more cosmopolitan and somewhat anomalous Elizabethan period:

> In that long period there were so many words that were chosen. Everybody was busy choosing words. . . . It was no longer just a song it was a song of words that were chosen to make a song. . . . and that is the important thing it was the specific word next to the specific word next it chosen to be next it that was the important thing. That made the glory that culminated in what is called Elizabethan. (207)

American life, even more given over to difference and complication than that of the Elizabethans, will of course also lead to a literature of "choosing" rather than "finding" words, and be even further from Chaucer's "whole thing" which "does not need explaining, it merely needs stating" (216).[16] For this reason Stein posits a privileged relationship between Elizabethan literature and American: "It has often been known that American literature in a kind of a way is more connected with English Elizabethan than with later and that if you remember was at a time when words were chosen to be next one to the other . . ." (220). American literature, above all that of Henry James, continues this tradition, but with a difference, as in America there is a supplementary "separation from what is chosen to what is that from which it has been chosen" (220); American literature "has to be without any connection with that from which it is choosing" (221). Thus, the importance of James:

> And so this makes it that Henry James just went on doing what American literature had always done, the form was always the form of the contemporary English one, but the disembodied way of disconnecting something from anything and anything from something was the American one. The way it had of often all never having any daily living was an American one. (222)

Stein goes on to insist, "Some say that it is repression but no it is not repression it is a lack of connection, of there being no connection with living and daily living because there is none" (222), before establishing herself as James' successor: "And then I went on to what was the American thing the disconnection" (222).

What emerges, then, is that the G.I.s who now "have this language that is theirs" (*Selected*, 706) have either completed the work of James or Stein, or become the rightful heirs to whom this labour is now bequeathed, as their language too consists above all of "choosing words." It is not so much that their spoken language might give rise to writing, as an "oral" or "vernacular" text like *Brewsie and Willie* could lead one to believe, as that their speaking is already a *form* of writing, the result of a writing which had to *choose*, to violently and deliberately supplement the lack of "natural" linguistic development, itself retarded, ironically, by the predominance of the written word. If *Everybody's Autobiography* privileges writing at the expense of speech, because "talking is not thinking or feeling at all any more, it used to be but it is not now but writing is" (33), the epilogue of "The Coming of the Americans" and *Brewsie and Willie* seem to celebrate the rediscovery of legitimate chat; where Lewis worries about writing opening its porous borders to the speech of "Beach-la-mar," Stein celebrates a new talking brought about by a literally literary "disconnect."

This privileging of disconnection shows why, for Stein, expatriation and expatriate writers are at the center of the American problematic. "There is something in this native land business and you cannot get away from it" (*Selected*, 697) Stein writes in "The Coming of the Americans," yet as she put it in *Everybody's Autobiography*, when still resisting encouragements to visit the US, "After all I am American alright. Being there does not make me more there" (94). William Carlos Williams said something very similar about her in 1930:

> Stein's pages have become like the United States viewed from an airplane—the same senseless repetitions, the endless multiplications of toneless words, with these she had to work.
>
> No use for Stein to fly to Paris and forget it. The thing, the United States, the unmitigated stupidity, the drab tediousness of the democracy, the overwhelming number of the offensively ignorant, the dull nerve—is there in the artist's mind and cannot be escaped by taking a ship. She must resolve it if she can, if she is to be. (*Imaginations*, 352)

Yet one must take issue with Williams' assumption that the flight to Paris was an attempt to forget; on the contrary, as the passage on the writer's "two countries" from *Paris France* makes clear, at the very least Stein wished to present expatriation as an *extension* of the "disconnect" at the heart of American writing as she saw it. This is clear throughout *Paris France*, where it is always the inappropriateness of France for the twentieth century and its innovations—innovations which Stein consistently associates with America and herself—which make it their inevitable locale:

> And that is what made Paris and France the natural background of the art and literature of the twentieth century. Their tradition kept them from changing and yet they naturally saw things as they were, and accepted life as it is, and mixed things up without any reason at the same time. Foreigners were not romantic to them, they were just facts, nothing was sentimental they were just there, and strangely enough it did not make them make the art and literature of the twentieth century but it made them be the inevitable background for it. (17)

and subsequently:

> So it begins to be reasonable that the twentieth century whose mechanics, whose crimes, whose standardisation began in America, needed the background of Paris, the place where tradition was so firm that they could look modern without being different, and where their acceptance of reality is so great that they could let any one have the emotion of unreality. (18)

Stein frequently asserts that America is the "oldest" nation as it was the first to enter the twentieth century; as a creature of that century herself, Stein needs the "unreality" of Paris—for her, still Benjamin's capital of the nineteenth century—as "background" for the revolutionary work of Spaniards in painting, herself in writing. Meanwhile, elements of Americanness are not only maintained but often cultivated and turned loose, yet precisely as *estranged* from any value they might have as onto-topological indices of subjective authenticity or coherence.[17] In this way, William Carlos Williams' description of Stein's writing as being like the "United States viewed from an airplane" is all the more apt, the airplane's view capturing not only the geometrical flattening of Stein's prose, but also the distanced, abstracted reappropriation and display of the "American" material. However, Stein's flight to Paris is part of her flight "over" the United States, and Paris, no less than America, finds itself "unreal." This complex negotiation with local grounding and its derealization is also key for another California writer, likewise given to a writing of displacements: Jack Spicer.

CHAPTER 6

JACK SPICER'S *AFTER LORCA*: TRANSLATION AS DELOCALIZATION

Jack Spicer—poet, bohemian, linguist, alcoholic, and early gay-rights activist—died of alcohol poisoning in San Francisco in 1965, at the age of forty. It is reported that his penultimate words, uttered in agony on his deathbed, were: "My vocabulary did this to me."[1] His inclusion in a study of expatriate Modernists may seem anomalous. Not only was he not an expatriate, he hardly even crossed the borders of the United States. Moreover, born in 1925, he is usually grouped with the "New American Poetry" poets, and more specifically, the San Francisco Renaissance coterie, which consisted largely of former students of the University of California at Berkeley, like Spicer, Robert Duncan, and Robin Blaser, and refugees from the experimental Black Mountain College, where Charles Olson had been rector. What I hope to demonstrate here, however, is the extent to which his aggressively regionalist poetics, in its dialectic with an "Outside" enacted notably through translation, is a clear inheritance of the expatriate modernists of the previous generation. Writing Spicer into the network of issues we have been studying is not meant to imply a seamless appurtenance to "modernism," but rather to stress how any "post-modernism" invoked regarding his work must mean a deep critical dialogue with those predecessors. In Spicer, the typically modernist double engagement with the foreign, implying a new elaboration of the domestic, could be said to come home. Spicer posits translation as central to his project in a manner wholly deriving from Pound, while his emphasis on the "Outside," on a regional grounding established through the necessity of its negation, jibes with much of what we have seen in our examination of Stein. As Michael Davidson and others have stressed, "community" was crucial to Spicer's poetics: until his death, almost all of his work was published independently, often in mimeograph form, and distributed free in local bars and coffee shops or sold for next to nothing, while at various points in his life, Spicer formally prohibited his work from being distributed outside the San Francisco Bay Area. Yet this sense of community, through the key tropes of haunting and translation, is one which also crosses languages, continents, and the grave.[2] Even more, this paradoxical grounding of "community" on the ruptures of death, geographical distance, and translation is inextricably tied to a reconsideration of the poetic object as such, or the poem as object, which parallels the deconstruction of poetic subjectivity and agency his well known theory of inspiration as "dictation" enacts. In order to examine this, we must look briefly not only at his extended translation project, *After Lorca*, but also at his subsequent book, *Admonitions* of 1958, which, working from an epistolary model, explicitly refers to the *After Lorca* of the year before.

Indeed, Spicer's key declaration from *Admonitions* has achieved canonical status in the small but growing body of criticism devoted to his work[3]; it is made in the course of anointing his previous book, *After Lorca*, the inauguration of his mature poetic production. Spicer writes, ". . . all my stuff from the past . . . looks foul to me." He goes on to explain:

> Halfway through *After Lorca* I discovered that I was writing a book instead of a series of poems. . . .
>
> The trick naturally is what Duncan[4] learned years ago and tried to teach us—not to search for the perfect poem but to let your way of writing of the moment go along its own paths, explore and retreat but never be fully realized (confined) within the boundaries of one poem. This is where we were wrong and he was right, but he complicated things for us by saying that there is no such thing as good or bad poetry. There is—but not in relation to the single poem. There is really no single poem.
>
> That is why all my stuff from the past (except the *Elegies* and *Troilus*) looks foul to me. The poems belong nowhere. They are one night stands filled (the best of them) with their own emotions, but pointing nowhere, as meaningless as sex in a Turkish bath. It was not my anger or my frustration that got in the way of my poetry but the fact that I viewed each anger and each frustration as unique—something to be converted into poetry as one would exchange foreign money. I learned this from the English Department (and from the English Department of the spirit—that great quagmire that lurks at the bottom of all of us) and it ruined

ten years of my poetry. Look at those other poems. Admire them if you like. They are beautiful but dumb.

Poems should echo and reecho against each other. They should create resonances. They cannot live alone any more than we can. . . .

Things fit together. We knew that—it is the principle of magic. Two inconsequential things can combine together to become a consequence. This is true of poems too. A poem is never to be judged by itself alone. A poem is never by itself alone. (*Collected Books*, 60–1)

This statement, and the practice it describes, are rightly seen as turning points in Spicer's poetics, marking his abandonment of the lyric as compositional unit, and his turn to what he would call the "serial poem" or "book" as an alternate structure. Robin Blaser, to whom the above statement was initially addressed as a letter, before being included verbatim by Spicer in *Admonitions*, accepts this turn to book-form as the break between Spicer's juvenile and mature work. Thus Blaser's posthumous edition of Spicer's poetry is titled *The Collected Books of Jack Spicer*, and omits nearly all of Spicer's pre-serial work. Likewise, Donald Allen's equally posthumous edition of Spicer's early poetry also takes its title largely from the above pronunciamento, calling itself *One Night Stand & Other Poems*, and quoting the passage I cited above in its preface.

What must be noted, however, is that this "admonition" to Robin Blaser admits of two different sets of implications, one more radical than the other. The less radical reading would cast Spicer's declaration as one bearing on form in the conventional sense, the short lyric being seen as too condensed, too resistant to the self-reflexive meanderings of repetition, echo, elaboration and self-correction which become increasingly important to him, and therefore in consequence being jettisoned for the more flexible, modulated, dialectical structure of the "book."[5] This is entirely valid and consonant with Spicer's own emphasis in his discussions of the "serial poem," but also, I think, an insufficient account of the full implications of his poetics. For what Spicer here "admonishes" against with the most force is the sort of expressive formalism of the "English Department" which demarcates, isolates, and seals literary works into coherent, self-contained units, each with a meaning, problem, or emotion its potentially very foreign currency can be translated back into. And this, as Spicer well knew, is no different with regard to a "book" than to a single lyric. In its most radical sense, then, Spicer's view that "there is really no single poem" is violated if the "book" is seen as simply a longer, more complex, but essentially equivalent self-identical signifying structure, for in this case the objections Spicer has to the "single poem" are in no way alleviated—the "book" will be "judged by itself alone" in exactly the same fashion. Rather, his poetics take on their full power when considered as a poetics of displacement and deferral: "there is really no single poem" must also imply "there is really no single book"—that poetry, to be poetry, must always be exceeding its own limits and falling short of its own demarcations. If Mallarmé, as Sartre suggests, put the world between parentheses,[6] Spicer on the other hand does similar violence not to the world but to the poem. His assault on the poem is the opposite of the phenomenology of the English department, as his work flattens poetry out into the world, spills poetry over. This is not Whitmanian elevation of a poetic quality inherent in all things, nor found poetry, but rather lost poetry, continual displacement, the constant pressuring or dispersal of poetry into its other, whether called "prose" (which incidentally comprises a great deal of the so-called poetry in many of Spicer's books), the "world," or the "real."

And it is in this context that we can see the key strategic role played by translation in Spicer's work, which attacks the conventional authenticity of the poetic experience on every level. If the serial poem assaults the idea of the poem as interpretive object or aesthetic artifact,[7] likewise, Spicer's extremist version of inspiration in which the poem is "dictated" to the poet by something entirely and magically other and Outside the poet (which he sometimes refers to as "ghosts" or "Martians"), if notoriously problematic, still manages to radically recuse the shared Beat and confessional emphasis on self-expression, taking us to a poetics, as Peter Gizzi has pointed out, much more in line with those of Beckett than either of these two groups.[8] Spicer often figures "dictation" as a form of possession or haunting, as he will in *After Lorca*, but also quite strikingly as radio broadcasting, in which, surprisingly, the poet is not the magnified and multiplied vocal source, but rather attributed the somewhat inglorious role of what Spicer calls the "receiver." That is, dictation as broadcasting implies not the potential "projection" of the poet's subjective voice into an ever expanding field, but rather the need for the poet to act as an antenna "tuning into" and adequately reproducing an utterly alien signal.[9] Thus, Spicer can say "I really honestly don't feel that I own my poems, and I don't feel proud of them," while acknowledging his role by asserting, "But at the same time you don't get the radio program if the radio set has static in it" (*House*, 15). Spicer's late poem "Sporting Life" is his most explicit treatment of the metaphor: "The trouble with comparing a poet with a radio is that radios don't develop scar-tissue" (*Collected Books*, 218).[10]

In fact, Spicer's sense of poetry as dictation and the poet as a "receiver" of a voice which is Other is a crucial explanation for a notable, and indeed noted, oddity: that *After Lorca*, the book through which Spicer himself felt he had reached his poetic maturity, was in its conception a book of translations.[11] As we have seen, the contradiction is only apparent, since for Spicer poetry is less a question of *finding* one's voice than of letting it be *lost*, just as "craft" consists less in polishing poetic objects than in wrenching language outside of a context which would allow it to objectified, or reified, into the status of "poem." But the mobilization of translation has additional implications, as it allows Spicer to inscribe himself into a complex network of modernist genealogies, particularly those pertaining to the relationship between the contingencies of any given language, subjective positioning, and American identity, the latter being minimalized by Spicer into the regional. Thus, *After Lorca* evolves into an intricate set of polemical negotiations—not only with Lorca and with a foreign language, but also with Lorca's own similar negotiation with another poet and foreign language, as the centerpiece of Spicer's collection is Lorca's famous "Ode to Walt Whitman." At the same time, Spicer's procedure is quite consciously in and of itself a homage to Ezra Pound's *Homage to Sextus Propertius*, as Spicer, like Pound, takes wild and deliberate liberties with his source text. While doubling Pound, Spicer "receives" Lorca voicing Whitman, inevitably raising the question of who is dictating to whom, and who is translated by what. This question of heritage becomes all the more complex when one remembers Pound's "A Pact," the famous poem addressed to none other than Walt Whitman, of which the thrust is precisely the difficulty of coming to terms with cumbersome heritages. Spicer's elaboration of his own belatedness with regard to these texts is the drama, to the extent that any exists, in *After Lorca*.

The book *After Lorca* consists of a "ghost-written" prose introduction by "Lorca" himself, six prose "letters" to "Lorca" from "Jack" interspersed among the thirty-three "translations," and a verse "postscript" for Marianne Moore titled "Radar." According to Clayton Eshelman, ten of the "translations" can only be considered as Spicer originals.[12] Among the Lorca texts which Spicer translated, the "Ode to Walt Whitman" is by far the most famous, and the longest. As commentators have noted, this is clearly a key text for

Spicer, as it is here that Lorca openly discusses the homosexuality that he and Spicer shared. But Pound too presides over the project as a tutelary spirit, as some of Spicer's letters make clear. He sounds Poundian indeed in a letter to Robin Blaser, when he claims:

> What I am trying to do is to establish a *tradition*. When I'm through (although I'm sure no one will ever publish them) I'd like someone as good as I am to translate these translations into French (or Pushtu) adding more. Do you understand? No. Nobody does.

Later in the same letter, Spicer writes "I can see why Pound got so angry at the reaction to his 'Propertius'" ("Letters to Robin Blaser," 48). Spicer, in fact, went beyond Pound in his treatment of Lorca, not only substantially altering words or lines in individual poems, but also quite simply including poems of his own in the book, at times Lorcaesque, at times not. "Tradition" for Spicer then means a preferably endless multilingual network of continual textual appropriation, reappropriation, and misappropriation, for which "translation" provides one important model.[13] However, as the "letters" make clear, translation also becomes *transubstantiation*, as the passing of one spirit or even body into another echoes and is echoed by the passing of languages. Translation and haunting are explicitly linked in *After Lorca*, which once again shows just how prescient a reader of Pound Spicer was.[14] If in terms of Spicer's work translation must be written into the greater chain of mediated discourses which came increasingly to define "poetry" both as act and inspiration, what is largely at issue in *After Lorca* is precisely the status of this "receptive" subjectivity of the translator, in its relation to its incorporation of the foreign. Spicer, rather than simply become the vehicle for Lorca's ghostly and Americanized voice, will in fact "talk back" to "Lorca," in a series of letters signed "Jack." Translation is refigured as dialogue, as has often been noted, but just as crucially, as epistolary dialogue—a series of entirely mediated messages and transmissions passed back and forth across borders of language, death, and the earth's cover. And for Spicer, the task of the translator consists not more in bringing the dead poet "to life" than in hauling the live translator, precisely, into death. Herein lies one of the true values of the act of translation for Spicer, and also, perhaps, much of his fascination with the myth of Orpheus. In his penultimate letter to Lorca, "Jack" claims that poetry freezes the instant the poet ". . . ceases to be a dead man" (48). The relationship between poetry and death, but also poetry and prose, obsess the book.

Indeed, the prose texts of *After Lorca*—"Lorca"'s introduction, and Jack's six letters to him—are rightly seen as cornerstones of Spicer's poetics.[15] Two points regarding them, however, have not been sufficiently stressed. First, if these texts often valorize "poetry" at the expense of "prose," they are written in prose themselves, and Spicer's subsequent books more often than not contained a significant portion of what is conventionally called "prose poetry." This forces us to ask to what extent these texts as performatives undo or at least complicate their constative claims. Second, little reflection has been given to the extent to which these reflections on "poetics" are also explicitly reflections on *translation*.

The first text in prose is the introduction to the volume, attributed to "Lorca." Here, the program of the book is clearly laid out:

> It must be made clear at the start that these poems are not translations. In even the most literal of them Mr. Spicer seems to derive pleasure in inserting or substituting one or two words which completely change the mood and often the meaning of the poem as I had written it,

and "Lorca" goes on to explain that Spicer also includes poems which are half translation, half originals, and others that are not by Lorca at all, without the reader being given any "indication which of the poems belong to which category" (11).[16] "Lorca" will wryly close his discussion of this matter with a metaphorical equivalence which underwrites the entire project—that of the human body and the literary corpus:

> Even the most faithful student of my work will be hard put to decide what is and what is not Garcia Lorca as, indeed, he would if he were to look into my present resting place. The analogy is impolite, but I fear the impoliteness is deserved. (11)

This figure is extended in Lorca's concluding sentences, which again treat of the strange "mixture" of Spicer and Lorca of which *After Lorca* consists. I quote in full:

> The dead are notoriously hard to satisfy. Mr. Spicer's mixture may please his contemporary audience or may, and this is more probable, lead him to write better poetry of his own. But I am strongly reminded as I survey this curious amalgam of a cartoon published in an American magazine while I was visiting your country in New York. The cartoon showed a gravestone on which were inscribed the words: "HERE LIES

AN OFFICER AND A GENTLEMAN." The caption below it read: "I wonder how they happened to be buried in the same grave?" (12)

That the dead are "notoriously hard to satisfy" points not only to the debt that the translator may be said to owe to the "original" which he parasites and exploits—it also recalls the manner in which the dead most classically express this dissatisfaction, to wit, as truculent ghosts. But the question left open is whether this act of translation is the transgression for which appeasement must be made, or the act of appeasement itself, extending as it does the "life" of the dead poet's text. In his work on Pound, Daniel Tiffany has stressed how translation can be seen as a sacrifice on the part of the translator, who would deliver himself over to the service of the alien "voice." In this way, translation appears as

> ... a process whereby the original author or text is brought to life, resurrected, through a depletion of the translator's vitality, or, more seriously, through a reification, a deadening, of his native language. There is a terrible risk, of course, in feeding the dead from the store of one's own vitality. (191)

Yet if the "original" text can be seen as a "succubus" or "parasite" feeding off the vitality of the living translator, the reverse is equally true, for the translator is a consummate "grave-robber," as Chamberlain has referred to Spicer in this context (427), stealing an alien "voice" through which to speak what is, after all, his own tongue. Thus, the importance of the introduction by "Lorca": in this book, not only will Lorca "speak" through the "voice" of Spicer, but the blatant forgery of the introduction reminds us that Spicer is also always speaking through the "mask" of "Lorca." The mixing of original poems with translations, the injection of original lines and words within the boundaries of the translations, is crucial for creating this sort of bidirectional dialogue. The officer and the gentleman indeed share the same grave, in the form of the patrician aristocrat Lorca and the seedy bohemian Spicer, and one melds into the other just as Lorca's corpse commingles with its resting place.

However, the letters "Jack" writes back to "Lorca" are largely built around a group of entirely predictable oppositions, heavily scripted by the dominant poetics of the last two hundred years at least: reality/language, poetry/prose, life/death, necessity/contingence, permanence/transience, and finally, self/other. All of these will be subtly interrogated by Spicer, and at times overturned, and even from the outset he signals his potential radicality in his treatment of an opposition he chooses to foreground: "invention" as opposed to "disclosure." Here, contrary to expectations, it is invention and imagination which are aligned with the devalorized category of "prose," while the seemingly pedestrian "disclosure" becomes the poetic act par excellence. "Invention is merely the enemy of poetry," Jack writes in the first letter, continuing, "Prose invents—poetry discloses" (15). If the recusal of invention, the imagination, and all attendant qualities of subjective self-expression represents a radical departure from the dominant modes of American poetry in the 1950s, such a stance also opens the door to a rather naive mimeticist form of objectivism, in which the poet and language would be asked to withdraw in favor of some sort of translinguistic "real." The linguistic texture of almost any Spicer poem makes it difficult to assume that that position was in fact his, but by the same token makes his very emphasis on "disclosure" and what he calls "objects" and the "real" all the more enigmatic. Therefore it is hardly surprising that much in Jack's letters to Lorca, in the wake of the valorization of "disclosure," is devoted precisely to the question of just what it might be that poetry "discloses," and what the role of language might be in this form of revelation which, whatever else, is also defined as "poetic." Regarding these questions, one of Spicer's most famous statements is this declaration, "I would like to make poems out of real objects. The lemon to be a lemon that the reader could cut or squeeze or taste—a real lemon like a newspaper in a collage is a real newspaper. . . . The imagination pictures the real. I would like to point to the real, disclose it, to make a poem that has no sound in it but the pointing of a finger" (33–4).

The implications of the above are quietly enormous. Spicer's vision of a "silent poem," first of all, breaks entirely with the logocentric ideality of the poem, based in the temporality of speech. Spicer here imagines a writing which would retain its full iconic properties, and resist resolution into the status of simple *representation* of the aural temporality of the expressive poetic "voice." However, this poetics is in no way "objective" as its very center consists precisely of a silent speech *act*—the deictic "pointing" towards the real which is disclosed. Subjective positioning remains the organizing principle of the poem. The result is a poetry which is almost a phenomenological reduction of the speech act into pure linguistic gesturality, a ceaseless pronominal stutter, sheer deixis, affirming nothing but the possibility of its own spacing. It is this poetics which leads inexorably toward

Spicer's increased emphasis on address, in the epistolary *Admonitions* and after, and which demonstrates again the complicity for Spicer of translation with all tropings of the epistolary and distancing, including radio.

But again, let us remember that these musings arise in the midst of a discussion explicitly devoted to translation, occurring within a book of translations. In this light, the point to be emphasized is simply that some sort of poem made out of "real objects" would necessarily be a poem which both obviated the need for *and* entirely resisted translation. What Spicer is concerned with here is not the relationship between the language of poetry and the "reality" that language is supposed to represent, but rather the conditions of translatability, of transferability, of text. The "collage of the real" would be an untranslatable text; Spicer here is interrogating not singularity, but that oddly unthinkable ideality which is able to resist the singularity of individual languages, and allow for transfer across them. At the same time, Spicer is wholly aware of language as object itself. Indeed, the choice of the "lemon" as example is surely not fortuitous, as in the second poem presented after the letter in question we find the following quatrain:

I carry the No you gave me
Clenched in my palm
Like something made of wax
An almost-white lemon. (36)

(Llevo el No que me diste,
en la palma de la mano,
como un limón de cera
casi blanco.)

The metaphorical construction found in these lines is notable: rather than highlight the capacity of "words" here to represent objects (for example, the English "lemon" and Spanish "limón" both standing in for an identical referent), Spicer's exemplary object—the lemon—metaphorically represents nothing other than the *word* "No," which is treated as an object itself, as the verbs "to carry" and "to give" remind us (as they do in Lorca's Spanish). Given the rhetorical logic of this stanza, a word would seem to be something which can be "pointed to" as much as anything else. Thus this poem, by having the "lemon" refer to the "No," does indeed replicate the logic of collage, in which the "real objects" which are appropriated can also function on an entirely different order as signifiers within the collage construct (thus, a piece of wallpaper, identifiable as such, is simultaneously a girl's face, etc.).

Moreover, if an actual lemon is untranslatable, it is worth noting that in this exchange between Lorca and Spicer there is one word which need not be rendered—precisely this "No," the object of transit *within* each poem, which happens to be identical in English and Spanish, and can be simply carried over from one poem to the next. This single word permits of a transit entirely different from everything else Spicer must undertake, and of course raises the specter of the most faithful translation of all—one in which Lorca's actual Spanish words could all simply be retained. The "No," handed from lover to lover, and now, from poet to poet, is that which Spicer has *not* translated, the bitter, wax lemon to which one can only, and need only, point.

This "No" thus stands at once for ultimate translatability, and ultimate resistance to translation, and in this respect seems representative of all language, as Spicer sees it. For as Spicer puts it in the letters, words neither "represent," nor "imagine" nor even "disclose"—rather, "Words are what sticks to the real. We use them to push the real, to drag the real into the poem. They are what we hold on with, nothing else. They are as valuable in themselves as rope with nothing to be tied to" (25). This radically metonymic sense of language at once objectifies language and acknowledges its radical contingency—a contingency which Spicer also feels affects the "real objects" language is asked to point to. Just as mimetic exactitude cannot generally be maintained in translation (aside from exceptional cases like that of the word "no," one must replace the poet's words with others, yet the poetic object is in essence nothing but words) so on the level of the signified, for Spicer "translation" is also necessary: "That tree you saw in Spain is a tree I could never have seen in California, that lemon has a different smell and a different taste, BUT the answer is this—every place and every time has a real object to *correspond* with your real object—that lemon may become this lemon, or it may even become this piece of seaweed, or this particular color of gray in this ocean. One does not need to imagine that lemon; one needs to discover it" (34, Spicer's italics). As translation becomes the search for "correspondences," on the level of both the signifier and the signified (as the example of "seaweed" rendering "lemon" indicates), it can only be effected through the sort of "correspondence" or exchange of voicings

Spicer punningly has in mind in these letters, as he makes clear in closing this one: "Even these letters. They *correspond* with something (I don't know what) that you have written (perhaps as unapparently as that lemon corresponds to this piece of seaweed) and, in turn, some future poet will write something which *corresponds* to them. That is how we dead men write to each other. Love, Jack" (34, Spicer's italics).[17] Translation is literally letter-writing, as Spicer sees each of his renderings as at once a *response* addressed to Lorca, prompted by his work, and also as a *correspondence*, re-placing that work in another time, language and context. Spicer sees himself as sending Lorca's work back to him as well as extending Lorca mediumistically. Ross Clarkson has pointed out that for Spicer, "Translation, as a correspondence with the dead, is more than transcribing a poem into another language; rather, translation is an instance of poetic community through communication between the living and the dead" (201). Clarkson is entirely right, but I would like to stress that the form this communication takes is figured not as dialogue but as epistolary exchange; for Spicer, the emphasis on mediation and remainder, the material inscription of the sign, and the gap between sender and receiver, remains paramount. If this mediation finds its supplement in Spicer's fantasm, issued by "Lorca," of the decomposing bodies melding seamlessly into each other, their materiality, like that of newspapers cut up and repasted in collage, is equally stressed.

Spicer's conceit, then, is that "Lorca" and "Jack" are translated into each other on every level, and in this way he attempts to rewrite translation as erotic exchange rather than as a complex book-keeping of indebtedness. Of course, what is most erotic about this mediumistic, ghostly dialogue is that one is spoken *by* the other as much as one speaks to him, in a sort of echolalic *mise-en-abyme* which both invokes and defeats the narcissism that Spicer alludes to in his translations of the two poems which García Lorca had titled "Narcissus." Crucially, in terms of these tropes yet another figure enters the discussion, and thus the grave: Walt Whitman. Indeed, the admixture of the archetypal American autochthonous poet opens the possibility that *After Lorca* is but a voyage through difference, language, and death ultimately home. Yet the mediating figure of Lorca will permit Spicer to position himself quite differently in the end, notably, through a shared rejection of Whitman's New York, coupled with an alternative emphasis on the literality of the name.[18]

The term "translation" emerges at several key points in *Leaves of Grass*, and is one of Whitman's favorite words for examining two related issues: the relationship between author and reader, and the relationship between the singularity of the individual subject, and the traces and remainders which it is capable of producing: writing, footprints, and the green grass itself which grows out of corpses above their graves. Whitman in fact first focuses on the idea of translation in his effort to decipher the mysterious writing of the "grass," whose proffered communication has given the title for his entire writing project. Shortly after "reading" what he calls the "hieroglyphic" of the grass as "the beautiful uncut hair of graves" (193) early in "Song of Myself," Whitman attempts to imagine the lives of the bodies which now "live" on in the form of the grass they literally nourish in their decomposition: "I wish I could translate the hints about the dead young men and women, / And the hints about old men and mothers, and the offspring taken soon out of their laps" (193). Given the figural economy established here and so heavily marked by the book's title, it could be suggested that *Leaves of Grass* is nothing other than a reflection on translation, "grass" signifying nothing but signification and mediation, or the world as foreign text. Here, it would seem that the bodies have themselves been "translated" biologically into grass, and Whitman now attempts to translate backwards towards the source corpus. As every book of Whitman's poetry is titled *Leaves of Grass*, and the idea of the "grass" is intimately linked to problems of translation, the centrality of the trope of translation for all of Whitman becomes strikingly apparent. Stressing this point, Whitman chooses this very trope to close "Song of Myself." The poem ends with the following lines:

> I bequeath myself to the dirt to grow from the grass I love,
> If you want me again look for me under your boot-soles.
>
> You will hardly know who I am or what I mean,
> But I shall be good health to you nevertheless,
> And filter and fibre your blood.
>
> Failing to fetch me at first keep encouraged,
> Missing me one place search another,
> I stop somewhere waiting for you. (247)

Whitman's poem thus ends with an assertion of supreme transmutability, but not necessarily perfect translatability—if he can be found bodily in the mud beneath one's bootsoles (as the dead of section 6 are found in the grass above the graves), nevertheless, "You will hardly know who I am or what I mean." This might explain why only a few lines above those I have just quoted, Whitman declares "I too am not a bit tamed, I too am untranslatable" (247). Translation, it seems, emerges as "impossible" but also inescapable: it is death that makes possible and necessary what Whitman calls "translation" in these places, as the term names the mediation between the singularity of the individual bounded by a lifespan, and the terrestrial general economy that ensures that all continues without irremediable loss—an idea Whitman expresses again in section 6: "The smallest sprout shows there is really no death, / And if ever there was it led forward life, and does not wait at the end to arrest it" (194). Whitman's abundant poetry on death almost always teeters vertiginously between exuberance at nature's ability to feed off and prolong what disappears (too often assimilated by critics to a transcendentalist "faith") and overwhelming anxiety before the irrecuperable singularity of the event of an individual life. These are precisely the mediations that Spicer interrogates by having "Lorca" trope the mixing of texts as a mixing of corpses. However, in both Whitman and Spicer, "translation" implies not only the mediation of what is living across the boundaries of death, but also the displacement of the origin of poetic authority and the lyric voice. Towards the very end of "Song of Myself" Whitman writes:

> I do not say these things for a dollar or to fill up the time while I wait
>   for a boat
> (It is you talking just as much as myself, I act as the tongue of you,
> Tied in your mouth, in mine it begins to be loosen'd.)
>
> I swear I will never again mention love or death inside a house,
> And I swear I will never translate myself at all, only to him or her who
>   privately stays with me in the open air. (243)

These remarkable lines set up a series of oppositions only to undermine them. First, of course, the crucial opposition between author/reader, sender/receiver is undone as the reader becomes the speaker of the Whitmanian text. Whitman presents himself here as a *medium* through which the reader's voice is re-turned to and towards himself or herself. Thus the eroticized moment of subjective union when two tongues merge in one mouth is also, and oddly, a moment of solipsism. This problem is perhaps recognized by some syntactic oddities in what follows: no sooner does the poet establish a category as unconditional regarding translation ("I will *never* translate myself *at all*") than he appends a condition to it ("*only to him or her...*"), a condition which in and of itself seems contradictory, involving both "privacy" and "the open air." Now, to speak with the tongue of another is after all the situation of the translator, and Whitman seems to be suggesting that the entirety of his poetry can be seen as a kind of translation—of the "hints" of the grass, but also of the bound tongues of his readers, of their "howls restrain'd by decorum" (195) as he puts it earlier in "Song of Myself." Of course, this scene is explicitly eroticized as the tongue is transferred from mouth to mouth, and this might be why so much precaution surrounds the more metaphorical "translation" of the lines cited above. For if Whitman is happy to posit himself as a sort of mediator, allowing his readers to speak to themselves through his intercession, he is more wary of being translated in turn. Indeed, this latter act seems torn between a complicity which requires "privacy" and intimacy on the one hand, and on the other an intersubjective transparency and "merging," to use another of Whitman's terms, that can only imply the "open air." "Translation" at once protects and reveals a secret, at once expresses and replaces whatever is "translated"; as affectionate and transgressive as a kiss, it openly proclaims an impenetrably private exchange. Spicer harks back to Whitman by figuring translation as an eroticized extension of bodies from beyond their resting places, with the text as something passed along, from poet to poet and language to language, without ultimate origin or destination.

All of the issues Spicer raises concerning translation, transferability, correspondence, and complicity, come to the fore in the centerpiece of the book, Spicer's translation of the "Ode to Walt Whitman," a poem itself incessantly worrying the relationship between eros, recognition, region and idiom. The publication history of Lorca's poem— privately printed and distributed only to friends—already mirrors the central tension of the work, which is to honor the double imperative to both reveal and conceal homoerotic investment, in the poetry of both Whitman and of Lorca. The poem is largely a complicated and at times contorted arabesque of identifications and repudiations, and most importantly, repudiations of identifications, for the poem's central questions are precisely who has the right to claim Whitman, and what his true legacy is. Whitman is clearly celebrated as a sort of patriarch for gay poets everywhere, yet Lorca also violently rails against certain sorts of homosexuals, whom he refers to by a standard Spanish derogatory term, "maricas," an obvious (and frequently chosen) translation of which might be "faggots." In excoriating the "maricas," Lorca revels in some of the most violently homophobic language in the canon, for example: "¡Maricas de todo el mundo, asesinos de palomas!/ Esclavos de la mujer. Perras de sus tocadores," which Greg Simon and Steven F. White render "Faggots of the world, murderers of doves!/ Slaves of women. Their bedroom bitches" (García Lorca, 234–5), and which Spicer gives as follows: "Cocksuckers of all the world, assassins of doves, /Slaves of women, lapdogs of their dressing tables" (31). A famous crux, however, is what distinguishes the "maricas," for whom Lorca implores, "Let there be no mercy" (31), from the "beautiful Walt Whitman" (31) of "hermosura viril" (manly beauty)? One traditional answer, which some of the lines quoted above imply, is that Lorca disapproves of "feminine" homosexual style which would render gay men as grotesque imitations and therefore "slaves" of women, while approving the more "macho" style (to use Lorca's own Spanish adjective) of the Whitman persona. This is certainly true up to a point, but such a conclusion is troubled by lines like these: "That is why I do not cry out, old Walt Whitman, /Against the little boy who writes/ A girl's name on his pillow, / Or the kid who puts on a wedding dress/ In the darkness of a closet/ Or the lonely men in bars/ Who drink with sickness the waters of prostitution/ Or the men with green eyelids/ Who love men and scald their lips in silence" (Spicer's rendering, 30). These lines, in fact, are usually cited as prime evidence of the other prevailing interpretation, to wit, that Lorca approves of homosexuals so long as they remain in "the darkness of a closet," as it were, denouncing those who act on their desire, or allow their sexuality to become visible.

In an interesting article, Eric Keenaghan, for example, argues that "marica" refers to those who are "sexually conspicuous" as opposed to the "silent and hidden individuals" whom Lorca tolerates (284). Keenaghan suggests that Spicer's consistent choice of outrageously sexualized diction for his translation deliberately undermined Lorca's ideal of "gay invisibility," constructing in its stead "Spicer's advocation of gay textual visibility" (286). The problem with this reading is that Lorca's poem itself is predicated on nothing other than Whitman's very "visibility" and "legibility" as a gay poet—it is because of these qualities that the poem is offered to him, and that the question of homosexuality is raised within it. Keenaghan in fact acknowledges this too, stating that Lorca does not associate Whitman with "absolute abstinence" (286), and quite rightly suggesting ". . . Whitman's sexuality is noticeably present but it is not ostentatious" (287). So it would seem the difference between "Whitman" and the "maricas" consists not in an opposition between invisibility and visibility but rather in sexual semiotics, that is, strategies and attitudes of marking and demarcating an identity which must nevertheless not be entirely effaced. What is at issue for Lorca would then be a sort of tact, that is, the problematics of context and address, of sexuality as event and text. Nowhere are problems of tact more heavily encoded than in language, and the diction of Lorca's text alternates painfully between elaborate metaphorical euphemism, in its descriptions of Whitman, and derogatory invective in those of the "maricas." Keenaghan is right to point out how Spicer consistently replaces euphemisms with obscene, explicit diction, but one should remember that in order to function a euphemism must always successfully name its object, in spite of its obscurantist thrust—it is not an encoding, on the contrary. What euphemisms imply, constructed as they so often are through metonymy, synecdoche, and metaphor, is that what is to be designated will be marked through trope, will be allowed to be symbolized so long as remaining essentially nameless, with no "proper" identity whatsoever. A sub-species of catachresis, euphemism renders not *invisible* but *anonymous*, and is in this sense the dialectical inverse of the pejorative invective, whose logic is that of total identity between the proper name (in theory, wholly arbitrary) and an "objective" negative predication. The pejorative term implies that to be what it names is to be abject in a manner and degree utterly resistant to—precedent to—adjectivisation; add the adjective "good" to any pejorative term, and the insult is only intensified. What concerns Lorca most, then, is neither the existence of the desire, nor its acting out, nor its suppression, but the manner in which it allows itself to be remarked or named, and it is this concern that Lorca both expresses as his "content" and enacts in his linguistic strategies.

    The complexity and occasional incoherence of these strategies are emphasized by John K. Walsh in an article whose stated goal is precisely to unravel the "logic" underlying Lorca's construction of valorized and abject categories of homosexuality in the "Ode." After arguing persuasively against readings based on oppositions between masculine and feminine style, or openness and secrecy, Walsh can only conclude that the sought after "logic" is not entirely to be found: "We have seen that the category [of homosexuals] Lorca wishes to condemn is never quite defined, or the definitions are dismantled by the poet as the poem moves along" (271). Yet Walsh does rightly stress that the homosexuality which Lorca abominates is consistently seen as "urban" (263, 271). Indeed, Lorca pointedly dubs his "maricas" as "maricas de las *ciudades*," literally, "of the cities" (English translations often render this as "urban") and Walsh reminds us that great portions of the "Ode," indeed, of *The Poet in New York* as a whole, are devoted not to homosexuality, but to the economic and spiritual impoverishment of urban life. For Walsh, much of the poem's difficulties derive from its "flawed syllogism that would force together two themes: one sociologic (Whitman's dream of a hearty America—his Mannahatta—against the present and tawdry, mechanical New York); one sexual (Whitman's virtuous and soaring homosexuality against the fetid and debased homosexualities of the cities)" (270). The syllogism is indeed flawed, as Lorca can never define what precise aspect of "urban" homosexuality makes it so decidedly abject, but such a classification is crucial not only for Lorca's sense of culture and ultimately ethics, but also for his sense of language and poetry. And it is in relation to these issues that Spicer's own regionalism takes succor in Lorca's, in a project which, as translation, must in some ways violate both.

It has become a critical commonplace that Lorca regarded the modern urban culture of rootless peripatetic wage-slavery and compensatory commodity fetishism as incompatible with poetry to such an extent that the title "Poet in New York" was meant to sound "paradoxical."[19] Lorca's poetry most often assumes an entirely coherent and shared cultural space, in which all forms of allusion are immediately understood. This raises serious problems for the outsider, and the reader of a translation is an outsider by definition. For example, it is difficult to understand much at all about a poem like "Sevillanas del Siglo XVIII" if one doesn't know that Triana and La Macarena are neighborhoods in Seville, Triana being traditionally associated with Flamenco. These *proper names* might very well function as *foreign nouns* for a reader from Hispanic Latin America or other parts of Spain, to say nothing of the linguistic foreigner. Then there are the numerous Lorca poems which take their names from different Flamenco forms. All this implies that for Lorca, the "poet in New York" is more than the poet as tourist—he is the poet who has been separated from that which gives his poems sense, on the most basic level. "Foreignness" here means breaking the link with a cultural continuum so seamless that the distinction between proper name and common noun is effaced. Naturally, this fanstasmatic space is one in which translation, in any form, is entirely unnecessary. More importantly, the valorizing of such a space can lead to a sense, which Lorca at times seems to have shared, that the sheer mediacy implicit in any act of translation is in and of itself "anti-poetic." Cosmopolitan New York, then, risks being poetically impossible, and the flitting urban "maricas" partake in a privileged manner of this impossibility which the body of Whitman, systematically assimilated by Lorca to a natural or geographical element (who has "dreamed of being a river" and who will "sleep on the banks of the Hudson/ With your beard toward the pole and your palms open" Spicer, 29, 31) is seen to militate against. To the extent that the "maricas" are indeed urban, their horror comes precisely from their anonymity, their essential namelessness. The panic they induce is as much linguistic as sexual, and faced with their menace Lorca resorts to an ultimate and ambivalent defense: he calls them by their names in an extraordinary list of regional derogatory epithets:

> Contra vosotros siempre,
> *Fairies* de Norteamérica,
> *Pájaros* de La Habana,
> *Jotos* de Méjico,
> *Sarasas* de Cádiz,
> *Apios* de Sevilla,
> *Cancos* de Madrid,
> *Floras* de Alicante,
> *Adelaidas* de Portugal. (García Lorca, 234)

The above list may seem at first universalizing, asserting as it does that every city, like New York, has its contingent of "maricas," differing only in the name used to excoriate them.[20] Yet at the same time, as *poetry* the list is anything but universalizing, as it is utterly untranslatable—it is precisely the *singularity of each regional name* that occupies each line, and not the group each name points to. In other words, in terms of translation the "referent" of this list is not a category or "group"; rather, the "referents" are plural, and are nothing other than a list of names. Here, the translator has no choice (or has the lucky chance, depending on how you look at it) but to preserve in its literality the very foreign body of the word it is his usual task to efface, as it is those words which this passage represents, and Spicer's version reads as follows: "Fairies of North America,/ Pajaros of Havana,/ Jotos of Mexico,/ Sarasas of Cadiz,/ Apios of Seville, /Cancos of

Madrid,/ Adelaidas of Portugal" (31).[21] Threatened by a New York that is dissolute, in every sense of the word, Lorca responds by rhetorically reaffirming an identity of proper name and common noun, as he had in his Andalusian poems. If following Walsh we accept that Lorca fails to establish any transcendental "category" capable of defining the "maricas," here he seems to abandon his failed project of categorization precisely by exploding any potential grouping into distinct, untranslatable nominalist fragments. The various groups are emphatically *not* subsumed under a single name; on the level of language, all possibility of equivalence and exchange is denied, including the referential exchange without which translation is impossible—the "matter" or referent of this particular passage is the singularity of a given name, in a given language, in a given place.

Lorca defeats the menace of the urban, rootless "maricas" precisely by regionalizing them, by tying them to local linguistic practices, by abandoning adjectival description, in favor of the luminosity of the name. In this respect, his poetics and perhaps his sexual politics are more progressive than they might appear, or than he might have thought. Despite the derogatory violence, Lorca calls out his address in the "nighest name," as Whitman might have put it.[22] And these names in their very variety might seem to indicate that ultimately, if the "category" he is seeking to define does not exist it is because it has no actual "existence" beyond its continual reinvocation through the repetition of derogatory interpellation. It is the ontological groundlessness of the derogatory epithet which the poem enacts here, in a strikingly violent example of what Judith Butler has called the "aesthetic enactment of an injurious word" which

> *uses* that word, but also *displays* it, points to it, outlines it as the arbitrary material instance of language that is exploited to produce certain kinds of effects. In this sense, the word as a material signifier is foregrounded as semantically empty in itself, but as that empty moment in language that can become the site of semantically compounded legacy and effect. (99)

Thus, Lorca has written a poem not only about displacement, rootlessness, and sexuality, but also about names—names which Spicer as translator can only receive and reproduce as such. Here Lorca's text functions exactly as Spicer's "real lemon," crossing all borders utterly intact. Thus the fantasy of a silent poem, which would only "point" is fulfilled, for Spicer simply "points" to Lorca's own words, words which themselves were engaged in pointing out, addressing, and interpellating through the singularity of the name. As identity fuses with the singularity of a given language or regional dialect, the derogatory epithet becomes the essence of poetic matter. A poetics of referentiality (and surrealism is nothing if not that) gives way before a poetics of pragmatics, as the cultural and contextual weighting of a word becomes the central poetic fact. This implies a poetics of both literal and cultural translation and citationality, and also one in which the hermeneutic horizon which the "serial poem" was meant to trouble recedes even further before the valency of poetry as act, interpellation, and event.[23] It is this realization that leads Spicer in *Admonitions* directly to the problematics of address, in a work whose form is explicitly epistolary, whose model is Dickinsonian rather than Whitmanian, and whose central rhetorical feature is obscenity. Spicer's labour of translation leads him to posit death as the space of utterance and utterance as letter-writing, in a manner consonant with both Dickinson's astonishing correspondence and her great poems on haunting.[24] Obviously, the book's conceit of a series of letters addressed to various individuals, mostly Spicer's friends, extends the relationship between translation and the epistolary sketched in *After Lorca*, in which every poem but one is also "for" someone or other. However, the reduction of all poetry to letter-writing *generalizes* the field of death, while also insisting on poetry as *event*, which paradoxically ties it to place, moment, and the unrepeatably singular. Indeed, the incorporation of Lorca, stressed through Spicer's trope of the dissolution of the bodies in the grave, needs to be read in the context of what Spicer, in one of *After Lorca*'s letters to Lorca, refers to as "encysting," and this in relation to an elimination of the "personal," which so much of Spicer's work, such as his dedications, "letters," and deliberately inflammatory, perlocutionary rhetoric seems to militate for.

Here, Spicer discusses how "any sudden personal contact, whether in the bed or in the heart" (48) disrupts the poet's essential "loneliness" and thrusts him into the anti-poetic space of life and the "big lie of the personal—the lie in which these objects [the "real objects" which Spicer had wished to build poems from, rather than words] do not believe" (48). Yet, Spicer continues,

> ... the loneliness returns. The poet encysts the intruder. The objects come back to their own places, silent and unsmiling. . . . And this immediate thing, this personal adventure, will not have been transferred into

the poem ... will, at best, show in the lovely pattern of cracks in some poem where autobiography shattered but did not quite destroy the surface. And the encysted emotion will itself become an object, to be transferred at last into poetry like the waves and the birds. (48)

In other words, "encysting" kills as it preserves, maintaining a "loneliness" while nevertheless breaching it, which in turn allows the "personal" to harden into a thing ready to take its place in the collage (rather than being seamlessly exchanged into poetry, without remainder). In this way, the "outside" becomes a way for the poet to turn himself inside out—as is translation—and to some extent, Spicer posits an hystericization of many of the issues we have seen heretofore, as the homology between textual body and physical body, the letter and the erotic encounter, is stressed. Likewise, through the often campy exchange with "Lorca," Spicer thematizes translation as the deconstruction (or here, decomposition) of authority and authorship, which we saw was the end result of the practice of Pound. Moreover, in a manner analogous to Stein's dialectical derealization of the immediate, estranged, surroundings, for Spicer "regionalism" has meaning only within a system which also militates for the systematic destruction of the proximate, notably that of the self-identity of both the poet and the poem, and which through "correspondence" posits the singular place as always also transposable. In regard to such paradoxes, one must note that it is above all the "prose" of the letters to Lorca which allow *After Lorca* to fully assume its status as "book." Indeed, henceforth Spicer's work will consistently feature prose, prose poetry, and a heavy prose inflection on "verse."[25] Not surprisingly, it is in the space of a novel that Spicer will conduct his most elaborate investigation of regionalism and homecoming, as if such concerns could only be broached through an excursion into what for a poet may be the foreign territory of prose.

CHAPTER 7

HOMECOMINGS: THE POET'S PROSE OF ASHBERY, SCHUYLER AND SPICER

Spicer's poetics, as we saw in the previous chapter, demonstrate an entirely Poundian emphasis on the centrality of translation for poetic production, along with positing a dialectics of locale and its derealization which is in many ways reminiscent of Stein. Unlike his two expatriate forerunners, however, he offers no extended meditation on Americanness or American identity as such, and gives little sense of a "cosmopolitan" shock before the untethering or relativizing of cultural practice. That said, the resolutely Californian Spicer's profound unhappiness in New York and Boston was certainly lived by him as a form of exile and cultural estrangement, and it is hardly coincidental that relatively soon after his return to the Bay Area he undertook the writing of a novel which foregrounds the high modernist trope of the return, while also remaining entirely Jamesian—not in its problematization of the foreign, but in its questioning of "home" as the promise of perfect fit and adequation, the final end to wandering and alienation. Spicer, as we shall see, rams boisterous, ebullient Beatnik San Francisco, already a media cliché by the time of his novel, against the impalpability of the Jamesian uncanny.

At roughly the same time, Spicer's contemporary, John Ashbery, had set off for Europe and was in most hallowed modernist fashion discovering the extent to which Parisian expatriation could turn into an American scene. Certainly, Ashbery in the 1950s was more worldly and cosmopolitan than Spicer in terms not only of his personal movements and contacts, but also his sense of literary and artistic space. If Spicer was in fact extremely well read and possessed of some proficiency in foreign languages, his allegiance to the community of San Francisco Bay Area poets and his sense of that as his enabling context went unquestioned. Ashbery, through his long residence in Paris, his intense interest in foreign writers such as Raymond Roussel, and above all, the concrete problems his poems pose, clearly invokes an international, largely French avant-garde as the context in which his work can be received. Perhaps surprisingly, however, Ashbery's sojourn abroad also led to speculations (sometimes somewhat anguished), on the relationship between expatriation, Americanness, and cultural identity—and especially, the ramifications of this for the artist or writer—which are entirely in keeping with the traditions of James, Pound, and Stein. At the same time, Ashbery fully recognizes his belatedness with regard to such issues, along with the drastically transformed transatlantic cultural space of the 1950s and 1960s. Indeed, such transformations form a considerable part of the subject of his collaborative novel, *A Nest of Ninnies*, co-written with his close friend, the poet James Schuyler, himself well traveled in Europe, especially in Italy, and the novel takes on a new legibility when read in the context of Ashbery's explicitly expatriate reflections, found primarily in the art criticism now collected in *Reported Sightings*. As coda, then, this chapter will examine the prose excursions of three post-War poets into the terrain of uncanny homecomings, perplexed exoticism, touristic consumption, and the ambiguities of cosmopolitanism, which has proved to be so central for the High Modernism of the first half of the twentieth century.

In 1958, shortly after finishing *After Lorca* and *Admonitions*, Jack Spicer embarked on a very different sort of project: a detective novel, meant to be viable commercially while also settling some literary scores. Spicer had left the Bay Area in June, 1955, for an unhappy eighteen-month sojourn in New York and Boston. Upon his return in November, 1956, he found the literary scene he had left behind significantly transformed by the artistic and media phenomenon of the Beats, whose spectacular arrival can be marked by Allen Ginsberg's historic reading of "Howl" at the "6" Gallery in San Francisco in October, 1955. Spicer, one of the six artists who cooperatively ran the gallery and gave it its name, would almost certainly have read too that night had he not been on the East coast—a fact which no doubt intensified his sense that he and his regional coterie had been upstaged by upstart East coast newcomers of inferior quality, as San Francisco and the "Beat" scene became increasingly famous over the course of 1957, with the "Howl" obscenity trial in San Francisco, and the publication of *On the Road* later that year. Spicer's revenge would be to make some money caricaturing for a gullible public a seedy underworld of art, literature, drugs, radical politics, and illicit sex, for which San Francisco was now nationally famous. The novel, which his editors have dubbed *The Tower of Babel*, was left unfinished, as after several months Spicer returned his focus to poetry, planning to finish the book once a publisher was found. Had it been completed, it would have represented a fascinating addition to post-War American prose; it is hard to believe it ever would have been the mainstream economic success Spicer at least professed to have envisioned.[1]

The novel's hero is one J. J. Ralston, a former student of the University of California at Berkeley who has left town almost a decade before the story begins to become an East coast college professor, husband, and published poet. Although his book "received an excellent review from Randall Jarrell" (10), Ralston feels something is missing in his work, and decides to return for the summer to the environs of his youth, where, he has heard tell, an entirely new movement in writing is in effervescence: ". . . you've come to dig the San Francisco Renaissance?" (4), asks a young woman in a bohemian bar, who immediately pegs him as the curious East coast cultural tourist after a glance at his suit and his copy of *Partisan Review*. Ralston will predictably find himself thrown into the middle of a crime mystery, which becomes a murder mystery, but the main mystery of the book is not whether Ralston will ever solve the crimes, but rather, if he will ever succeed in writing a truly good poem. Thus, the novel's premise wittily echoes and allegorizes classic conventions of the detective genre which Spicer knew very well and greatly enjoyed, as Ralston returns to the scene of his youth in search of personal redemption and a restoration of his early convictions, for he can no longer deny the horror he has become: not a jaded, dirty cop, or a mercenary private dick, but, "an, face it, academic poet [sic]" (10). One can imagine a potential publisher's dismay, as the mysteries of poetics, inspiration, and revision become increasingly dominant, at the expense of the crime story. That said, Spicer also closely follows significant elements of the hard-boiled paradigm, as Ralston, with an occasional detour to Berkeley or Sausalito, acts as a Virgil-like guide leading the reader-Dante down into a seething urban underworld just below the sensory horizon of the city, albeit one populated not by gangsters, drug-dealers, prostitutes, numbers-runners, and cops on the take, but by eternal graduate students, hotheaded young literary rebels, Zen Buddhists, disabused cultural critics, political activist lawyers, and bohemian homosexual antique dealers. The novel's main concern—whether Ralston succeeds in writing the poem he came "home" to write—remains an open question, given where the manuscript leaves off. Very late in the text, Ralston, after a morning spent in grueling ascents of some of San Francisco's hills, interrupted by occasional pauses to compose, certainly feels he has, and as a result he is ready to leave the city, along with the intrigue in which he has found himself embroiled; one might be tempted to speculate that it is the resolution of Ralston's creative impasse that robbed Spicer of the desire to finish his story. However, it is crucial to note that Ralston's "breakthrough" only comes at a high price.

The key event of the entire novel occurs in the first chapter, when Ralston, seated at one of the new bars in San Francisco on the day of his arrival, encounters a very young and strangely attractive poet named Rue Talcott. When Ralston dismisses Rue's visionary conception of poetry, the latter angrily tears to shreds the copy of *Partisan Review* Ralston had on the table before him, in which one of his poems was printed. Rue storms out of the bar only to return shortly thereafter with a large live fish, which he slaps down on the bar next to Ralston. Rue points to its mouth, where Ralston detects a tightly folded piece of paper that turns out to be a poem Rue is offering him. Ralston tears it to tatters in reciprocation without so much as reading a line, after which Rue, on the verge of tears, takes his fish and leaves. But in the following hours Ralston is haunted by the scene, feeling slightly guilty but even more, anxious at the possibility that the poem of Rue's he refused might just have been what he was returning to San Francisco to find. Still, when Rue tracks Ralston down the next evening and hands him a sheaf of poems, eagerly enjoining him to read them, rather than seize the opportunity he will spend the rest of the novel finding ways of not so doing, despite Rue's repeated insistence. When Ralston finally manages to write his poem, then, it is accompanied by a kind of declaration of independence, which I find equivocal at best:

> He opened the notebook and glanced at it again with satisfaction. It was one of *his* poems. A little alien perhaps, just as the face he looked at in the bureau mirror in his hotel room in San Francisco was not quite the same face that he had looked at in the bathroom mirror in Boston, a little changed, but *his*. All of this crap . . . all of this having a fish slammed at you was just the outer edges of the poem that you would really write. I am myself, Ralston thought with surprise, and my poems are my poems. (152–3)

Clearly, the emphasis on possession and self-identity are somewhat at odds with the poetics of "dictation," the "outside," "correspondences," and haunting which we saw in the previous chapter, to say nothing of Spicer's pronouncement, "I really honestly don't feel that I own my poems" (*House*, 15). But even restricting ourselves to the context of the novel, Ralston's accomplishment is thrown seriously into doubt. In "the moment of his triumph" (154), just after knocking on the door of Rue's crashpad to return his poems, still unread, Ralston suddenly realizes he has lost them somewhere, in the course of the long stroll through the city during which his own poem was composed. Shaken, he thinks to himself that his wife, a psychiatrist, is "undoubtedly right about the reason for people losing things" (156), and we are told "He [Ralston] had a horror of things lost, a certainty, whether they were a pencil or a sheaf of poems, that they could never be found, were, in fact, cunningly hidden by the very process of being lost" (155). Although Ralston's subsequent conclusion that he must find Rue's poems before leaving town will be shaken, and then forgotten, in a dramatic turn the crime mystery takes in the very few remaining pages before the end of the manuscript, it is difficult to accept that Ralston's creative impasse has been overcome, given that the resolution occurs only thanks to a deliberate and symptomatic avoidance of the encounter with Rue, an encounter which seems increasingly likely to be sexual. On the contrary, the "creative" act we are given seems predicated on the kind of timid inability to take risks that Ralston had returned to San Francisco to counter.

Similar uncertainties can be found in terms of the architectonics of the plot, such as we have it, as the manuscript leaves off precisely at the point of an important structural interruption or reversal. That is, with Ralston thinking that his problem is finally solved (his poem written), and that he has extricated himself from the crime mystery (concluding that his appearance as a somewhat spurious character witness in an assault case will not be required), he is poised to leave home, for home, allowing the story to be brought to a close. Yet no sooner do these resolutions present themselves in their clarity to Ralston, than their premise is overturned: if Ralston has "found" his poem, he has lost those of Rue and must recover them prior to his departure, while, as a newspaper article spied by Ralston in the book's last pages tells us, it is no longer a question of determining whether the affable black, bohemian wire-sculptor Washington Jones is in fact guilty of assault or rather has been slandered, but of discovering if his fatal fall from his hotel room was in fact murder. If Spicer broke off the novel where he did, it is perhaps because he had led it to the verge of its second movement, in which, the conclusive certainties of Ralston now ironically undone (his "creative triumph" nothing but a repetition of his previous failures, the crime question no longer whether Jones was the *perpetrator* of a minor assault, but whether he was the *victim* of a murder), an entirely new narrative sequence would have to be generated to revisit the very same arena of concerns but from the inside out.[2]

Such a framework is entirely Jamesian. In fact, we have something similar near the middle of *The Ambassadors*, where Strether, surprised to learn that he has successfully persuaded Chad to return from Paris to Woollett and thereby accomplished his mission, suddenly and astonishingly reverses course and encourages him to stay, which among other things, gives the novel reason to continue and rewrite itself through an inverted second half, in which he and Chad largely exchange positions. These elements might help explain why, revisiting the "regions of nostalgia" of the city as he walks through it while running the errand of another, Ralston "felt rather like a sympathetic character from one of the novels of Henry James" (93), prior to worrying that he has been trapped in a "false position" (100), which, as Julie Rivkin has made clear, is an eminently Jamesian phrase, and also one James applies to Strether in his New York edition preface.[3] In fact, just before this, in a designation that is far from innocent, Ralston describes himself to Rue and Sonia (the woman who claims Jones assaulted her, and who will later be revealed as Rue's lover), as being sent "as a kind of ambassador" (96). It would seem that Ralston's journey through San Francisco largely repeats Strether's visit to Paris, a half-century later.

Both Strether and Ralston return to an earlier scene of youthful hopes, trying to recover in some way what seems lost; both end up staking much on an encounter with the authentic, and both fear they are too old for such an encounter to register in their lives (while Strether is fifty-five and Ralston only thirty-one, the considerable age difference between the latter and the "kids" of the new scene, Rue among them, is something Ralston often harps on). "What one loses one loses" (153) Strether crucially proclaims in *The Ambassadors*, even if his ultimate faith in that credo remains one of that novel's central questions. We cannot know if Spicer would have led Ralston to a similar conclusion, or given him a chance at redemption instead, but the novels parallel each other in their posing of these problems.[4]

However, a key difference between them is that if Strether is indeed returning to a Paris he had visited in his youth, it is nevertheless a visit to the entirely and hopefully revivifying *foreign*, as the novel's obsessions with exoticism, touristic consumption, and authenticity emphasize. Ralston, on the other hand, returns to a space which if troped as foreign in a similar vein is nevertheless also stressed as being his *home*—the site of his birth as a poet, as the novel reminds us in various places—and Ralston arrives with a nearly explicit desire to experience the home *as* foreign, to reinvest it with difference, to recover it as other (the inverse of one valency of Strether, ultimately thwarted, that would make a "home" of the foreign). This is seen as soon as the novel's first page, which emphasizes the "strangeness" of the bar Ralston has found compared not only to Boston, but also to the San Francisco he remembers. His green bottle of ale looks somehow unfamiliar to him: "But it shouldn't look unfamiliar, he thought, I used to drink it when I lived here" (1), and the measuring of these differences becomes a constant of the book. In other words, the pleasure that San Francisco now offers to Ralston is its lack of transparency, its insistence that it now needs to be *read*, as emblematized by the letters themselves of Rue's poems, on which Ralston refuses even to cast his gaze, leaving them safely in their envelope before losing them, most safely of all. Crucially, much of Ralston's reluctance to read the poems is portrayed not only as his fear of actually facing the difference in search of which he had come, but even more, as his anxiety concerning the meaning of Rue's desire for him, as he seems the least likely sort of audience that Rue would be interested in;[5] when Ralston firmly resolves to leave San Francisco, he seems to be fleeing not only the question of his attraction to the city, but also that of the city, as personified by Rue in an obvious play on the French, to him. Following Laplanche, we can say that Ralston has succeeded in reconstructing San Francisco as the transferential space of the enigma, and that much of the novel consists of Ralston's successive ambivalences regarding the imperative to read, interpret, translate. At stake is nothing less than the source of the poetic, and Ralston's moment of "triumph" is not one of reified exoticization of an "authentic" encounter,[6] but on the contrary, the oddly similar attempt to assimilate into the known what threatens to be significantly other, captured neatly in the tautological annihilation of difference and affirmation of coherent identity conveyed by the phrase "My poems are my poems." Such a perspective not only precludes the kind of "collaboration" that Spicer enjoyed in *After Lorca*, but also that work's sense of how "correspondence" can reinvest Spicer's utterly local California seaweed or shade of gray in the Pacific with Lorca's Andalusian lemon.

As he spies the bay while crossing the bridge from San Francisco to Berkeley, Ralston reflects, with a nod to William Carlos Williams, as follows: "and it occurred to him that a return to the past, however pleasing, was in no sense a renewal," because "the past was no threat to John J. Ralston and this specious present [the encounter with Rue in the bar] was" (30).[7] The questions left suspended by Spicer's failure to finish the manuscript are whether the loss of the locus of the past and thus the impossible return become productive for poetry or not, along with whether such a loss is only the prelude to a dialectical recovery that would extend the "groundedness" which plays so equivocal a role in Spicer's regionalism. The description of Rue's poems as "cunningly hidden by the very process of being lost" is in no way a redundancy, as the need to investigate the role of loss as a strategy of preservation is as strong an element of Spicer's cartographies as it was those of Dickinson, whose "Door ajar/ That Oceans are" Spicer closes on the other coast.[8] Late in the book, immediately following some predictable, unspoken meditations of Ralston on the endlessness of the Pacific Ocean as opposed to the Atlantic, Madelaine remarks "It's beautiful, isn't it. . . . I've always wondered how it would look to someone returning to it" (132). "Revisiting it," Ralston corrects her, before changing tack: "It looks fine. A little too much like a harbor at the end of the world. A little too much of a wall out there maybe" (132), as if the difference between the half-open door and the ultimate wall hinged on the distinction between the revisit and the return, the endlessness of repetition and the finality of arrival, in their failure to be parsed. Finally, as Ralston gazes in the opposite direction from his new New England home and the Europe beyond it, Spicer brings transatlantic American modernism to the edge of the latent possibility always within it, occasionally surfacing: the other coast. It is here that he begins his penultimate book, *Language*, with the ear of poetry straining not toward the Europe of cultural authority and mythic origins, but pressed up against the deafening shell of the ill-named "Pacific":

This ocean, humiliating in its disguises
Tougher than anything.
No one listens to poetry. The ocean
Does not mean to be listened to. A drop
Or crash of water. It means

Nothing.
It
Is bread and butter
Pepper and salt. The death
That young men hope for. Aimlessly
It pounds the shore. White and aimless signals. No
One listens to poetry. (*Collected Books*, 217)

∼

If John Ashbery is routinely placed at the center of discussions of "postmodern" American poetry, his reflections on expatriation and art, clearly fueled by the ten years or so he spent in Paris in the 1950s and 1960s, hearken back directly to those of modernists Stein, Pound and James. Sounding like the second discussing the third, Ashbery writes "A certain kind of American sensibility had to extricate itself from America in order to realize itself" (*Reported Sightings*, 299) and "This perhaps is the real reason why younger American painters take to Europe: a feeling of wanting to keep their American-ness [sic] whole, in the surroundings in which it is most likely to flourish and take root" (*Reported*, 96–7); as forcefully as Pound or Stein, Ashbery points to European expatriation as a particular expression and preserve of Americanness, rather than its abandonment. In fact, in reference to Stein, he posits a sense of the importance of her expatriation very similar to that she expressed herself: "One feels there must be a connection between her decision to install herself in Paris at the age of twenty-nine and the beginning of a period that saw . . . her first masterpieces of narrative prose" (*Reported*, 109). Ashbery goes on to stress the "distance from America," the "insulation" provided by the ambient foreign language, and her solitude within the "traditionally conservative esthetic climate of official Paris" (109) as key for the "American" *Three Lives* and *The Making of Americans*. In other discussions, Ashbery goes well beyond Stein's emphasis on Parisian "unreality," to insist that the city's "indifference" (99), conservatism, and anti-Americanism are bracingly productive for both American artistic identity and artistic self-reliance in general, in statements which can sometimes be quite hyperbolic: "What is especially moving in the work of the Americans abroad [in France] is a general resolution in the face of apathy and apartheid to determine their individuality, to create something independent of fashion" (91).[9] Yet, this affirmation of the independence of identity runs parallel to a more

Jamesian tonality, in which Ashbery also portrays expatriation as a salutary destruction of all stable identities altogether, in a problematic very much like that which James works through in his discussion of the "cosmopolite." Thus, in his key article on American artists in Paris, "American Sanctuary in Paris," published in 1966, at the end of his own expatriation, Ashbery offers a long passage from Hawthorne to illustrate the situation of his subjects:

> The years, after all, have a kind of emptiness when we spend too many of them on a foreign shore. We defer the reality of life, in such cases, until a future moment when we shall again breathe our native air; but, by and by there are no future moments; or, if we do return, we find that the native air has lost its invigorating quality, and that life has shifted its reality to the spot where we have deemed ourselves only temporary residents. Thus, between two countries, we have none at all, or only that little space of either in which we finally lay down our discontented bones. (*Reported*, 90)

Ashbery fails to specify that the above is one of the closing passages of *The Marble Faun*, or that he has cut his excerpt just before its concluding sentence: "It is wise, therefore, to come back betimes—or never" (*Marble*, 358). This is because Ashbery replaces Hawthorne's injunction to make a determining choice with quite the opposite, remarking immediately following the above:

> The redeeming feature of this pessimistic tableau is, for an artist, precisely the inability of identifying anywhere. The feeling of being a stranger even in moments of greatest rapport with one's adopted home is the opposite of the American 'acceptance world' which so often ends up by stifling an artist's originality. (90–1)

Rather than either stay or return, the artist is enabled by doing neither, by, much like James' cosmopolite, remaining nowhere, despite the risk that Hawthorne evokes: that the only place this "nowhere" can be grounded is the grave where we lay down our bones, or where Spicer and Lorca meet in a poetry of death.[10] However, this cultivation of betweenness, placelessness, and cultural interference is explored not with solemnity but hilarity in the novel Ashbery co-wrote with James Schuyler, *A Nest of Ninnies*, a work which also would seem relevant to another of Ashbery's remarks on the question: ". . . with today's communications and transportation, nobody is an expatriate" (*Reported*, 88); an affirmation which also implies nobody is ever completely at home.

Started as a game to alleviate the boredom of a long car trip in 1952, Ashbery and Schuyler wrote *A Nest of Ninnies* over a seventeen-year period, the novel being first published in 1969 by E. P. Dutton. Standard practice for the poets was to compose sentence by sentence in alternation, each trying to outdo the other for allusive and outrageous wit.[11] The title is stolen from the Elizabethan "jest book" by Robert Armin, who was Shakespeare's main comic actor during the latter part of the Bard's career. The plot—ruled by whimsy under the guise of outrageous coincidence—is certainly not the novel's main organizing feature (understandably, given the circumstances of its composition), while characterization in any realist sense is also readily and cheerfully sacrificed to the principle of impossibly witty and bizarre repartee, within a novel consisting preponderantly of dialogue. Be this as it may, it is important nevertheless to note that events do occur, and that characters, if not actually "evolving" in any traditional novelistic sense, are subjected to significant changes in situation. The book begins by introducing us to two young couples, both of whom are living in a state of cohabitation in suburban New York—Marshall and Alice Bush, and Fabia and Victor Bridgewater. In the earliest scenes of the novel, the cordial relations between the two sets of two take on troubling undertones for the reader, as a certain flirtation between "very pretty" (11) Fabia Bridgewater and Marshall Bush makes itself apparent, unsettlingly well tolerated by Alice. This is, however, not a novel of adultery, not a belated revenge tragedy—as gradually becomes clear, the Bushes and Bridgewaters are not married couples, but in each case, a pair of siblings, and the two pairs are engaged in a burgeoning double courtship. As we witness the tentative exchanges of something like romantic affection passing between Alice Bush and Victor Bridgewater, Fabia Bridgewater and Marshall Bush, the revenge tragedy gives way to the marriage comedy, and the question of adultery is replaced by that of exogamy—will the consanguineous Bush and Bridgewater households be disbanded, allowing new and different forms of exchange to take place? But things hardly remain so simple, as exogamy in this novel will take the hyperbolic form of exoticism; for many characters in the book, romantic adventure is found beyond the confines of suburban "Kelton," and implies the venerable expatriate haunts that are France and Italy. As Fabia, Alice, Victor, Marshall's boss Irving Kelso, and possibly Marshall himself find bliss with partners culled abroad, the question of the relationship of affect to the exotic is posed with increasing insistence, especially in contrast to the book's initial presentation of sibling relationships as the originary model of domestic partnership. A structural implication of the novel is that claustrophobic, suburban Kelton is narrow to the point of incestuousness when measured against cosmopolitan, densely historical sites like Paris, Rome, and Palermo, yet the book also engages in a non-systematic but omnipresent remapping of the usual circuits of exchange of cultural capital. In the end, the book is far less a satire of a clichéd, pre-fab suburbia, bereft of historical rootedness and tradition and thriving on American vulgarity, than a reflection on this suburbia's putative others, and the plenitude they are often assumed to possess: the cosmopolitan metropolis and European authenticity, the real real, compared to which suburbia would be no more than a poor relative and embarrassing imitation—in other words, the hyperbolic American space.

The sense of suburban marginality is voiced by Alice Bush on the novel's first page: "I dislike being fifty miles from a great city. I don't know how many cars pass every day and it makes me wonder" (9), yet the novel will never allow the exoticized, valorized other stages it presents to become the measure of any ultimate authenticity, even their own. Beginning and ending in Kelton, the book dismantles the elsewheres its characters seek, while the exoticist desire for authenticity, if not subjected to the intricacies of James' dismantlings, is ruled by schemas of recognition and resemblance wholly dictated by the touristic transformation of "experience" or the "encounter" as such into a consumer object, leading to a series of casual disappointments. The book often seems an illustration of the following corrective to Benjamin's theory of the aura, which Dean MacCannell proposes in *The Tourist*:

> Benjamin believed that the reproductions of the work of art are produced because the work has a socially based 'aura' about it, the 'aura' being a residue of its origins in a primordial ritual. He should have reversed his terms. The work becomes 'authentic' only after the first copy of it is produced. The reproductions *are* the aura, and the ritual, far from being a point of origin, *derives* from the relationship between the original object and its socially constructed importance. (47–8)

We are shown this search for an authenticity to match that of a reproduction regularly. In Florida, Fabia remarks, " 'I'm disappointed. . . . I expected the sea to be bluer. I know it's quite blue, but I expected it to be even bluer' " (45), and we are told that "both sky and sea grew pale beside Irving Kelso's shirt, on which azure and indigo nightjars were at work and play" (45), in a scene whose humor comes not from subordinating "nature" to "artifice," but rather from portraying the *figure* for a particular space (Irving's tropical shirt) as acting more forcefully than the disappointing site (Florida) it is meant to signify. The shirt is more "Florida" than Florida "itself." In similar fashion, James' complex reversal of the relationships between painting and landscape, image and frame, representer and represented, in the Lambinet scene of *The Ambassadors* is now effected by a single laconic observation at the Roman forum: "Alice yawned and turned toward the view. In the sultry light, it was looking remarkably like a sepia reproduction of itself" (103). At the same time, the common denominator of all exotic tourist destinations for the Keltonians— their status as exotic tourist destinations—can sometimes lend them all a strange and dreamlike similarity, despite their outstanding differences: " 'Somehow,' Fabia was saying to Claire, 'I had not expected Paris to be quite so much like Florida' " (93); the reification of *difference* as structuring category ironically leads to its flattening.

In addition to the mechanics of the construction of the foreign, then, the book also addresses the question of its objectification and consumption, and this in the most literal ways. In fact, tourism as form of "conspicuous leisure" as MacCannell puts it, borrowing from Veblen, plays a major role in one of Ashbery's first famous poems, "The Instruction Manual," which closes its imaginary journey to Mexico as follows:

> How limited, but how complete withal, has been our experience of Guadalajara!
> We have seen young love, married love, and the love of an aged mother for her son.
> We have heard the music, tasted the drinks, and looked at colored houses.
> What more is there to do, except stay? And that we cannot do.
> And as a last breeze freshens the top of the weathered old tower, I turn my gaze
> Back to the instruction manual which has made me dream of Guadalajara. (*Mooring*, 10)

The title of the poem refers not only to the boring text from which the speaker turns in his musings, but also to the subject of the poem, for the work does nothing so much as "instruct" the reader as to how to have an exotic vacation.[12] From this follows the cheerfully oxymoronic juxtaposition of the terms "limited" and "complete," implying not only that our touristic appropriation of the foreign may very well be utterly "complete" despite its being limited, but even more, that such "completion" may necessitate these very limitations, as Guadalajara is reduced to a few romanticized sentimental relationships and a digestible series of typical sounds, tastes and colors. In his case study of sight-seeing in San Francisco, MacCannell suggests, "Sightseers do not, in any empirical sense, *see* San Francisco. They see Fisherman's Wharf, a cable car, the Golden Gate Bridge, Union Square, Coit Tower.... As elements in a set called 'San Francisco,' each of these items is a symbolic marker" (111). The poem's wistful realization that staying is the thing "we cannot do" is crucial in such a framework: only by leaving, by remaining a tourist, can such a form of parcellated appropriation manage to function. But the wistfulness is also tied to a real problem, and one which interests *A Nest of Ninnies*: how to exploit the experience after one has left, that is, not only how to "have" the touristic experience, but how to transport it "back home" and preserve it there. It is important to remember that this is a question at which Strether throws up his hands, insisting on returning only to *loss*. The denizens of *A Nest of Ninnies* are more cheerfully pragmatic, packaging and enjoying their Europe in the form of sexual partners, food, and antiques. Yet we are hardly in the realm of the pure products, "the real thing," that Strether so longed for and attempted to thrill to. For example, Alice's Italian catch, Giorgio, brings a little bit of Italy back home to Kelton, where he opens an Italian restaurant. However, this Northern Italian first encountered in Sicily and bearing the family name of Grossblatt decides that his restaurant, The Trentino, will mix both Italian and Tyrolean fare, thereby allowing him to attract "both the German food lovers and the Italian" (131). The joke here is double: first because it reminds us that within the opposition "domestic" and "foreign," all the different "foreigns" are rendered in some ways equivalent and interchangeable, the actual particularities of the exoticized targets being merely anecdotic. But secondly, the Trentino Alto Adige region of Italy, near the Austrian border, in terms of gastronomy, language, and other "markers" would indeed strike most Americans as more "German" or "Austrian" than Italian. What Giorgio presents as American market savvy—offering the customers choice—might be just the opposite, as a large component of his venue would almost certainly *not* correspond to what the average Keltonian would be hoping to find in an "Italian" joint. Here, it is precisely Giorgio's authenticity which prevents him from being the "real thing," but throughout the novel, local produce and culinary tradition—those internalizable synecdoches of place and culture, like the sublime omelet Strether ingests during his lunch with Marie—find themselves no longer attached to an entity they might encapsulate. Witness the French Mrs. Turpin in an earlier chapter: " 'A New England boiled dinner!' Mrs. Turpin exclaimed shrilly. 'I haven't had one since we left Honolulu' " (73).

What the novel often seems pointedly to realize, is the degree to which "authenticity," once accepted as a legitimate category, automatically gives added-value to anything, including inauthenticity. The absurdities of the situation operate bidirectionally in the novel. One example is found when Fabia's Italian beau Memmo invites her and her parents to the "bleak modernity" (104) of the family abode, where Mrs. Bridgewater gushes "It is nice to be in a home again" (104). Subsequently, Memmo's mother praises the Bridgewaters precisely for their fidelity to authenticity, for going beyond the clichéd tourist haunts:

> "Memmo has been telling me what wonderful tourists you are," the baroness said. "Most Americans, when they come to Rome, want to see only the Forum and the Spanish Steps. You have seen parts of the city that many Romans never see."
> Dr. Bridgewater swelled a little. "I find standing here, in Parioli, just as interesting as standing in the Pantheon. The one is the world of today; the other, of yesterday."
> Baroness Oscari looked at him with incredulity. After a long pause she said, "Well, there is no accounting for tastes." (105)

This little comedy is entirely predicated on assumptions regarding touristic exoticism. In MacCannell's account of "Staged Authenticity" (91–107), he discusses how the sophisticated traveler, unlike the vulgar tourist, aims at going beyond the attractions designed specifically for touristic consumption, hoping to "see life as it is really lived, even to get in with the natives" (94), as the Bridgewaters are doing here. Still, Mrs. Bridgewater may very well exclaim on how nice it is to be in someone's home, but presumably one travels to an ancient city to stay in a charming hotel near the historic center, not to find oneself in a suburb very much like the one whence one came. Even more importantly, if the Baroness praises the Bridgewaters for going "beyond" the tourist sites and seeing the "real" Rome, she obviously takes no pleasure in being grouped with that "Roman authenticity" herself—such a gesture removes her status as gracious hostess and recasts her as an ethnographic curiosity, to be classed, one imagines, with Venetian Gondoliers and Neapolitan urchins, in a manner again consonant with the danger constantly menacing Strether's fascination with Marie de Vionnet, who, as we have seen, at certain points tumbles into the category of ethnographic specimen. It is, of course, Dr. Bridgewater's hyperbole which gives the whole game away, forcing everyone to ponder just what structure of desire it takes to make Parioli as interesting as the Pantheon.

In terms of "Frenchness," however, in *A Nest of Ninnies* we move from Marie de Vionnet to the elegant Claire Tosti, roving international perfume saleswoman, cast in the role of emissary of all things French to her newfound American friends. At a dinner held in her honor and meant to be "typically American" for her benefit, she is plied with American mixed cocktails:

> "Do they have things like this in France?" Mrs. Bridgewater asked Claire, as she accepted a frosted mug from Irving.
> "Yes," said Claire, "and then again, no." (68)

"Yes, and then again, no," in addition to being nearly an exact citation of Chad's response to Strether when asked if the Vionnets are French,[13] is another emblem of the novel's obsession with the semiotics of the foreign and the exotic, and its simultaneous refusal to grant these signs any indexical authority whatsoever. This is felt particularly strongly in the novel's handling of idiom, regarding which Claire plays a highly strategic role. While the American characters speak a collage of television sit-com chatter, mail-order catalogue adjectival excess, corporate or journalistic jargon and mock baroque eloquence, as required, the foreign characters' incursions into English are treated in no generally consistent way, in terms of marking their foreignness. Thus, while we have every reason to believe that Giorgio's English would be weak, he usually speaks an exaggerated comic-book regular-New-York-guy kind of lingo, while the sophisticated Claire speaks a stilted, caricatured generically foreign idiom, but one which allows for frequent bilingual joking: "What strangeness. . . . I too am of Limoges. Or at least, I sometimes as a child passed my Easter vacation there, visiting my great aunt, a Limousine" (49), "Limousine" being the substantivized feminine adjective referring to the city, and therefore the correct term for a female denizen of Limoges. In fact, perhaps the most significant role she plays in the novel is as a semiotic breach in its linguistic surface, as yet another pretext for prying the language from the claims of the idiomatic mimeticism that some readers find conveyed by the book's dialogues.[14] In other words, Claire provides a sort of audibility for signifying production beyond the scope of props such as "characters" and "intentions," along with yet another occasion for subversions of the "realistic" American English the book is toying with throughout—an American idiom no less generically "real" than Claire's is generically "foreign." In terms of the book's poetics, Claire's foreignness and the speech to which it gives rise are in some ways analogous to what the scene of translation allows Pound to perpetrate in English.

However, in reference to James, the distance traveled can in part be measured by the extent to which America and Americanness are themselves now commodities. When Victor takes up with Claire's younger sister Nadia, the two decide to go into the business of selling American antiques in Paris, which draws forth the reply from Dr. Bridgewater "I have heard of bringing coals to Newcastle . . . but this takes the cake" (122), yet he misses the point: whatever the charm of American handicrafts will be for Parisians, it will hardly derive from their being "antique." As Claire remarks in her first appearance in the novel, "What excites me about America is the modern architecture" (50), but Old, or perhaps Olde World authority such as hers, cannot impede Kelton from running after the cachet of antique Europe. Not only have the owners of Sir Toby Belch's Pub brought in a genuine English architect to "make it look authentic" (160), but part of Giorgio's renovation of the soon to be opened Trentino consists of "antiquing the beams" (131), which raises a series of interesting questions: is the phony antique part of the American modernity that Claire prizes? Would Giorgio's antiqued beams be viable in Nadia and Victor's Paris store, or would they be seen as a piece of Italian handicraft rather than authentically American? Would a lapse of time increase or decrease their value? Having been "antiqued" at the origin, might they finally acquire value only when old enough to start to look new? The novel repeatedly asks how and when suburbia's imitation authenticities can become "authentic" expressions themselves, implying that a mystified Europe is in the end nothing more than a slightly older and thereby more palimpsestic America, in a world where "nobody is an expatriate."

In such a context, the autochthonous American scene finds itself with another grounding, circling back through exoticism to the impossible affirmation of the familiar. This happens because the over-investment in both temporal and geographical exoticism (the former implied by the valorization of antiques as such) leads to an astonishing conclusion: the mark of real "presence," of an actual "thereness," is invisibility. Thus in the book's final scene, Nadia takes Claire to task when her sister criticizes the decor of the newly opened Trentino for its lack of "profile" and "definition":

> "Oh no, Claire. This time you are wrong. It is just right: it is so 'with it' as to be invisible; one cannot see it until its time is past. More definition would crush some part of the public—make them self-conscious. As it is, all types and ages can come and rub along together. You see they are all having what our friend Giorgio calls, 'one hell of a good time.'"
>
> Irving was mildly puzzled. "I don't see anything wrong with it. I mean, it's what restaurants are like, isn't it?" (181)

Irving, of course, proves Nadia's point: the decor is entirely anonymous to him, being simply what restaurants look like; despite or because of its mix of Tyrolean and Italian features and antiqued beams, it is familiar to the point of transparency, and a realization of the "everyday" in its historical moment implies nothing so much as Irving's undiscriminating gaze. Does this lead us back to a valorization of *estrangement* in all its forms as the necessary condition for encounter and experience? Yes, to a certain extent, but it also implies, as strongly as James, or Pound's temporally disjunct idiom, the impossibility of being one's own contemporary, spatially or temporally, or at the very least, the sacrifice it entails. Thus, this invisibility of the everyday needs to be considered alongside the correlative hypervisibility of the banal, evident as soon as the latter is thrust into the position of sign of the authentic. Thus in Florida, Alice rejects the Crocodile Room, which we shall shortly learn is dear to Claire Tosti's heart: "Oh, I'm not going there.... It's too modern and garish. I'm going to that place we passed this morning, with the ceiling fans. It's like a real old-fashioned drugstore" (47). For Alice, the temporal exoticism implied by "old-fashioned" plays the same role that the geographical and cultural variety plays for Claire, enamored of the pure products of "garish" American kitsch vulgarity. However, returning to Alice's designation—"like a real old-fashioned drugstore"—I would like to suggest that one of the central questions of the novel is precisely the degree to which the category of the "real" can admit of similitude. To be "like" something real is to be neither real nor its other, while making the real itself serial; it is to offer entry into a space in which James's "real things," rather than ever elusive, are unavoidably everywhere, again raising the question of place.

In Giorgio Grossblatt's uncle's Italian restaurant in New York's Bowery, the guests are offered a bottle of "Est Est Est" in honor of the young newlyweds, Giorgio and Alice (137). This wine, which in fact exists, takes its name from a legend regarding the German cardinal Johann Fugger, who, around 1110 and on his way to the coronation of Henry V, sent a servant ahead of him to scour the Roman countryside in search of good wine, asking him to mark the door of any inn which provided it with the notation "Est !" In Montefiascone, the story goes, the cardinal came upon the decisive door marked iteratively with the exclamatory "Est ! Est !! Est !!!," expressing his servant's sense of the wine's superlative quality, and bestowing the name by which the wine is known to this day (the exclamation marks forming part of the name, though omitted by Ashbery and Schuyler). Wines, with their endlessly controlled and negotiated geographical denominations, are a striking emblem of the manner in which a mystified notion of place and origin can be turned into a value-added consumer product, and all the more when the sacred places are located in Europe and marketed to American consumers. To a certain degree, the label on all expensive wines reads "Est Est Est," while the ultimate extension of the trope is the ultimate luxury wine: the mythical one which "doesn't travel," implying, of course, that the dedicated consumer must have the leisure capital and time to do so in the wine's stead. This is a trope that Hawthorne exploits, in the anxieties concerning the dangers of geographical and cultural displacement which dominate *The Marble Faun*, in his account of the marvelous white wine "Sunshine," whose savor illuminates the ancestral house of Monte Beni: "The finest Orvieto, or that famous wine, the Est Est Est of Montefiascone, is vulgar in comparison" (174) notes the sculptor Kenyon, shortly before learning that if the wine is not better known it is because it "is so fond of its native home, that a transportation of even a few miles turns it quite sour" (174). The Monte Benis' faithful old servant continues:

> And yet it is a wine that keeps well in the cellar, underneath this floor, and gathers fragrance, flavour, and brightness, in its dark dungeon. That very flask of Sunshine, now, has kept itself for you, Sir Guest, (as a maid reserves her sweetness till her lover comes for it,) ever since a merry vintage-time, when the Signor Count here was a boy! (174)

For Hawthorne, the "Sunshine" is echoed by Donatello of Monte Beni himself, who loses his prelapsarian natural glow when forced out of the environs of his ancestral home (and to which Sin will prevent him from any sort of return, geographical proximity or no), itself a trope of the Garden of Eden and what is for Hawthorne the original exile. Meanwhile, in the dark bowels of the castle lurks the bottled Sunshine ready to open itself like a maiden to her lover, in a topography of open, sunny illumination and dark, subterranean concealment that could illustrate Freud's speculations on the Unheimlich.

A Nest of Ninnies ends on no such note of "hereness" and geographical and cultural continuity, as one might well imagine. Rather, at the novel's close, the characters exit Kelton's new favorite nightspot, the Trentino; the New Yorkers "moved off toward the parking area," that exemplary space of a culture of transience, as the Keltonians decide to make their way to the Gay Chico for some refried beans. As the novel ends, the "country cousins" of suburbia, we are told, "bent their steps toward the partially rebuilt shopping plaza in the teeth of the freshening foehn" (191), the latter being a term which Ashbery has himself defined as "a kind of warm wind that blows in Bavaria that produces a fog." In this way, it is as much a regional term and proper noun as those derogatory terms mobilized by Lorca, and it cannot, by definition, be found in Kelton, unless the latter be joined to Bavaria or relocated to the Alps.[15] The buried sunshine of mystical locale has given way to the virtual, suburban, enveloping American-Bavarian fog, as it sweeps over the parking lot and shopping mall, carried across the page by a word whose "native atmosphere and circumstance," as James put it in reference to the American idiom in "The Question of Our Speech," are inevitably neither here nor there. In Spicer, Ashbery, and Schuyler, we see where American transatlantic cosmopolitan modernism also invariably, dialectically tended—the suburbs and the other coast—while the museum, with walls or without, fades into its other which since James at least has also been its double: the shopping mall, which Europe's ghosts ask no better than to haunt.

NOTES

Introduction

1. I hope it is obvious that in the context of the twenty-first century, the linguistic space I'm evoking far surpasses the identifications I mention above; those are merely the ones I will be concerned with here.
2. In the context of a different argument, Wendy Stallard Flory made a similar point in 1989, "... the international perspective of the American expatriate writers of the early twentieth century need not be thought of as in any way 'un-American'" (5). Or as Shari Benstock observed in 1986 concerning Stein and Joyce, "... their writing compulsively reexamined cultures they had left behind: the locus of Stein's writing was always America just as Joyce's was always Ireland" (18). Later, Benstock suggests that Stein "became increasingly aware of the necessity to separate herself from America in order to write about it" (157). In this, she was hardly alone. In a similar vein, Ulla Dydo also asserts that when Stein returned to America for her lecture tour after thirty years abroad, "she presented herself not as an estranged expatriate but as a quintessentially American writer" (619), a position somewhat different from, but not contrary to that of James, as we shall see.
3. One way Giles presses this point is by considering writers of the most obviously problematic "nationality," such as Nabokov, Sylvia Plath, and Thom Gunn.
4. Ramazani's extraordinary essay exhaustively and cogently demonstrates the enormous variety of twentieth-century poets for whose work a transnational critical perspective must certainly figure as "primary rather than incidental," while also noting how, on the contrary, the critical trend concerning poetry in English over the last fifteen years has been "more nationally or regionally focused than cross-cultural, as if

literary critics have been elegiacally recathecting the national at a time when the globalizing processes of a century ago have multiplied and accelerated" (334).

5. Giles warns of the dangers of the "older critical styles of comparative literature" which "were predicated ultimately on the notion of simply transcending national cultures, cultures it loftily viewed as parochial and intellectually irrelevant" (17). Ramazani calls for a *"translocal poetics,"* neither "localist nor universalist," which would highlight "dialogic intersections," in contrast to the "international modernist" paradigm of Ellman and Kenner, for example, whose "internationalism was not always particularized" (350). Such a position is not without its paradoxes, as Ramazani is well aware: "a cross-cultural poetics depends on the identitarian paradigms it complicates" (351), and Ramazani realizes the extent to which a translocal poetics finds itself caught in a dialectical double-bind, albeit one he rightly sees as more productive than the regionalist and universalist alternatives: "To highlight these transnational and cross-ethnic ironies is, ultimately, to reassert the very national and ethnic categories of identity that a cross-cultural poetics is meant to outstrip.... And yet recently proposed alternatives run the risk of still greater reductionism" (353). Similarly, while I wholly endorse John Carlos Rowe's recent contention that Henry James "would be horrified by this commodification of him as an 'American author' rather than a figure who forces us to recognize the inherent *problems* of 'national authorship' (231), as Rowe's account shows very well, a consideration of such "problems" cannot be conducted without attention to the specific context within which James was led to pose them. Indeed, regarding such "problems," we are very much where James Baldwin leaves his American narrator in relation to his French entourage in *Giovanni's Room*, in a statement which one imagines must also have had pertinence to Baldwin's experience as a black man in white America: "And I resented this: resented being called an American (and resented resenting it) because it seemed to make me nothing more than that, whatever that was; and I resented being called *not* an American because it seemed to make me nothing" (85–6). The negotiation of the space between these two annihilating interpellations will be a major focus of this book.

6. Regarding Eliot, Crawford's intriguing pages in *Devolving English Literature* already point the way.

Chapter 1

1. "Not quite citizens and yet Americans... Negro Americans are in desperate search for an identity. Rejecting the second-class status assigned them, they feel alienated and their whole lives have become a search for

answers to the questions: Who am I, What am I, Why am I, and Where? Significantly, in Harlem the reply to the greeting, 'How are you?' is very often, 'Oh, man, I'm *nowhere*'—a phrase revealing an attitude so common that it has been reduced to a gesture, a seemingly trivial word" ("Harlem is Nowhere," 284–5).

2. The equating of expatriation, cosmopolitanism, new-found freedom, subjective rebirth, and increased artistic prowess is a cliché of modernism—sometimes foregrounded as such—and is omnipresent among both writers and their critics. Thus, in Ezra Pound's "What I feel about Walt Whitman," for example, Pound exults in his "world citizenship" (*Selected Prose*, 145); Joyce's *Portrait* famously ends with Stephen Dedalus's impending departure for France, the site where, perhaps surprisingly, he will embark on an eminently Jamesian project: to "forge in the smithy of my soul the uncreated conscience of my race" (276), although *Ulysses* qualifies this; Samuel Beckett's adoption of the French language is routinely described as indispensable for his finding his "true voice," while Gertrude Stein, in her *Autobiography of Alice B. Toklas*, certainly implies that the serious business of her life, both with Alice and as a writer, could only begin once in cosmopolitan Paris. As for recent critics, Donald Pizer's discussion of American writers in Paris talks of the expatriate desire to leave the "inadequacies and limitations" of home for "another world [which] seems to be free of these failings and to offer a more fruitful way of life" (1). While J. Gerald Kennedy stresses more heavily than Pizer the "risks" of "exile" in Paris, he also stresses how the city offered the expatriate American writer "freedom from the constraints and inhibitions of American life" culminating in "the opportunity for metamorphosis" (240–1). Meanwhile, Alex Zwerdling, focusing rather on London, finds that American writers flocked there to avoid an increasingly multi-ethnic United States, in which traditional patrician privilege was beginning to erode (ix–xvi). In all these cases, expatriation is linked to a clear and unequivocal new empowerment.

3. James surely knew that the term "Dutchman" was generally used to refer not to Dutch but to German immigrants, through a misunderstanding of the German "Deutsch." Similarly, "Dago" is apparently derived from "Diego," and was originally applied to Spaniards and Portuguese before designating primarily Italians.

4. In this essay, James meticulously distinguishes "speech" from the language or "idiom" which is spoken in a manner entirely consonant with the distinctions between "parole" and "langue" which Saussure was elaborating at roughly the same time.

5. Herder, quoted in Berman, *L'épreuve*, p. 67 (p. 39 in the English edition). My translation.

6. The association of "native language" with the "maternal" does not necessarily imply comfort and succor; *Le Schizo et les langues*, the

autobiographical account of Louis Wolfson's refusal of his native English, shows how this rejection is motivated by his sense of English as an almost physical extension of his mother's body, penetrating his own. His psychosis, however, is perhaps no more than the hyperbolic effect of the cultural linking of the maternal to the "native," and the native to the native language, in general.

7. See Cheryl Torsney for a reading of translation in *The American* in this light.
8. Berman defines ethnocentric translation as that which "carries out a systematic negation of the foreignness of the foreign work" (*L'épreuve*, 17, *Experience*, 5, translation slightly modified)—a violence not unlike the governess' negation of the otherness of her charges' desire, ending by her opposition to their very being.
9. for which Freud's original German is the word "Unheimliche"—a substantivized negation of the root of Schleiermacher's "heimische," which means homey, homelike, and domestic, as well as "native."
10. For a primarily narratological investigation of some of these issues, see Susan E. Honeyman.
11. As Eliot famously put it in "East Coker": And so each venture/ Is a new beginning, a raid on the inarticulate/ With shabby equipment always deteriorating/ In the general mess of imprecision of feeling,/ Undisciplined squads of emotion" (*Collected Poems*, 189).
12. Laplanche's work on "originary seduction" has been among the most discussed in the French psychoanalytic scene of the last twenty years, and I cannot provide a detailed account of it here. The reader in search of one would do well to consult Geyskens and Van Haute's *Confusion of Tongues*, which does an excellent job of situating Laplanche's theories within the history of psychoanalysis.
13. My translation; this passage is found on p. 126 of the English version of *New Foundations*.
14. Letter of October 29, 1888. I have chosen to retain throughout James' frequent use of ampersands and abbreviations of auxiliaries.
15. See Zwerdling for this anecdote, p. 133.
16. I do not have space to analyze the exchange in detail here, but Ralph and the reader learn from Isabel that not only had the former misunderstood Henrietta's remarks, he had also failed to perceive that her subsequent action was her comment upon Ralph's misconstruction. In this novel, where the failure to "read" one's lover, as Isabel puts it in Chapter 42, leads to catastrophe in marriage, Henrietta proves a better reader than Ralph and she will outread Isabel throughout. In terms of the ironies surrounding Henrietta, it is also worth emphasizing Deborah Parsons's recent work on the late nineteenth and early twentieth-century tendency to cast American women as the archetype of the vulgar tourist: "Women and Americans, and most anathema of all, female Americans,

were thus open to construction as patronising 'vulgar' tourists by the self-consciously cultural elite" (229). This context only reinforces how James here both profits from *and* subverts the clichés he can expect his readers to bring to his work.

17. Ralph Waldo Emerson makes precisely the same point in "Self-Reliance," to which the portrayal of the stereotypically "American" Henrietta could well be indebted: "If malice and vanity wear the coat of philanthropy, shall that pass? If an angry bigot assumes this bountiful cause of Abolition, and comes to me with his last news from Barbadoes, why should I not say to him, 'Go love thy infant; love thy wood-chopper; be good-natured and modest; have that grace; and never varnish your hard, uncharitable ambition with this incredible tenderness for black folk a thousand miles off. Thy love afar is spite at home'" (179). This is of course the same essay where Emerson famously rails against European travel, declaring, "It is for want of self-culture that the superstition of Traveling, whose idols are Italy, England, Egypt, retains its fascination for all educated Americans" (197).

18. Ross Posnock consistently emphasizes the later James' deep commitment to the dissolution of ego boundaries and subjective certainties as an essential part of both the reception of "impressions" and their expression in writing, notwithstanding his considerable ambivalence regarding such dispersals. See especially Posnock's chapter on *The Ambassadors* and *The American Scene*.

19. Paul Giles has also called attention to this text, but I cannot follow him in asserting that it shows "little sense . . . of James inquiring into the overall coherence or validity of national identity as a category of affiliation" (102). On the contrary, this piece seems an integral part of the Jamesian project Giles admirably defines elsewhere as that of "stripping nations of their inherited sacral aspects" and fostering a "more perverse pleasure in being strangers everywhere" (117).

20. Hana Wirth-Nesher has also made this point with regard to James, noting ". . . there is no recognition of home without the leaving of it" (243). Indeed, leaving home could be said to constitute the very construction of it.

21. Gert Buelens has provided an incisive critical overview of recent ethical and political criticisms of *The American Scene*, showing the need to rethink many of the terms in which this important debate is couched. See Sara Blair for a very subtle account of the ambivalent "logic of incorporation" (172) in play in James' speculations on the immigrants' possible place within a national body.

22. Given the passionate insistence of this motif, it is odd indeed that James is not more often invoked as stern critic of the culture of finance capitalism, of "conspicuous consumption" in Veblen's sense, though this link has recently been suggested by Posnock (250). Moreover, if James'

constant harping on the destructive force of capitalist competition in terms of architecture and the arts leads him to rather stereotyped "high modernist" lamentations concerning rampant imbecility as arbiter of public taste, it is clearly the vulgarity of the rich and not the ignorance of the poor which concerns him in this context.

23. Or as Cornelius Crowley has elegantly put it, in his discussion of this passage: "... être américain, c'est être exposé à cette étrangeté originaire. ... C'est en ces termes qu'une fraternité peut se nouer entre l'immigrant et le natif, par un partage de la commune dépossession" (369) ["... to be American is to be exposed to this originary foreignness. ... It is in these terms that the immigrant and the native can be joined in fraternity—through their sharing of the dispossession common to both"].

Chapter 2

1. Deborah Parsons has noted how Strether's meal in the countryside in Book Eleventh—a scene which, as we shall see, clearly dialogues with the one discussed above—also asks food and drink to figure as "motifs of Frenchness" and guarantees of "an authentic experience of France" (235). In the passage above, this insistence is magnified by not translating the name of the dish.

2. It could be objected that I over-stress the importance of Marie's "Frenchness" for Strether, as she more generally represents for him a "Europe" which her mixed background would in no way impede. I would counter this objection on two grounds: first, prior to the lunch scene I have discussed above, Strether sees Marie praying in the cathedral of Notre Dame, and Marie's inscription in what is for Strether also a particularly *Catholic* romance—and one which Strether can't help but link to Hugo's novel—already makes it hard to think of her as embodying some sort of vague "Europeanness" which could encompass English protestant tradition. The second point, perhaps more important, is that from the American perspective a mystified "Europeanness" is nothing but a clear, seamless, cultural cohesion and unity; the very introduction of the idea of confusion and difference, even if among European elements, makes it no longer by that token "European." In terms of the figural logic governing the relation between Marie and Frenchness, I would resist the temptation to call her a synecdoche as the "totality" to which she would then need to refer does not seem to exist outside of her incorporation of it. As not a sign of but a substitute for something which can not in itself exist, she is more properly a fetish.

3. Karen Scherzinger, in her fine reading of the scene, also notes the landscape's overinvested status as the "thing" (172), along with its equivocal relationship to the "exhibition room in Boston that lies behind and beyond it" (173).

4. On this note, it is worth recalling that despite his Gallic name, Lambinet was in fact an American painter.
5. Among many examples of James' use of "position" in this sense, we can remember this, from "The Question of Our Speech" : "Every language has its position, which, with its particular character and genius, is its most precious property. . ." (53). "Point of view" also often indicates the adopting of a particular cultural perspective as enabling of vision, as in this 1879 letter to William: "I am sinking also rapidly into that condition of accepted & accepting Londonism when impressions lose their sharpness & the idiosyncrasies of the place cease to be salient. To see them, to feel them, I have to lash my flanks & assume a point of view" (*Selected Letters*, 122–3).
6. Phyllis van Slyck makes interesting points concerning Strether's construction of Chad and Marie's union as a "fantasy object" (566), though I differ with her sense of this being dependent on Marie's "multiplicity" (567). In the context of the rise of consumer culture, Claire Oberon Garcia has also noted the sly complicity between the seemingly opposed values of vulgar, mercantile America and sophisticated, aesthetic Europe. For an extended reading of Chad's Parisian displays as rehearsal for his Woollett career in advertising, see William Greenslade.
7. Sara Blair's incisive reading of the cosmopolitan Miriam Rooth in *The Tragic Muse* suggests some of the dangers that Marie may or may not skirt.
8. "If I have called the whole idea of the presence and effect of Hilda in the story a trait of genius, the purest touch of inspiration is the episode in which the poor girl deposits her burden. She has passed the whole lonely summer in Rome, and one day, at the end of it, finding herself in St. Peter's, she enters a confessional, strenuous daughter of the Puritans as she is, and pours out her dark knowledge into the bosom of the Church . . ." (*Literary Criticism*, 446).
9. In a fascinating article on the dialogue James entertains with Hawthorne in *Roderick Hudson* and *William Wetmore Story*, Sheila Teahan discusses James' consistent annoyance with Hawthorne's aversion to nudity in sculpture, along with questions of textual veilings in both authors. I would add that Hawthorne's puritan insistence on self-disclosure necessarily *commands* the nudity that returns to haunt him when embodied in marble or bronze.
10. In an intriguing article, Eileen T. Bender also touches on James' use of an "English lightly seasoned with Gallic" (128), while additionally closely examining Marie's key shift into French. Though I don't agree with Bender's parsing of artificiality and authenticity, "spontaneity" and pretense, this is an incisive account of the relationship between multilingualism and cosmopolitanism in the novel.

11. A compelling recent account of Marie as "elusive image of ambiguity and mystery" can be found in Phyllis van Slyck's "Knowledge and Representation in *The Ambassadors*: Strether's Discriminating Gaze" (567).
12. Claire Oberon Garcia is one of the few to note the clear parallel drawn between these characters she dubs the "two 'Marys'" (9), though she doesn't read them in relation to their biblical template. Posnock also stresses the filial aspect of Strether's relationship to Maria, referring to her as his "maternal confidante" (235).
13. If the novel doesn't harp on the motif of the "older woman" as much as it might, James warns in his preface that the difference in age between Marie and Chad was "liable to be denounced as shocking" (xxxii).
14. See Siobhan Peiffer for an interesting account of debt in James, particularly in *The Ambassadors*.
15. Van Slyck also notes the importance of this passage (574), though drawing different conclusions from it.
16. Crowley's neologism refers to the foreign voices and accents which call to and haunt James throughout his stay in New York, as recorded in *The American Scene*, and his article provides a brilliant analysis of James' confrontation with the "annonce de la langue maternelle, telle qu'en une langue toute autre le temps la change" (373) ["the proclamation of the mother tongue, as the entirely different language into which time is transforming it"].
17. It is worth mentioning that this model of the transition from virginity to maternity through the alterity of sexuality as a privileged figure of the German "Bildung," that is, the attainment through difference of a form which rests programmed in potentio, can be linked to the view of translation as a necessary alienation of a national literature, which ends by leading it to its ultimate universal destiny, as specific cultural product. For a brilliant analysis of this, see Chapter 3 of Berman, *The Experience of the Foreign*.
18. In fact, to read him in this light is to read him as Mrs Newsome and Strether at the outset insist on reading Chad, presumed to be the victim of a "horrible woman" and "quite helpless in her clutches," as James' prospectus for the novel puts it (*Notebooks*, 388).

Chapter 3

1. For a brilliant reading of catachresis in Pound, see Rabaté, 173–82.
2. So Alex Zwerdling, borrowing from James, names what he sees as the American modernist expatriate attempt to achieve cultural pre-eminence in an England in which class boundaries and cultural homogeneity seemed more secure than in America: "That Britain still seemed, comparatively speaking, a society in which class distinctions were fixed, men

in firm control, and the Anglo-Saxon legacy not seriously threatened by other races and religions made it more appealing to these disaffected writers in their flight" (xiv). For Zwerdling, the investment of Pound or Eliot in literary London is literally reactionary, a defensive gesture enacted in the face of the changes America was undergoing at the time, and Pound's great frustration during the London years would be his failure to impose himself as "the literary dictator of London" (235).

3. The phrase also seems to echo, or be echoed by, Eliot's horticultural metaphor from "The Hawthorne Aspect," one of Eliot's two contributions on James to the same number of *The Little Review*. There, Eliot suggests that James' "transplantation" in Europe was in fact what "improved" and gave a "chance" to James' "strong native taste," the flavor deriving from the "soil of his origin" (47–8). Again, expatriation becomes a scene of, or fertile soil for, Americanness.

4. James Baldwin has given one of the most incisive post-war accounts of this paradox, suggesting precisely that the African-American's doubled and divided identity makes him or her in fact the very hyperbole of Americanness: "They face each other, the Negro and the African, over a gulf of three hundred years—an alienation too vast to be conquered in an evening's goodwill, too heavy and too double-edged ever to be trapped in speech. This alienation causes the Negro to recognize that he is a hybrid. Not a physical hybrid merely: in every aspect of his living he betrays the memory of the auction-block and the impact of the happy ending. In white Americans he finds reflected—repeated, as it were, in a higher key—his tensions, his terrors, his tenderness. Dimly and for the first time, there begins to fall into perspective the nature of the roles they have played in the lives and history of each other. Now he is bone of their bone, flesh of their flesh; they have loved and hated and obsessed and feared each other and his blood is in their soil. Therefore he cannot deny them, nor can they ever be divorced.

The American Negro cannot explain to the African what surely seems in himself to be a want of manliness, of racial pride, a maudlin ability to forgive. It is difficult to make clear that he is not seeking to forfeit his birthright as a black man, but that, on the contrary, it is precisely this birthright which he is struggling to recognise and make articulate. Perhaps it now occurs to him that in this need to establish himself in relation to his past he is most American, *that this depthless alienation from oneself and one's people is, in sum, the American experience*" (*Notes*, 118, my emphases).

5. As published in the *Selected Prose*, "Patria Mia" represents a 1913 revision made by Pound of two serialized articles which had appeared in *The New Age*: "Patria Mia," which ran in eleven installments from September 5 to November 14, 1912, and "America: Chances and Remedies," which ran in six installments from May 1 to June 5, 1913. Interestingly, the

1913 revision omits a companion piece, "Through Alien Eyes," which ran in four installments, from January 16 to February 6, 1913. Pound's June 3, 1913, letter to his father presents him as "finishing" the revised version (*Seleceted Letters*, 21), while according to Carpenter (167), Pound would have met James himself in February, 1912—about six months before the serial version of "Patria Mia" began to appear. It is worth noting how much temporal overlap there is between both of Pound's "James" pieces, focusing on America, and his work on translation, particularly from the Chinese. Just three months after finishing the revisions to "Patria Mia," that is, in September 1913, Pound would begin his work on Fenollosa's papers. About five years later, while preparing the "Henry James" number of *The Little Review* in the spring of 1918, he was already foreseeing the subsequent publication of *The Chinese Written Character* in the pages of the same journal. The James number turned out to be that of August, 1918, while the latter text, completed much earlier, would finally appear in installments in *The Little Review* between September and December, 1919.

6. Pound differs with James on the value of the skyscraper, but like him, places an extended description of the approach to New York harbour in a strategically central spot. Likewise, when James claims that "the machinery is colossal" (92) for transforming the children of very foreign-seeming immigrants into "the stuff of whom brothers and sisters are made," and regarding whom "the idea of intimacy of relation may be as freely cherished as you like" (92), Pound laconically throws off, "People marvel that foreigners deluge America and 'lose their own nationality almost at once'; that 'their children all look alike'" (*Selected Prose*, 101).

7. James writes, "One of these denotements is that social democracies are unfriendly to the preservation of *penetralia*; so that when *penetralia* are of the essence, as in a place of study and meditation, they inevitably go to the wall" (185). Pound includes this header in a list of other headers and phrases which he highlights from *The American Scene*: "Newport, the standardized face, the Capitol, Independence Hall, the absence of penetralia, innocence, essential vagueness, etc., language 'only definable as not *in intention* Yiddish,' the tabernacle of Grant's ashes, the public collapse of the individual, the St Gaudens statue" (*Literary Essays*, 327).

8. Almost 100 years later, Jacques Derrida defined democracy in surprisingly similar terms, arguing that it cannot but be vacant, absent, deferred, and in abeyance, given its defining relationship to alterity and plurality: "C'est le sens propre, le sens même du même. . . c'est le soi-même, le même, le proprement même du soi-même qui fait défaut à la démocratie. Il [the "double renvoi" Derrida sees as constitutive of democracy] définit la démocratie, et l'idéal même de la démocratie, par ce défaut du propre et du même" [It is the proper meaning, the meaning

itself of the same. . . . it is the oneself, the same, the proper self of the oneself, which democracy lacks. It [the double relay] defines democracy, the ideal of democracy itself, by this lack of the proper, the same, the itself] (*Voyous*, 61).

9. "The tree picks up its roots and turns them inward to walk. How convenient to stick one's foot into the earth and be nourished? At sacrifice of the freedom to be nomadic?. . . . My predisposition (at least in youth) being nomadic. It is not for me to rebuke brother semite for similar disposition. Happy the man born to rich acres, a saecular vine bearing good grapes, olive trees spreading with years" (243).

10. These statements can be compared to Eliot's from "In Memory," published in the same issue of *The Little Review*: "I do not suppose that any one who is not an American can *properly* appreciate James" (44). Note how Pound inflects this into the question of displacement: for him, the "proper" reader is the American gone *abroad*, or the "exile" reading from "both sides of the Atlantic."

11. The editors' annotations from Pound's correspondence with Margaret Anderson indicate that the section of "Henry James" titled "The Middle Years" was a reprint from a contribution to the January, 1918, issue of *The Egoist*, while "The Notes to 'The Ivory Tower'" was "recast' from an April, 1918, piece written for *Future* (this latter piece was not printed in its entirety in the "Henry James" number). See *Pound/Little Review*, p. 204, for further details. As printed in *Literary Essays*, "Henry James" contains numerous and for the most part minor revisions of *The Little Review* contributions. In these pieces, Pound also freely lifted phrases from his "Provincialism the Enemy," first published in *The New Age* in four installments, between July 12 and August 2, 1917, and currently available in the *Selected Prose*.

12. Pound's apposition of "abysmal" and "maternal" in evoking "Louisa Pallant" is hardly insignificant. In her brilliant study of the figure of the abyss in the late James, Evelyne Labbé notes that for James "*fascinante et souvent dangereuse, la femme sera, dès l'origine, la profondeur même*" (10) [fascinating and often dangerous, from the outset woman will be depth itself]; one would only add no woman more so than the mother and her supplements.

13. See Richard Sieburth's "In Pound We Trust" for a brilliant reading of Poundian "circulation" in its erotic, economic, political, and poetic dimensions.

14. Additionally, of course, in both "Notes on Elizabethan Classicists" and "How to Read" Pound unambiguously identifies translation with the motive force in the development of English literature, writing in the former "A great age of literature is perhaps always a great age of translations; or follows it" (*Literary Essays*, 232), and in the latter, again invoking Chaucer, "After this period English literature lives on

translation, it is fed by translation; every new exuberance, every new heave is stimulated by translation, every allegedly great age is an age of translations, beginning with Geoffrey Chaucer, Le Grand Translateur, translator of the *Romaunt of the Rose*, paraphraser of Virgil and Ovid, condenser of old stories he had found in Latin, French, and Italian" (*Literary Essays*, 34–35).

15. A similar metaphorics governs the erotic schema which Pound sees as underpinning the poetics of the troubadours, and their followers, Guido and Dante. In *The Spirit of Romance* Pound writes, "Man is—the sensitive physical part of him—a mechanism, for the purpose of our further discussion a mechanism rather like an electric appliance, switches, wires, etc." (92). For Pound, it is the unattainability of the poet's love object that makes flow between them the charge or current productive of poetry. As he puts it, "The electric current gives light where it meets resistance" (97). The technological sense of "translateur" is entirely consonant with some of Pound's preferred terminology of the period for explaining the relationship between erotics and poetics. Indeed, in the troubadour tradition the poem is often addressed itself by the poet who has written it, notably in the convention of the "envoi," which emphasizes how the very poem is also a kind of "translateur," linking the highly charged poles which are the poet and his (in Pound's examples) beloved.

16. See Chapter 4 of Michael North's *The Dialect of Modernism* for an indispensable discussion of "black face" dialect in Pound and Eliot.

17. The entirety of Chapter 5 of *Reading Pound Reading*, "Kulchural Graphics," is extremely illuminating on these questions.

Chapter 4

1. Notable examples of this trend would include Daniel Tiffany's *Radio Corpse* (1995), Robert Kern's *Orientalism, Modernism, and the American Poem* (1996), Ming Xie's *Ezra Pound and the Appropriation of Chinese Poetry*, Yunte Huang's *Transpacific Displacement* (2002), and above all, Steven Yao's *Translation and the Languages of Modernism* (2002). Note also that Richard Sieburth's Library of America edition of Pound's work other than the *Cantos* bears the title "Poems and Translations," and publishes virtually the entirety of the latter, including renderings of Greek drama, Noh plays, and other work which could be classified as "prose."

2. My use of "heliotropic" is derived from Jacques Derrida's "White Mythology: Metaphor in the Text of Philosophy."

3. "... the Chinese ... attained the known maximum of *phanopoeia*, due perhaps to the nature of their written ideograph ..." (*Literary Essays*, 26–7). If Pound is officially the "editor" of Fenollosa's *The Chinese Written Character as a Medium for Poetry*, as Yunte Huang has recently

suggested he is apparently quite an intrusive one, and the critical practice of treating him as a co-author, at least regarding answerability for the claims staked therein, seems justified. See Huang, pp. 43–50, and 60–92, for interesting discussions of the appropriations of both Fenollosa and Pound.
4. See Yao for an excellent recent acount of this.
5. "Also he was so accustomed to observe the dominant line in objects that after he had spent what could not have been more than a few days studying the subject at the museum, he could understand primitive Chinese ideographs (not the later more sophisticated forms), and he was very much disgusted with the lexicographers who 'hadn't sense enough to see that *that* was a horse,' or a cow or a tree or whatever it might be. . . ." (*Gaudier-Brzeska: A Memoir*, 46). Note that if here Pound does indeed gesture towards a distinction between radicals and compound ideographs, his insistence on the essentially visual nature of Chinese writing will not significantly waver. See *Chinese Written Character*, 30–1, for the same story.
6. Robert Kern, for example, has devoted much space to establishing the importance of Emerson for Fenollosa, yet he too agrees that this aspect of Fenollosa's thought does "depart" from "the Swedenborgian Emerson of *Nature* at least" (126–7). It seems to me that this departure is not incidental, but absolutely crucial.
7. This emphasis on dynamic process and relation also shows "imagisme" already hurtling into the "vorticism" of 1914.
8. Several recent studies, notably those by Yao, Huang, and Xie, provide illuminating and indispensable discussions of the Chinese source-texts Pound was appropriating, within Chinese poetic tradition. Here, I shall focus primarily on how the Chinese becomes, literally, a "pretext" for interventions in English.
9. Robert Kern notes something similar, remarking that Pound "allows his English to be reordered or even *dis*ordered" and that certain turns of phrase in *Cathay* correspond "to little we can imagine actually being said in English" (186). However, I differ from Kern when he argues that such transfer of "otherness" represents an attempt to recover a "transcendental signified" by taking us "out of our own time limits and space limits" (187). Rather, it is these very limits which are brought to the foreground in such a process. Meanwhile, Daniel Tiffany points out that the "Cathay" tone can be found elsewhere in Pound, and more precisely in haunted "crypt poems." "The plaintive voice of 'The River Merchant's Wife,'" Tiffany argues, can be heard in "The Tomb at Akr Çaar" (143).
10. See p. 39 for other examples. For Fenollosa's argument concerning the active force of metaphoricity in Chinese, see pages 21–6.
11. Eric Hayot, for example, praises Pound for managing to "retain the double characters that begin each line" of the Chinese original (520).

See Yao for an excellent, detailed account of Pound's rendering of the poem, including transcriptions of the Chinese characters from Fenollosa's notes (39–42).

12. Pound is certainly unidiomatic elsewhere in the sense of not basing himself on contemporary spoken English, but none of his other invented Englishes seem to willfully dwell on distortion, the bent half-tone, as does his "Chinese."
13. The original French reads, "La traduction, c'est cela : *chercher-et-trouver le non-normé de la langue maternelle pour y introduire la langue étrangère et son dire*" (*La traduction*, 131, original emphasis).
14. And in this way, Pound clearly belongs among those Robert Crawford calls "provincial" modernists: "cultural ec-centrics who liked to confront the English cultural centre with material pointedly foreign to it" (254). His entire chapter "Modernism as Provincialism" is an indispensable account of the variety of such strategies and practices in relation to modernist negotiation with the English cultural center generally.
15. According to Carpenter, Pound translated the *Ta Hio*—from French, and not Chinese—in the autumn of 1927 (460). As a section of what would later become the "Cavalcanti" essay was published in the *Dial* in March, 1928, it is safe to say he was immersed in Guido at about the same time. This concatenation of Confucius and Guido is anything but random.
16. The essay "Cavalcanti," now available in the *Literary Essays*, was first published in this form in *Make It New* in 1934. Its various sections, however, had all been published in various combinations by 1929, and according to David Anderson, left unaltered thereafter. See Anderson, p. 203 *et passim*, for details. Pound's early *Sonnets and Ballate of Guido Cavalcanti* was published in 1912.
17. "Rossetti's translations were perhaps better than Rossetti," Pound suggests in "How To Read" (*Literary Essays*, 36); he never argues to the contrary.
18. Tags are common throughout the reminiscences of the *Pisan Cantos*, in both Italian and Pound's English. See, for example, "formato locho" in LXXIV (446), "dove sta memora" in LXXVI (452), and the same phrase, a few pages later, preceded by a translation and paraphrase of the lines in the *canzone* which explain the phrase: " nothing matters but the quality/ of the affection—/ in the end—that has carved the trace in the mind" (457).
19. Pound quotes "F. Z."—the editor of the Italian edition of Guido he was using—to the effect that the "canzone solely on the nature of Love was so celebrated that the rarest intellects . . . set themselves to illustrating it with commentaries. . ." (*Poems*, 189), without mentioning the poem's title.
20. The task of sorting out Pound's evolving sense of Cavalcanti is still further complicated by the fact that the translation of the "Donna mi

Prega" which he offers in the "Cavalcanti" essay is *not* one that reflects the turn to "pre-Elizabethan" clarity, but rather, one which renders the height of Pound's emphasis on the "musicality" of Cavalcanti's verse, therefore translated into high "Elizabethan" idiom (as the "dedicace" of the translation to "Thomas Campion his ghost" (155) makes clear). For the "pre-Elizabethan" rendering, in conformity with the sample translations of shorter works Pound offers at the essay's close, one must turn to the very different version in *Canto XXXVI*. This version also reflects Pound's latest conclusions regarding the cruxes of the Italian text which he evokes in the essay, whereas the rendering printed therein often features completely contradictory readings.

21. For a brilliant account of the complicity of Guido and Confucius in the "Adams" *Cantos*, see Rabaté, pp. 122–9. More recently, Yao has provided an extremely incisive account of Pound's appropriation of the Confucian "rectification of names," pp. 162–88. Yao points out that the appearance of the "ch'ing ming" characters "coincides exactly with the shift in Pound's actual mode of poetic production from lyrical (and narrative) evocations of his social and political views to explicitly didactic transcriptions of 'historically grounded' examples of governmental action (both wise and foolish)" (170). It is interesting to note that Cavalcanti's poem is used by Pound precisely as a historical transcription in this sense, its tags operating as material examples.

22. And of course he was. For accounts of the critical reception of Pound's Cavalcanti translations, see both David Anderson's introduction to his edition, and Lawrence Venuti's more recent *The Translator's Invisibility*.

23. See Venuti, pp. 195–8.

24. Daniel Tiffany's insightful analysis of Pound's work on Cavalcanti powerfully argues for the centrality of the latter, in terms precisely of a view of translation as *debt*. Tiffany points both to Pound's emphasis on "extreme literalism" in terms of his renderings of Guido, and to the fact that these seem to yield more "speculative innovations" for Pound than any of his other translating projects (206).

25. See Tiffany, Venuti, and Sieburth, "Channeling Guido." I would broadly agree with Venuti's general assessment that, "The dense archaism [of Pound's later Cavalcanti translations] hardly produces the illusionistic effect of transparency that he valued in the *dolce stil novisti*" (197). But one must note that "precision" and "transparency" are not the same thing, even if Pound at times seems to forget this. Indeed, as we shall see, whatever gains in "precision" the later style achieves are made precisely through their rejection of an easy transparency of "sound and sense" to which the earlier style may be seen to appeal.

26. Richard Sieburth says something very similar in his "Channeling Guido," suggesting that the archaisms of *Canzoni*, for example, create

an "a-chronistic" dialect, which "calls into question what exactly it might mean to speak as a 'contemporary.'" This question of temporal incoherence is of entirely the same order as those translation poses on the level of subjective affirmation, or responsibility in the literal sense, and linguistic interference.

27. Crawford incisively, if briefly, evokes the key role of "translatorese" in the *Cantos*, rightly seeing it as yet another means of a "provincial" bypassing of "both English culture and the 'proper' language of 'standard English'" (243). Crawford also uses the term to account for MacPherson's similar practice in the Ossian poems, and thus begins to sketch the shape of an historical account not only of translation, but also of translatorese, in the construction of modern literary "Englishes."

28. *Ripostes* contains as appendix "The Complete Poetical Works of T. E. Hulme," and several short poems which announce Pound's "imagist" moment.

29. Throughout Dante's work, the poet portrays the network of his body and senses as literally reconfigured by love, while suffering aches, pains, fever, illness, and even temporary blindness when confronted with his beloved, to the point that, in Rossetti's translation, Dante is asked this very reasonable question: "To what end lovest thou this lady, seeing that thou canst not support her presence? Now tell us this thing, that we may know it: for certainly the end of such a love must be worthy of knowledge" (201). It is this question which largely provokes the poem, "Donne ch'avete intelletto d'amore."

30. In his edition, Anderson lists two other early translations of this sonnet, one unpublished (43–5).

Chapter 5

1. Stein's consistent emphasis on this unreality should inflect critical accounts of the importance of the texture of everyday life and domestic habit in Stein's representations of Paris and France, as found, for example, in Lisi Schoenbach's recent article. To the extent that such elements are grounding, it is due to their groundlessness at least as much as to being a "rich soil of daily life" in which the exotic plants of "philosophical thought and literary experimentation flourish" (256).

2. Robert Crawford makes interesting remarks on the structural importance for modernism of the *Odyssey* as the story of a "return," and more precisely, a return effected by "no Agamemnon returning to the culturally dominant Greek mainland, but a provincial returning to his island of Ithaca" (242).

3. "The Geographical History" is also very concerned with writing, which is at times posited as the prime characteristic of the "human mind" which allows for a break both with "human nature" and the ubiquitous

"little dog" of identity: "writing has nothing to do with the human speech with human nature and therefore it has something to do with the human mind," and shortly thereafter, "But the human mind can write and so cannot any dog and so human writing is not human nature it is the human mind" (*Writings1932–1936*, 382).

4. See North, Chapter 3, and especially pages 72–6, for this account.
5. In his insightful chapter on Stein in *Imagining Paris*, J. Gerald Kennedy stresses Stein's dialectic of home and foreign, inside and outside throughout, paying considerable attention to Stein's affirmation of the need for the writer to have "two countries." I quite agree with Kennedy's sense of the way Stein annuls both her "homeland," by leaving it, and Paris, by consistently harping on its unreality, and would subscribe to his sense of Stein's enactment of an "auto-displacement" (44). However, while Kennedy argues that this is part and parcel of her commitment to an "absolute interiority" (44), I will argue here that the result of Stein's practice is also a turning inside out of these sorts of borders.
6. The reference to Mérimée is less baffling when we remember that his *Carmen* is key for Nietzsche in his late rejection of Wagner.
7. In his fascinating discussion of Stein, Hemingway, and James in the context of "queer modernity," Eric Haralson convincingly shows how Van Wyck Brooks' excoriation of James as in some way castrated *because* expatriated was a very common trope, endorsed by Hemingway, but not only: "The project of making 'expatriation and castration' (or cognates such as feminization and sexual inversion) appear all but synonymous in James's case was a *group* project among Anglo-American authors" (196). Lewis, like Stein, hints that Hemingway's hypermasculinity, of which his American persona is a component, is a form of overcompensation. Yet the thrust of Lewis' argument is that this overcompensation only exacerbates the impotence it could be seen to counter, as it is the American scene itself in which castration is most perilously threatened. The English Lewis enters this network in an intriguing manner, one complicated even further by Shari Benstock's suggestion that Stein's "weakness" for Hemingway was specifically erotic, a contention certainly supported by Lewis' own discomfort regarding his mimetic weakness for the same ambiguous object.
8. Mencken's derisive reference to Jewish business acumen as opposed to linguistic facility, offensive as it is, is also counter-balanced by other sections of the study, and just a few pages prior to it he writes, "The Italians, the Slavs, and above all, the Russian Jews, make steady contributions to the American vocabulary and idiom" (205). He also has some interesting pages on Yiddish in America (416–19), and in his chapter on "Proper Names in America" speaks sympathetically of the immigrant's distress when confronted with xenophobia, and his or her subsequent desire to

anglicize the family name. Evoking not only "linguistic hostility" but also the "deeper social enmity" facing the immigrant, he suggests that "a concept of inferiority has come to be attached to mere foreignness" (341), and goes on to discuss "Abraham, Silberer and other German psychoanalysts" (342) who have contributed to studying what we would now call the "interiorization" of this hostile sentiment which attaches to the family name. He gives many examples of assimilated Jewish names, and shows not the slightest anxiety at the thought of Jews thereby hiding their origins and melting invisibly into the pot, as one would imagine Lewis would have. Also of note in this section is Mencken's long list of racist and xenophobic epithets (341–2), which he offers as evidence of the hostility facing the immigrant: "Our unmatchable vocabulary of derisive names for foreigners reveals the national attitude" (341).

9. Things are rarely easy with Lewis. Though here "hand made" seems to be used with a positive valuation, elsewhere in the book Lewis declares, ". . . art consists among other things in a *mechanizing* of the natural. It bestows its delightful disciplines upon our aimless emotions. . . it substitutes for the direct image a picture. And, ultimately. . . it substitutes *a thing* for *a person* every time" (129, Lewis' italics). One would think such ideas might have implications for Lewis' discussion of Hemingway's automatisms.

10. The Pétain translations were largely brought to public attention through Wanda Van Dusen's discovery and publication of Stein's draft of an introduction to them. In her "Portrait of a National Fetish," she also provides an overview of various accounts of Stein's politics, as does Barbara Will in her "Lost in Translation." Though by no means downplaying Stein's disturbing sympathies for far-right thought, Will sees signs of resistance and ambivalence in Stein's use of language in the Pétain renderings, and concludes by suggesting that "Stein may well have decided to undertake the Pétain translation project largely as an insurance policy to guarantee her and Toklas's survival" (664–5). Also see John Whittier-Ferguson's "Stein in Time," for an attempt at dedramatizing Stein's political commitments.

11. Stein makes this claim repeatedly throughout the piece: "Now Henry James had two ways in one" (166), "Henry James is a combination of the two ways of writing and that makes him a general a general who does something. Listen to it" (166), "Remember that there are two ways of writing and Henry James being a general has selected both, any general has selected both otherwise he is not a general and Henry James is a general and he has selected both" (168). In his careful reading of "Henry James," Charles Caramello also emphasizes the importance of the "two ways" of writing of which James was capable, and working from the opposition between "present knowledge" and the "distortive act of remembrance," nevertheless concludes that "James saw that he

could write both ways at once, and Stein saw that she had to do likewise" (183), while also affirming that the Hugnet translation project was crucial in this effort (184).

12. Barbara Will, for example, argues that for Stein "changing a text from its original into another form seemed to her to be, ultimately, a passive rather than a creative act," thus rendering "translation" the "signifier for a mode of writing that threatened the nature of what she called 'genius'" (654), along with contending that for Stein the "translated text" is "killed" by "the relentless pressures of an 'outside,' an audience, demanding that the writer write not 'his way' but 'some way of somebody's'" (655). Ulla Dydo also suggests a similar dichotomy between "genuine poetry" and "fakery," also arising from Stein's experience of translating Hugnet (322). These valuations are perhaps more consonant with Wyndham Lewis' condemnation of "influence" and demands for subjective autonomy than with Stein's more pliable views. Meanwhile, it if is true that in "What is English Literature" Stein aligns the difference between serving "god" and serving "mammon" with that between "writing the way it is being written" and "writing the way it has been written" (222), one must note that these categories are *not* identical with those in "Henry James," where *Before the Flowers* and the sonnets are assimilated to works "written as they were going to be written," which if in some way prescriptive, is far from the damning writing "that *has been* written" of "What is English Literature."

13. Caramello makes a similar point, affirming: "This dichotomy of outside/inside encapsulates the analogous relationships of audience/writer, translator/writer, writer as self-observer/writer as self-observed" (184), while also calling attention to Stein's key statement on the relation between *The Flowers* and *The Autobiography* in *Lectures in America*: ". . . for the first time in writing, I felt something outside me while I was writing, hitherto I had always had nothing but what was inside me while I was writing" (312). This "outside" being presumably the words of another poet, the perspective of another person, writing itself.

14. See her "We are Americans" for a helpful account of the "identifications" Stein proposes between herself, the G.I.s, and "America" in general, "all via language" (514), in *Brewsie and Willie* and other related texts.

15. For excellent close readings which show this process in action, see Marjorie Perloff, "Poetry as Word-System: The Art of Gertrude Stein," in *The Poetics of Indeterminacy*. The young Beckett, impressed with Stein's ability to hollow out language, referred to her "logographs" (*Disjecta*, 172).

16. Ulla Dydo reproduces a fascinating typescript, attributed to the fingers of Alice Toklas, which gives the heading, "The Contrast between the

Notes

English Daily Life and the American Lack of a daily Life," and lists a series of seven contrasted pairs, among them Carlyle and Emerson, Wordsworth and Whitman, and George Meredith and Henry James (625).

17. I take this term from Jacques Derrida: "By ontopology we mean an axiomatics linking indissociably the ontological value of present being (*on*) to its *situation*, to the stable and presentable determination of a locality, the *topos* of territory, native soil, city, body in general (*Specters*, 82).

Chapter 6

1. Immediately followed by "Your love will let you go on." For this story, see Robin Blaser's "The Practice of Outside," published in Spicer's *Collected Books* (287–8, 325), which is also an indispensable study of Spicer's work. Ellingham and Killian also relate this anecdote (357), along with other accounts of his last days, in their fascinating biography, *Poet Be Like God*.
2. See Michael Davidson's pathbreaking *The San Francisco Renaissance: Poetics and Community at Mid-Century* for more on this, as well as Ross Clarkson's more recent contribution.
3. Although Spicer was published in Donald Allen's enormously influential *New American Poetry* anthology in 1960, and has long aroused interest among practicing poets, both in America and abroad, it is only recently that his work has begun to receive the academic attention bestowed on that of his close friend Robert Duncan, or other "New American" poets such as Ginsberg, O'Hara, and Ashbery. Along with Davidson's important work, Maria Damon's *The Dark End of the Street: Margins in American Vanguard Poetry* has been crucial in establishing the importance of a non-Beat San Francisco poetry community in the fifties, along with Spicer's key place within it. In fact, Ellingham and Killian use Spicer's life as a nexus to trace the simultaneous emergence of literary, artistic, and gay subcultures in the post-war, pre-hippy San Francisco Bay Area.
4. That is, poet, friend, and sometime mentor, Robert Duncan.
5. The question of "serial form" is recurrent in the correspondence of Blaser, Duncan, and Spicer in 1957 and 1958, with Duncan commonly acknowledged as the major instigator. Spicer refers to these questions repeatedly in his letters to Blaser of 1957 and 1958 ("Jack Spicer: Letters to Robin Blaser"), while in a letter dated June 16, 1957, Blaser writes Duncan, "As to 'serial composition'—this is what I've been learning most from you. I call it unfolding because it does not require thematic development." (BANC MSS 79/68c, Bancroft Library, University of California, Berkeley).

6. "Non, il ne fera pas sauter le monde : il le mettra entre parenthèses" ("No, he will not blow the world to pieces: he'll put it between parentheses"), p. 5.
7. Behind this discussion would seem to lurk a quarrel with the New Critical appropriation of Eliot's "objective correlative," which might well have been at the height of its authority at this time.
8. ". . . dictation also works as a joust with culturally sanctioned myths of poetic authorship that were definitive in Spicer's time, from confessional poetry to the Beat aesthetic. . . . Spicer's description of dictation . . . curiously resonates with the opening of Beckett's late work *Company*: 'A voice comes to one in the dark. Imagine' " ("afterword" in Spicer, *House*, 176). Gizzi's long essay is an essential contribution to criticism on Spicer.
9. This move allows Spicer to distance himself both from the "projective verse" of Charles Olson, a key elder statesman for Spicer's circle, and from the oracular, authoritarian implications of Pound's radio broadcasts.
10. In a related move, Spicer will take a metaphor from baseball, and designate the poet neither as the batter nor the pitcher but rather as the catcher—another sort of "receiver," crouching at the mercy of unpredictable pitches (see, "Four poems for the St. Louis Sporting News," *Collected Books*, pp. 256–8, and *House*, pp. 101–147, especially 117). It is surprising that Spicer did not turn to American football, where "receiver" is an established position. When he does draw on football as allegory for poetic creation in his unfinished novel, the key figure is the quarterback; however the allegory is proffered by a character whose poetics are anything but reliable, as we shall see in Chapter 7 (*Jack Spicer's Detective Novel*, 5–7).
11. Burton Hatlen has discussed this "curious fact" very effectively, quite rightly emphasizing the crucial example of Pound (119–20), and in her excellent study of *After Lorca*, Lori Chamberlain begins with this paradox .
12. Eshelman's "The Lorca Working" is an indispensable piece of scholarship for all but the Lorca expert, briefly reviewing as it does the relationship to the source of every poem in *After Lorca*.
13. Revealingly, in his letters to Blaser he often refers to his own renderings as "untranslations," encloses the word "translation" in scare quotes, or even proposes the term "transformations" as more apt. See "Letters to Robin Blaser."
14. For an important reading of the link between translating and haunting for Pound, see Daniel Tiffany's groundbreaking *Radio Corpse: Imagism and the Crypthaesthetic of Ezra Pound*. Lori Chamberlain also notes the link between haunting and translation in Spicer, as her title's reference to "ghostwriting" suggests.
15. In fact, Spicer chose one of them as his "statement on poetics" for Donald Allen's *New American Poetry* anthology (413–14).

16. Critics have pointed out that this introduction in fact significantly inflates the non-Lorca element of the book when "Lorca" claims that there are "an almost equal number of poems that I did not write at all" (11), but it is nonetheless accurate in its statement of the basic program.
17. As Chamberlain has pointed out (430), Spicer's emphasis on "seaweed" as a corresponding object is probably also a comment on why he chose to place it prominently in the first translation of the book, "Juan Ramon Jimenez," where it mistranslates "nardo" (literally, "spikenard") much to the annoyance of Clayton Eshelman, who overlooks the theory of "correspondences" throughout his discussion of Spicer's mistranslations.
18. See Chapter 3 of Ellingham and Killian for Spicer's virulent dislike of New York.
19. See Christopher Maurer's introduction to the *Selected Verse* (p. xiv) for more on this.
20. Keenaghan, for example, stresses this universalizing dimension: "This list of epithets is transnational and transcultural, reducing all visible, sexually active gays to a series of one-dimensional names that condemns their homosexual practices and traps them in a chain of stereotypes" (285).
21. I have no explanation as to why Spicer's list omits the "Floras de Alicante."
22. See "Crossing Brooklyn Ferry," where Whitman describes the erotics of complicitous recognition precisely through the figure of the intimate name, as in these lines and elsewhere: "Was call'd by my nighest name by clear loud voices of young men as they saw me approaching or passing,/ Felt their arms on my neck as I stood, or the negligent leaning of their flesh against me as I sat,/ Saw many I loved in the street or ferry-boat or public assembly, yet never told them a word" (311).
23. Regarding "cultural translation," Butler writes: "The contemporary scene of cultural translation emerges with the presupposition that the utterance does not have the same meaning everywhere, indeed, that the utterance has become a scene of conflict. . . . The translation that takes place at this scene of conflict is one in which the meaning intended is no more determinative of a "final" reading than the one that is received, and no final adjudication of conflicting positions can emerge. That lack of finality is precisely the interpretive dilemma to be valued. . ." (91–2).
24. Spicer's negotiations with Dickinson deserve more space than I can give them here; his 1956 review of the Johnson edition of her poetry shows the depth of his engagement with her work at the very moment when his conceptions of "seriality" and the "book" begin to emerge, while also anticipating some of the most interesting work on Dickinson's correspondence by over thirty years. See *The House that Jack Built*, 231–7, for the review.

25. I have in mind here Spicer's mobilization of a syntax that breaks with the primacy of the line of verse, while still employing it. In his excellent study of the subject, Ron Silliman argues that Spicer "became the first truly sentence-centered poet in the American language" (164), for whom the "sentence became the unit of composition, and the line . . . a means for locating stress within the sentence" (165).

Chapter 7

1. The above information is taken from Ellingham and Killian; see above all Chapters 4 and 5 of *Poet Be Like God*.
2. Likewise, it seems reasonable to assume that the slow-moving flirtation with Madelaine, the young wife of older poet and cultural impresario Arthur Slingbot, would fail to advance, being replaced by the possibility of an affair with Rue.
3. "it would take a felt predicament or a false position to give him so ironic an accent" (xxxv), and again, "The false position, for our belated man of the world—belated because he had endeavoured so long to escape being one, and now at last had really to face his doom—the false position for him, I say, was obviously to have presented himself at the gate of that boundless menagerie primed with a moral scheme of the most approved pattern which was yet framed to break down on any approach to vivid facts" (xxxvii). It is a very similar sort of break down which continually threatens—or promises to rescue—Ralston's poetics throughout Spicer's novel.
4. *The Ambassadors*, like much of James, is also very much a detective novel in its way: its protagonist has an over-riding mystery to solve, which the reader shares (the nature of the relationship of Chad and Marie de Vionnet) and, no less than a conventional detective, must be constantly on the alert for clues and quick and canny in interpreting them. For that matter, what detective fiction presents more pressingly than James characters who urgently need to think on their feet, read the signs, plan their moves, and cultivate their contacts, if not to stave off a literal death, then to protect themselves from the symbolic annihilation which James has the gift of making seem every bit as final? Meanwhile, if Slavoj Zizek is right that the "noir" text is distinguished from the older detective novel in that in the former the detective's task can no longer be taken at "face value," since "as a rule, it turns out that the client who hires the detective is part of a game which differs radically from what appears to be the case" (188), then both novels qualify: the motives of both Mrs. Newsome and Arthur Slingbot, the caricature of Kenneth Rexroth who sends Ralston on his "errand," are far from clear.
5. "Why me? Why on earth do you pick me?" (75), Ralston asks Rue, and he repeatedly expresses annoyance and mystification at Rue's dogged

persistence to be read by him. Regarding one potential answer, if the novel refers to homosexuality frequently, presents a few gay characters, and takes us to a gay bar, what we are shown of Rue's love life, to say nothing of Ralston's, is strictly heterosexual, though Ralston's discomfort at Rue's naked torso, appearing in the final scene, seems a portent of things that were to come.

6. A poetics of the encounter seems closer to Rue's, as he rejects Ralston's appeal for literary clarity as no more than just "better glasses to wear" as opposed to his own goal: "a different room" to look into (19).

7. The opening poem of Williams' 1954 collection, *The Desert Music and Other Poems*, is "The Descent," of which the first lines read "The descent beckons/ as the ascent beckoned./ Memory is a kind/ of accomplishment,/ a sort of renewal/ even" (*Pictures*, 73).

8. See Dickinson's "I cannot live with You—/ It would be Life— (317–18).

9. Ashbery elsewhere mentions "the reluctance of the Paris public to contemplate anything new, especially of American origin" (104), refers to Paris as the city "famous for its angry inhabitants, high living costs and lack of any sustained excitement in the contemporary arts" (99), and evokes a new category of American artists who are "not expatriates but *apatrides*," regarding whom, "Far from dreading the day when their money runs out and they have to go back to America, many of them look forward disgruntledly to it" (98). This is not jingoism, of course, but the grumpy, displaced resentment of the foreign culture which James evokes in his discussion of the "cosmopolite" (see Chapter 1 of the present study), as well as a preservation of its foreignness through an emphasis on its *costs*—costs which are to be paid "back home" too. Indeed, a disgruntled *attentisme* is an entirely plausible response to the double xenophobia to which the expatriate is subject, and which Ashbery cogently exposes in an article on R. B. Kitaj, where he evokes the "precarious fate" of voluntarily expatriated American artists, "confronted with the xenophobic indifference of both their adopted country and their homeland, always suspicious of its émigrés" (299).

10. For expatriate artists, Ashbery also evokes their more mundane "greater risk of living out obscure careers than their compatriots who stay put" (299).

11. However, Ashbery has said that as the novel progressed, they began to allow themselves more than a single sentence when inspiration so dictated (Ashbery and Ford, 38). David Lehman notes that the poets tried collaborating by letter while Ashbery was in France, but found it less satisfactory (83). Additional information about the evolution of the project can be found in James Schuyler's fascinating letters to Ashbery, collected in *Just the Thing*.

12. See Shoptaw, pp. 36–8, for an acute glance at the poem as a parody of the "travelogue" and the "touring gaze."

13. "Yes. That is no!" (*Ambassadors*, 136). See Chapter 2 of this study for an account of the scene.
14. Lehman suggests that the dialogue is "a celebration of the American suburban vernacular, which is accurately mimed in the spirit not of ridicule but of 'respect for things as they are'" (81), but I would argue that in this respect too, the novel refuses the logic of mimeticism that the term "mime" invokes.
15. Ashbery's account is cited and discussed by John Vincent, who notes that the novel "does not take place in Bavaria, where foehns generally occur" (173), and quite rightly suggests this disturbs the novel's "closural traction" (173). A survey of dictionaries and encyclopedias suggests that "foehn" is now commonly extended into a generic term for katabetic winds, but it does also have specific regional links to Bavaria and the Alps.

BIBLIOGRAPHY

Abraham, Julie. " 'We are Americans': Gertrude, *Brewsie and Willie.*" *Modern Fiction Studies* 42, no. 3 (1996): 508–27.
Adorno, Theodor. *Minima Moralia: Reflections from Damaged Life.* Translated by E. F. N. Jephcott. London: Verso Press, 1974.
Alighieri, Dante. *Vita Nuova.* Milan: Garzanti editori, 1995.
Allen, Donald, editor. *The New American Poetry: 1945–1960.* Berkeley: University of California Press, 1999.
Anderson, David. *Pound's Cavalcanti: An Edition of the Translations, Notes, and Essays.* Princeton, NJ: Princeton University Press, 1983.
Ashbery, John. *The Mooring of Starting Out: The First Five Books of Poetry.* Hopewell, NJ: The Ecco Press, 1998.
———. *Reported Sightings: Art Chronicles, 1957–1987.* Edited by David Bergman. Cambridge, MA: Harvard University Press, 1991.
Ashbery, John, and Mark Ford. *John Ashbery in Conversation with Mark Ford.* London: Between the Lines, 2003.
Ashbery, John, and James Schuyler. *A Nest of Ninnies.* London: Paladin, 1987.
Baldwin, James. *Giovanni's Room.* London: Penguin, 2001.
———. *Notes of a Native Son.* London: Penguin, 1964.
Beckett, Samuel. "Dante ... Bruno. Vico .. Joyce" in *James Joyce/Finnegans Wake: A Symposium.* New York: New Directions, 1972.
———. *Disjecta: Miscellaneous Writings and a Dramatic Fragment.* Edited by Ruby Cohn. New York: Grove Press, 1984.
Bender, Eileen T. " 'The Question of His Own French': Dialect and Dialectic in *The Ambassadors.*" *Henry James Review* 5, no. 2 (Winter, 1984): 128–34.
Benstock, Shari. *Women of the Left Bank: Paris, 1900–1940.* Austin: University of Texas Press, 1986.
Berman, Antoine. *L'épreuve de l'étranger: Culture et traduction dans l'Allemagne romantique.* Paris: Editions Gallimard, 1984. Translated by

S. Heyvaert under the title *The Experience of the Foreign: Culture and Translation in Romantic Germany* (Albany: State University of New York Press, 1992).

———. *La traduction et la lettre ou l'auberge du lointain*. Paris: Editions du Seuil, 1999.

Blair, Sara. *Henry James and the Writing of Race and Nation*. Cambridge: Cambridge University Press, 1996.

Buelens, Gert. "Possessing the American Scene: Race and Vulgarity, Seduction and Judgment." *Enacting History in Henry James: Narrative, Power, and Ethics*. Edited by Gert Buelens. Cambridge: Cambridge University Press, 1997.

Butler, Judith. *Excitable Speech: A Politics of the Performative*. London: Routledge, 1997.

Caramello, Charles. *Henry James, Gertrude Stein, and the Biographical Act*. Chapel Hill: University of North Carolina Press, 1996.

Carpenter, Humphrey. *A Serious Character: The Life of Ezra Pound*. London: Faber and Faber, 1988.

Chamberlain, Lori. "Ghostwriting the Text: Translation and the Poetics of Jack Spicer." *Contemporary Literature*, vol. 26, no. 4 (1985): 426–42.

Clarkson, Ross. "Jack Spicer's Ghosts and the Immemorial Community." *Mosaic*, no. 34, vol. 4 (2001): 199–211.

Crawford, Robert. *Devolving English Literature (revised second edition)*. Edinburgh: Edinburgh University Press, 2000.

Crowley, Cornelius. "*The American Scene*: Henry James et la joie de l'altération ultime." *Les langages des dépravés*. Edited by Anne Tomiche. Clermont-Ferrand: Presses Universitaires de Clermont-Ferrand, 2003.

Damon, Maria. *The Dark End of the Street: Margins in American Vanguard Poetry*. Minneapolis: University of Minnesota Press, 1993.

Davidson, Michael. *The San Francisco Renaissance: Poetics and Community at Mid-Century*. Cambridge: Cambridge University Press, 1991.

De Gourmont, Rémy. *The Natural Philosophy of Love*. Translated and with an introduction by Ezra Pound. London: Quartet Books, 1992.

Derrida, Jacques. *Specters of Marx: the State of the Debt, the Work of Mourning, and the New International*. Translated by Peggy Kamuf. London: Routledge, 1994.

———. *Voyous*. Paris: Editions Galilée, 2003.

———. "White Mythology: Metaphor in the text of Philosophy." *Margins of Philosophy*. Translated by Alan Bass. Chicago: University of Chicago Press, 1982.

Dickinson, Emily. *The Complete Poems of Emily Dickinson*. Edited by Thomas H. Johnson. Boston: Little, Brown & Company, 1960.

Dydo, Ulla, with William Rice. *Gertrude Stein: The Language that Rises: 1923–1934*. Evanston: Northwestern University Press, 2003.

Eliot, T. S. *Collected Poems: 1909–1962*. New York: Harcourt, Brace & Company, 1968.
——. "The Hawthorne Aspect." *The Little Review* (August, 1918): 47–53.
——. "In Memory." *The Little Review* (August, 1918): 44–7.
Ellingham, Lewis, and Kevin Killian. *Poet Be Like God: Jack Spicer and the San Francisco Renaissance*. Hanover: Wesleyan University Press, 1998.
Ellison, Ralph. "Harlem is Nowhere." *Shadow and Act*. New York: Signet, 1966.
Emerson, Ralph Waldo. "The Poet." *Selected Essays*. New York: Penguin, 1982.
——. "Self-Reliance." *Selected Essays*. New York: Penguin, 1982.
Eshelman, Clayton. "The Lorca Working." *Boundary 2*, vol. 27, no. 1 (1977): 31–49.
Fenollosa, Ernest. *The Chinese Written Character as a Medium for Poetry*. Edited by Ezra Pound. San Francisco: City Lights Books, 1983.
Flory, Wendy Stallard. *The American Ezra Pound*. New Haven: Yale University Press, 1989.
Freud, Sigmund. *Art and Literature* (Penguin Freud Library, vol. 14). London: Penguin, 1990.
Garcia, Claire Oberon. "The Shopper and the Shopper's Friend: Lambert Strether and Maria Gostrey's Consumer Consciousness." *The Henry James Review* 16.2 (1995): 153–71.
García Lorca, Federico. *Selected Verse: A Bilingual Edition*. Edited by Christopher Maurer. New York: Farrar, Strauss & Giroux, 1997.
Geyskens, Tomas, and Philippe Van Haute. *Confusion of Tongues: The Primacy of Sexuality in Freud, Ferenczi, and Laplanche*. New York: Other Press, 2004.
Giles, Paul. *Virtual Americas: Transnational Fictions and the Transatlantic Imaginary*. Durham: Duke University Press, 2002.
Greenslade, William. "The Power of Advertising: Chad Newsome and the Meaning of Paris in *The Ambassadors*." *ELH* 49, no. 1 (Spring, 1982): 99–122.
Haralson, Eric. *Henry James and Queer Modernity*. Cambridge: Cambridge University Press, 2003.
Hatlen, Burton. "'Crawling into Bed with Sorrow': Jack Spicer's *After Lorca*." *Ironwood*, no. 14, vol. 2 (1986): 118–35.
Hawthorne, Nathaniel. *The Marble Faun*. Edited by Susan Manning. Oxford: Oxford University Press, 2002.
Hayot, Eric. "Critical Dreams: Orientalism, Modernism, and the Meaning of Pound's China." *Twentieth Century Literature* 45, 4 (Winter, 1999): 511–33.
Higginson, Thomas Wentworth. "Letter to a Young Contributor" in *Army Life in a Black Regiment and Other Writings*. London: Penguin, 1997.

Honeyman, Susan E. "*What Maisie Knew* and the Impossible Representation of Childhood." *The Henry James Review* 22 (2001): 67–80.

Huang, Yunte. *Transpacific Displacement: Ethnography, Translation, and Intertextual Travel in Twentieth-Century American Literature*. Berkeley: University of California Press, 2002.

James, Henry. *The Ambassadors*. Oxford: Oxford University Press, 1985.

——. *The American Scene*. London: Penguin, 1994.

——. *Collected Travel Writings: The Continent*. New York: Library of America, 1993.

——. *Literary Criticism: Essays on Literature, American Writers, English Writers*. New York: Library of America, 1984.

——. *The Notebooks of Henry James*. Edited by F. O. Matthiessen and Kenneth B. Murdock. New York: Oxford University Press, 1961.

——. *The Portrait of a Lady*. New York: W. W. Norton & Co., 1995.

——. "The Question of Our Speech" in *Henry James on Culture: Collected Essays on Politics and the American Scene*. Edited by Pierre A. Walker. Lincoln: University of Nebraska Press, 1999.

——. *What Maisie Knew*. London: Penguin, 1985.

James, Henry and William. *Selected Letters*. Edited by Ignas Skrupskelis and Elizabeth M. Berkeley. Charlottesville: University Press of Virginia, 1997.

Joyce, James. *A Portrait of the Artist as a Young Man*. London: Penguin, 1992.

Keenaghan, Eric. "Jack Spicer's Pricks and Cocksuckers: Translating Homosexuality into Visibility." *The Translator*, vol. 4, no. 2 (1998): 273–94.

Kennedy, J. Gerald. *Imagining Paris: Exile, Writing, and American Identity*. New Haven: Yale University Press, 1993.

Kern, Robert. *Orientalism, Modernism, and the American Poem*. Cambridge: Cambridge University Press, 1996.

Labbé, Evelyne. *Ecrits sur l'abîme: les derniers romans de Henry James*. Lyons: Presses universitaires de Lyon, 1990.

Laplanche, Jean. *Entre séduction et inspiration : l'homme*. Paris: Quadrige / Presses Universitaires de France, 1999.

——. *Nouveaux fondements pour la psychanalyse*. Paris: Quadrige / Presses Universitaires de France, 1987. Translated by David Macey under the title *New Foundations for Psychoanalysis* (Oxford: Basil Blackwell, 1989).

Lehman, David. *The Last Avant-Garde: The making of the New York School of Poets*. New York: Doubleday, 1998.

Lewis, R. W. B. *The Jameses: A Family Narrative*. New York: Farrar, Straus & Giroux, 1991.

Lewis, Wyndham. *Men Without Art*. Santa Rosa: Black Sparrow Press, 1987.

Lindberg, Kathryne. *Reading Pound Reading: Modernism After Nietzsche*. New York: Oxford University Press, 1987.

MacCannell, Dean. *The Tourist: A New Theory of the Leisure Class*. Berkeley: University of California Press, 1999.

Mencken, H. L. *The American Language: An Inquiry into the Development of English in the United States (third edition revised and enlarged)*. New York: Alfred A. Knopf, 1926.

Michaels, Walter Benn. *Our America: Nativism, Modernism, and Pluralism*. Durham: Duke University Press, 1995.

North, Michael. *The Dialect of Modernism: Race, Language & Twentieth-Century Literature*. New York: Oxford University Press, 1994.

Parsons, Deborah. "The Note/Notion of Europe: Henry James and the Gendered Landscape of Heritage Tourism." *Symbiosis: A Journal of Anglo-American Literary Relations* 2, no. 2 (1998): 225–40.

Peiffer, Siobhan. "Commerce and Freedom in *The Ambassadors*." *Henry James Review* 23 (2002): 95–104.

Perloff, Marjorie. *The Poetics of Indeterminacy: Rimbaud to Cage*. Evanston: Northwestern University Press, 1983.

Pizer, Donald. *American Expatriate Writing and the Paris Moment: Modernism and Place*. Baton Rouge: Louisiana State University Press, 1996.

Posnock, Ross. *The Trial of Curiosity: Henry James, William James, and the Challenge of Modernity*. Oxford: Oxford University Press, 1991.

Pound, Ezra. *ABC of Reading*. New York: New Directions, 1960.

———. *The Cantos*. New York: New Directions, 1986.

———. *Gaudier-Brzeska: A Memoir*. New York: New Directions, 1970.

———. *Guide to Kulchur*. New York: New Directions, 1970.

———. *Literary Essays of Ezra Pound*. Edited and with an introduction by T. S. Eliot. New York: New Directions, 1968.

———. "Patria Mia." *The New Age*, September 5, 1912, p. 445 (available in electronic facsimile at: www.modjourn.brown.edu/mjp/newage.html).

———. *Poems and Translations*. Edited by Richard Sieburth. New York: Library of America, 2003.

———. *Pound/The Little Review: The Letters of Ezra Pound to Margaret Anderson*. Edited by Thomas L. Scott and Melvin J. Friedman, with the assistance of Jackson R. Bryer. London: Faber and Faber, 1988.

———. *Selected Letters of Ezra Pound, 1907–1941*. Edited by D. D. Paige. New York: New Directions, 1971.

———. *Selected Prose 1909–1965*. Edited, and with an introduction by William Cookson. New York: New Directions, 1973.

———. *The Spirit of Romance*. New York: New Directions, 1968.

———. *Translations*. New York: New Directions, 1963.

Rabaté, Jean-Michel. *Language, Sexuality and Ideology in Ezra Pound's Cantos*. Albany: State University of New York Press, 1986.

Ramazani, Jahan. "A Transnational Poetics." *American Literary History*, vol. 18, no. 2 (Summer 2006): 332–59.

Rivkin, Julie. *False Positions: The Representational Logics of Henry James's Fiction.* Stanford: Stanford University Press, 1996.

Rossetti, Dante Gabriel. *The Early Italian Poets from Ciullo d'Alcamo to Dante Alighieri.* London: Routledge and Sons, 1914.

Rowe, John Carlos. "Henry James and the United States." *The Henry James Review* 27 (2006): 228–36.

Sallis, John. *On Translation.* Bloomington: Indiana University Press, 2002.

Sartre, Jean-Paul. "Préface" to *Poésies*, Stéphane Mallarmé. Paris: Gallimard, 1945.

Scherzinger, Karen. " 'Lurking Ghosts': Metaphor, *The Ambassadors*, and Henry James's Population of the American Scene." *The Henry James Review* 24 (2003): 168–79.

Schleiermacher, Friedrich. "On the Different Methods of Translating." *Theories of Translation: an Anthology of Essays from Dryden to Derrida.* Edited by Rainer Schulte and John Biguenet. Chicago: University of Chicago Press, 1992.

Schoenbach, Lisi. " 'Peaceful and Exciting': Habit, Shock, and Gertrude Stein's Pragmatic Modernism." *Modernism/Modernity*, vol. 11, no. 2 (2004): 239–59.

Schuyler, James. *Just the Thing: Selected Letters of James Schuyler, 1951–1991.* Edited by William Corbett. New York: Turtle Point Press, 2004.

Shoptaw, John. *On the Outside Looking Out: John Ashbery's Poetry.* Cambridge: Harvard University Press, 1994.

Sieburth, Richard. "Channeling Guido: Ezra Pound's Cavalcanti Translations." *Cavalcanti tra i suoi lettore.* Edited by Maria Louisa Ardizzione. Florence: Cadmos, 2003.

———. "In Pound We Trust: The Economy of Poetry/The Poetry of Economics." *Critical Inquiry* 14 (Autumn 1987): 142–72.

Silliman, Ron. *The New Sentence.* New York: Roof Books, 1987.

Spicer, Jack. *The Collected Books of Jack Spicer.* Edited by Robin Blaser. Santa Barbara: Black Sparrow Press, 1980.

———. *The House that Jack Built: The Collected Lectures of Jack Spicer.* Edited by Peter Gizzi. Hanover: Wesleyan University Press, 1998.

———. "Jack Spicer: Letters to Robin Blaser." *Line*, vol. 9 (1987): 26–55.

———. *Jack Spicer's Detective Novel: The Tower of Babel.* Hoboken: Talisman House, 1994.

———. *One Night Stand & Other Poems.* Edited by Donald Allen. San Francisco: Grey Fox Press, 1980.

Stein, Gertrude. "An American and France" in *What Are Masterpieces?* New York: Pitman, 1970.

———. *Everybody's Autobiography.* London: Virago Press, 1985.

———. *Paris France: Personal Recollections.* London: Peter Owen, 2003.

———. *Selected Writings of Gertrude Stein.* Edited by Carl Van Vechten. New York: Vintage, 1972.

———. "A Transatlantic Interview" in *A Primer for the Gradual Understanding of Gertrude Stein*. Edited by Robert Bartlett Haas. Los Angeles: Black Sparrow, 1971.
———. *Writings 1903–1932*. Edited by Catharine R. Stimpson and Harriet Chessman. New York: Library of America, 1998.
———. *Writings 1932–1946*. Edited by Catharine R. Stimpson and Harriet Chessman. New York: Library of America, 1998.
Teahan, Sheila. "My Sculptor/My Self: A Story of Reading." *The Henry James Review* 23 (2002): 246–54.
Tiffany, Daniel. *Radio Corpse: Imagism and the Cryptaesthetic of Ezra Pound*. Cambridge: Harvard University Press, 1995.
Torsney, Cheryl B. "Translation and Transubstantiation in *The American*." *The Henry James Review*, 17.1 (1996): 40–51.
Van Dusen, Wanda. "Portrait of a National Fetish: Gertrude Stein's 'Introduction to the Speeches of Maréchal Pétain' (1942)." *Modernism/Modernity* 3, no. 3 (1996): 69–92.
Van Slyck, Phyllis. "Knowledge and Representation in *The Ambassadors*: Strether's Discriminating Gaze." *Criticism* 39, no. 4 (1997): 557–79.
Venuti, Lawrence. *The Translator's Invisibility: A History of Translation*. London: Routledge, 1995.
Vincent, John. "Reports of Looting and Insane Buggery Behind Altars: John Ashbery's Queer Poetics." *Twentieth Century Literature*, vol. 44, no. 2 (Summer, 1998): 155–75.
Walsh, John K. "A Logic in Lorca's *Ode to Walt Whitman*," in *¿Entiendes? Queer Readings, Hispanic Writings*. Edited by Emilie L. Bergmann and Paul Julian Smith. Durham: Duke University Press, 1995.
Whitman, Walt. *Complete Poetry and Collected Prose*. Edited by Justin Kaplan. New York: Library of America, 1982.
Whittier-Ferguson, John. "Stein in Time: History, Manuscripts, Memory." *Modernism/Modernity* 6, no. 1 (1999): 115–51.
Will, Barbara. "Lost in Translation: Stein's Vichy Collaboration." *Modernism/Modernity* 11, no. 4 (2004): 651–68.
Williams, William Carlos. *Imaginations*. New York: New Directions, 1971.
———. *Pictures from Brueghel and Other Poems*. New York: New Directions, 1962.
Wirth-Nesher, Hana. "If This Is Liberty, It Must Be Paris: Landmarks and Home in *The Ambassadors*." *Homes and Homelessness in the Victorian Imagination*. Edited by Murray Baumgarten and H. M. Daleski. New York: AMS Press, 1998.
Wolfson, Louis. *Le Schizo et les langues*. Paris: Editions Gallimard, 1970.
Xie, Ming. *Ezra Pound and the Apppropriation of Chinese Poetry: Cathay, Translation and Imagism*. New York: Garland Publishing, 1999.
———. "Pound as Translator." *The Cambridge Companion to Ezra Pound*. Edited by Ira B. Nadel. Cambridge: Cambridge University Press, 1999.

Yao, Steven G. *Translation and the Languages of Modernism: Gender, Politics, Language*. New York: Palgrave Macmillan, 2002.

Žizek, Slavoj. *Enjoy Your Symptom! Jacques Lacan in Hollywood and Out*. London: Routledge, 1992.

Zwerdling, Alex. *Improvised Europeans: American Literary Expatriates and the Siege of London*. New York: Basic Books, 1998.

INDEX

Abraham, Julie, 112
Adams, John, 88
Adorno, Theodor, 10–11, 13, 14, 33
   Minima Moralia, 10–11, 33
Alighieri, Dante, 7, 82–5, 86, 92, 108, 171n15
   Il Convivio, 82
   The Divine Comedy, 82
   Vita nuova, 88, 92
   De Vulgari Eloquentia, 82–5
Allen, Donald, 120, 179n3, 180n15
Anderson, David, 173n16, 174n22, 175n30
Anderson, Margaret, 63
Anderson, Sherwood, 95
Armin, Robert, 150
Ashbery, John, 6, 8–9, 140–1, 148–59, 179n3
   "The Instruction Manual," 152
   A Nest of Ninnies, 9, 141, 149–59
   Reported Sightings, 141, 148–50

Baldwin, James, 161n5, 168n4
   "Encounter on the Seine," 168n4
   Giovanni's Room, 161n5
Barnes, Djuna, 9
Bataille, Georges, 11
Beckett, Samuel, 5, 84–5, 121, 162n2, 178n15, 180n8
   Company, 180n8

"Dante ... Bruno. Vico .. Joyce," 84–5
Bender, Eileen T., 166n10
Benjamin, Walter, 117, 151
Benstock, Shari, 160n2, 176n7
Berman, Antoine, 5, 14, 15, 16, 81–2, 85, 163n8, 167n17
Blair, Sara, 164n21, 166n7
Blaser, Robin, 118, 120, 123, 179n1, 179n5
Brooks, Van Wyck, 176n7
Buelens, Gert, 164n21
Burns, Robert, 104, 105
Butler, Judith, 137, 181n23

Caramello, Charles, 177–8n11, 178n13
Carlyle, Thomas, 178–9n16
Carpenter, Humphrey, 168–9n5
Cavalcanti, Guido, 82, 83, 85, 86–9, 93–4, 171n5
   "Donna me prega," 86–9
Chamberlain, Lori, 125, 180n11, 180n14, 181n17
Chaucer, Geoffrey, 67–8, 108, 114, 170–1n14
Clarkson, Ross, 129, 179n2
Confucius, 84
Crawford, Robert, 3, 4, 161n6, 173n14, 175n2, 175n27

Crowley, Cornelius, 51, 165n23, 167n16

Damon, Maria, 179n3
Daniel, Arnaut, 82
Davidson, Michael, 118–19, 179n2
de Gourmont, Rémy, 67
de Saussure, Ferdinand, 81, 162n4
Derrida, Jacques, 84, 169–70n8, 171n2, 179n17
  Specters of Marx, 179n17
  Voyous, 169–70n8
  "White Mythology," 171n2
Deschamps, Eustache, 68
Dickinson, Emily, 29, 109, 138–9, 147
Duncan, Robert, 118, 179n3, 179n5
Dydo, Ulla, 160n2, 178–9n16

Eliot, T. S., 3, 9, 69, 73, 98, 161n6, 163n11, 168n3, 170n10, 180n7
  "East Coker," 163n11
  "The Hawthorne Aspect," 168n3
  "In Memory," 3, 170n10
  "Tradition and the Individual Talent," 98
Ellingham, Lewis and Killian, Kevin, 179n1, 179n3, 181n18, 182n1
Ellison, Ralph, 11, 161–2n1
  "Harlem is Nowhere," 161–2n1
Ellman, Richard, 161n5
Emerson, Ralph Waldo, 77, 109, 164n17, 178–9n16
  "The Poet," 77
  "Self-Reliance," 164n17
Eshelman, Clayton, 122, 181n17

Faulkner, William, 3, 101
Fenollosa, Ernest, 64, 76, 77, 78, 80, 81, 168–9n5
Ferenczi, Sandor, 19
Flaubert, Gustave, 54
Flory, Wendy Stallard, 160n2
Ford, Mark, 183n11
Freud, Sigmund, 16, 19, 28, 30, 31, 159, 163n9
  "The Uncanny," 16, 28
Frobenius, Leo, 68, 69
Frost, Robert, 3

Garcia, Claire Oberon, 166n6, 167n12
García Lorca, Federico, 122–39, 159
  "Ode to Walt Whitman," 122–3, 132–9
Gaudier-Brzeska, Henri, 73, 76
Geyskens, Thomas, and Van Haute, Philippe, 21, 163n12
Giles, Paul, 3–4, 160n3, 161n5, 164n19
Ginsberg, Allen, 141, 179n3
Gizzi, Peter, 121, 180n8
Greenslade, William, 166n6
Gregory, Augusta, 108
Gunn, Thom, 160n3

Haralson, Eric, 176n7
Hatlen, Burton, 180n11
Hawthorne, Nathaniel, 6, 41–8, 51, 52, 149, 158–9
  The Marble Faun, 6, 41–8, 51, 149, 158–9
Hayot, Eric, 172–3n11
Hemingway, Ernest, 7–8, 95, 101–11
  The Sun Also Rises, 103
Herder, Johann Gottfried, 14
Higginson, Thomas Wentworth, 23, 109–10
  "Letter to a Young Contributor," 109
Honeyman, Susan, 163n10
Huang, Yunte, 2, 72, 171n1, 171–2n3
Hugnet, Georges, 111
Hulme, T. E., 175n28
Hyde, Douglas, 108

James, Alice, 27, 34
James, Henry, 1, 2, 3, 6, 7, 8, 9, 10–52, 53–70, 74, 81, 85, 95, 108–9, 111–12, 114, 115, 141, 145–6, 148, 149, 151, 152, 156–9, 161n5, 162n3, 176n7, 183n9
  The Ambassadors, 1, 6, 19, 33, 34–52, 145–6, 152–5
  The American Scene, 6, 7, 22–3, 24, 31–3, 51, 54–60, 108, 167n16
  "The Beast in the Jungle," 52
  Hawthorne, 42, 166n8

"The Jolly Corner," 16, 29, 31
Notebooks, 1, 167n18
"Occasional Paris," 6, 26–8, 32–3, 34, 47
The Portrait of a Lady, 6, 23–31
"The Question of Our Speech," 12–15, 18, 33, 49, 108, 159, 166n5
The Turn of the Screw, 15, 18, 19, 31
What Maisie Knew, 17–19
James, William, 22, 27, 34, 166n5
Jarrell, Randall, 142
Joyce, James, 84, 86, 160n2, 162n2
  Finnegans Wake, 84, 86
  A Portrait of the Artist as a Young Man, 162n2

Keenaghan, Eric, 133–4, 181n20
Kennedy, J. Gerald, 162n2, 176n5
Kenner, Hugh, 161n5
Kern, Robert, 171n1, 172n6, 172n9
Kitaj, R. B., 183n9

Labbé, Evelyne, 170n12
Laplanche, Jean, 6, 19–22, 29, 47, 146, 163n12
Lehman, David, 183n11, 184n14
Lewis, Wyndham, 7–8, 80, 94, 95–6, 101–11, 113, 115
  Men Without Art, 95–6, 101–10
Lindberg, Kathryne, 69
Luther, Martin, 81–2, 84, 108

MacCannell, Dean, 9, 151–4
MacPherson, James, 175n27
Mallarmé, Stéphane, 121
Maurer, Christopher, 181n19
Mencken, H. L., 105–10, 112
  The American Language, 105–10
Mérimée, Prosper, 103
Michaels, Walter Benn, 72–4, 76, 90
Moore, Marianne, 122
Mussolini, Benito, 67

Nabokov, Vladimir, 160n3
Nietzsche, Friedrich, 103
North, Michael, 69, 99, 171n16

O'Hara, Frank, 179n3
Olson, Charles, 118, 180n9
Ovid, 170–1n14

Parsons, Deborah, 163–4n16, 165n1
Peiffer, Siobhan, 167n14
Peirce, C. S., 76
Perloff, Marjorie, 178n15
Pétain, Philippe, 110, 111
Pizer, Donald, 162n2
Plath, Sylvia, 160n3
Posnock, Ross, 32, 164n18, 164n22, 167n12
Pound, Ezra, 2, 7, 8, 52, 53–94, 110, 113, 118, 122–3, 125, 139, 141, 148, 156, 157, 162n2, 180n9
  ABC of Reading, 67–8, 69, 74
  "America: Chances and Remedies," 168–9n5
  "The Beautiful Toilet," 79–80
  The Cantos, 86, 87
  Canzoni, 89–90
  Cathay, 71, 77–81, 89
  "Cavalcanti," 85–9, 93–4
  The Chinese Written Character..., 76–9, 168–9n5
  Gaudier-Brzeska, 172n5
  Guide to Kulchur, 61, 69, 170n9
  "Henry James," 54–6, 62–70, 169n7
  "Homage to Sextus Propertius," 8, 89, 122–3
  "How to Read," 74–6, 85, 170–1n14, 171–2n3, 173n17
  "Hugh Selwyn Mauberley," 56
  "I Gather the Limbs of Osiris," 68
  "Murder by Capital," 53
  "National Culture," 73–4
  "Notes on Elizabethan Classicists," 85, 170–1n14
  "A Pact," 122
  Patria Mia, 7, 54, 55, 56–62, 64, 67, 68
  Pisan Cantos, 173n18
  "Provincialism the Enemy," 65–6, 73–4, 170n11
  Ripostes, 90–1
  Sonnets and Ballate, 86, 89, 91, 92, 93

Pound, Ezra (cont.)
    The Spirit of Romance, 86, 171n15
    "Through Alien Eyes," 168–9n5
    "Troubadours: Their Sorts and Conditions," 87
    "A Virginal," 90–4
    "What I Feel about Walt Whitman," 83, 162n2

Rabaté, Jean-Michel, 167n1, 174n21
Ramazani, Jahan, 3, 4, 160–1n4, 161n5
Rivkin, Julie, 18, 52, 145
Rossetti, Dante Gabriel, 82–3, 85–94
    "Donne ch'avete intelletto d'amore" (translation of), 92
    Early Italian Poets, 87
Roussel, Raymond, 141
Rowe, John Carlos, 161n5

Sallis, John, 17–18
Sartre, Jean-Paul, 121
Scherzinger, Karen, 165n3
Schleiermacher, Friedrich, 16
    "On the Different Methods of Translating," 16
Schoenbach, Lisi, 175n1
Schuyler, James, 6, 9, 141, 149–59
    A Nest of Ninnies see Ashbery, John
Shakespeare, William, 83, 111–12, 150
Shoptaw, John, 183n12
Sieburth, Richard, 170n13, 171n1, 174n25, 174n26
Silliman, Ron, 182n25
Simon, Greg, and White, Steven, 133
Spicer, Jack, 6, 8, 94, 117, 118–39, 140–8, 159
    After Lorca, 8, 118–39, 141, 146
    Admonitions, 119–21, 127, 138–9, 141
    "Dictation and *A Textbook of Poetry*," 121, 144
    Jack Spicer's Detective Novel, 8, 141–7, 180n10
    Language, 147–8
    "Sporting Life," 122
Stein, Gertrude, 7–8, 94, 95–117, 118, 139, 140, 141, 148, 160n2, 162n2
    "An American and France," 100–1
    The Autobiography of Alice B. Toklas, 112, 162n2
    Before the Flowers of Friendship..., 111
    Brewsie and Willie, 99, 115, 178n14
    "The Coming of the Americans," 112–13, 115
    Everybody's Autobiography, 96–7, 98, 99, 115–16
    The Geographical History of America, 98, 175–6n3
    "Henry James," 97, 111–12
    Lectures in America, 178n13
    The Making of Americans, 97, 148
    "Melanctha," 97, 99
    Paris France, 96–100, 116
    QED, 99
    "Transatlantic Interview," 112
    "What are Masterpieces...," 97–8
    "What is English Literature," 114–15, 178n12
Synge, John Millington, 105, 108

Teahan, Sheila, 166n9
Tennyson, Alfred, Lord, 83
Theocritus, 83
Tiffany, Daniel, 2, 94, 125, 171n1, 172n9, 174n24, 174n25, 180n14
Toklas, Alice B., 112, 178–9n16
Torsney, Cheryl, 163n7

Van Dusen, Wanda, 177n10
Van Slyck, Phyllis, 166n6, 167n11, 167n15
Veblen, Thorstein, 152, 164n22
Venuti, Lawrence, 72, 174n22, 174n23, 174n25
Villon, François, 83
Vincent, John, 184n15
Virgil, 170–1n14

Walsh, John K., 134–5
Whistler, James McNeill, 58
Whitman, Walt, 7, 55, 58–9, 83–4, 108, 109, 122, 129–39, 178–9n16

"Crossing Brooklyn Ferry," 181n22
"Song of Myself," 129–32
Whittier-Ferguson, John, 177n10
Will, Barbara, 177n10, 178n12
Williams, William Carlos, 9, 116–17, 147
"The Descent," 183n7
Imaginations, 116–17
Wirth-Nesher, Hana, 35, 164n20
Wolfson, Louis, 162–3n6
Wordsworth, William, 178–9n16

Xie, Ming, 71, 78, 171n1

Yao, Steven, 2, 71, 171n1, 172n4, 172n8, 172–3n11, 174n21

Žižek, Slavoj, 182n4
Zwerdling, Alex, 162n2, 167–8n2